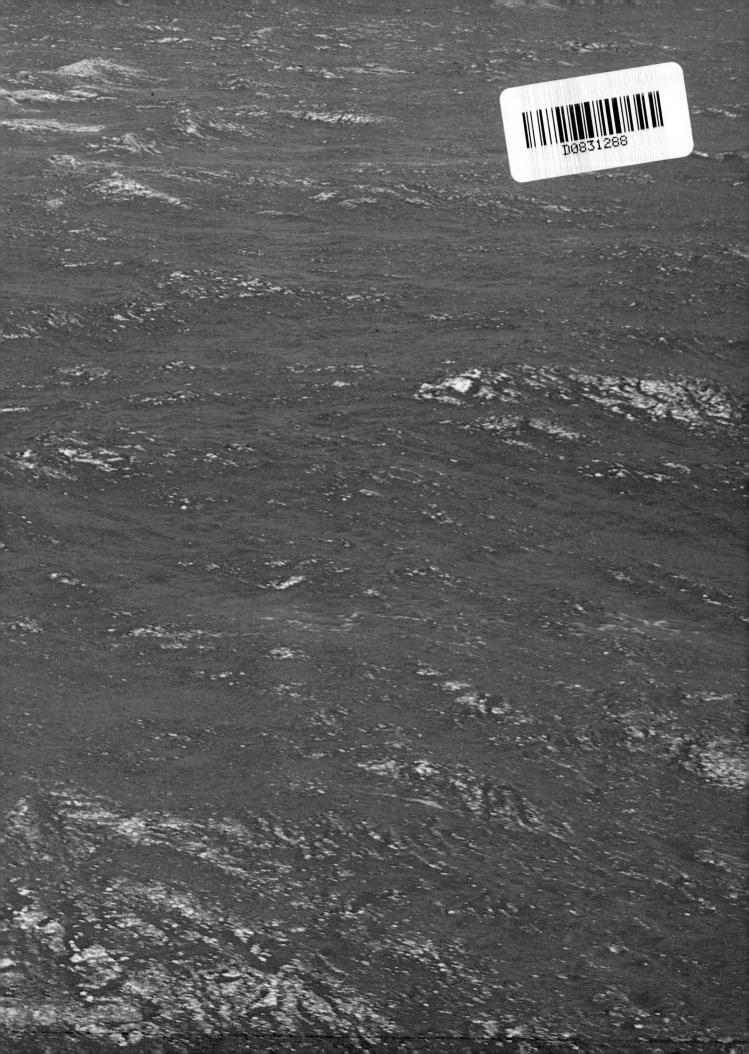

D0831288

Sailing Companion

Sailing Companion

Arthur Somers

Hamlyn
London · New York · Sydney · Toronto

Author's Acknowledgements

I would like to acknowledge with thanks the help of
Douglas Sanders and John Perrot who kindly
checked the chapters on Navigation and Meteorology
respectively; G. Dixon of Electronic Laboratories
who painstakingly answered my questions; Peter
Price of Aptell Marine who patiently explained some
electronic mysteries to me; David Bartlett of Reeds
Nautical Publication for permission to reproduce the
foreign glossary from the Almanac; and finally my
wife who contributed the recipes and the information
on provisioning.

Published by The Hamlyn Publishing Group Limited.
London · New York · Sydney · Toronto
Astronaut House, Feltham, Middlesex, England.

Copyright © The Hamlyn Publishing Group Limited, 1979

ISBN 0 600 383 628

All rights reserved, No part of this publication may be
reproduced, stored in a retrieval system, or transmitted,
in any form or by any means, electronic, mechanical,
photocopying, recording or otherwise, without the
permission of The Hamlyn Publishing Group Limited.

Phototypeset by Tradespools Ltd, Frome, Somerset.

Colour separations by Culver Graphics, Limited, Lane End, Bucks.
Printed in Italy by Group Poligrafici Calderara, Bologna

Contents

Introduction

The mere fact that you are reading this introduction indicates an interest in sailing. This may be prompted by mere curiosity, or more likely it is the stirring of a desire to introduce some adventure – or even a sense of purpose – into what may be a rather humdrum existence. If you have sailed before, you may wish to increase your knowledge of ships and the sea, in order to voyage further abroad. It is difficult adequately to explain to the newcomer to the sport the fascination of sailing the sea in its many moods, or the sense of achievement and satisfaction you feel by dealing competently with a potentially dangerous situation. Equally fascinating is the wide cross-section of people who become cruising yachtsmen. Although they are drawn from all nationalities, professions and walks-of-life they are united in a love of getting away from the artificial existence that the majority of us have to live.

This book is addressed to the "young of all ages" and especially to the family man who wants to take up an outdoor sport in which his family can participate. Sailing is a sport in which, racing apart, he will not necessarily be seen to be successful by other people but it is one in which he may nevertheless win the satisfaction of being able to think well of himself . . . An attempt has been made to explain the basic principles of sailing and boat-handling so that the beginner may start to sail with a certain amount of theoretical knowledge, while at the same time to provide guide lines for the man or woman who has sailed locally for a year or two and is about to embark upon that most rewarding of achievements – one's first trip 'foreign'. Life offers many exciting experiences and it is fair to say that, to a yachtsman, his first foreign landfall is a never-to-be-forgotten event: one which will always be looked back upon with nostalgia, no matter how widely he roams thereafter. No recommendations or advice are given on making long sea voyages; this highly-specialised subject is properly covered in other more advanced books. One of the best of them is by that doyen of cruising men, Eric Hiscock, in '*Voyaging under Sail*' (Oxford University Press 1970), which covers a wide range of seafaring knowledge in an interesting and competent manner.

Inevitably the more experienced sailor may become a little impatient at times at what may appear to him to an overstatement of the obvious. On reflection he will remember that to the beginner, sailing matters and even the language are strange, and so I have included a short glossary of nautical terms.

Much of what is written here applies equally to power-craft as it does to sail. Indeed seamanship, navigation, and safety at sea are all common subjects. Therefore, the motor-cruiser man who has a basic knowledge of sailing will not only be more understanding of the yachtsman's problems but he will inevitably be a better seaman himself. Even in this age of vast highly-mechanised, fully-automated leviathans of the sea, some perceptive nations still wisely spend money on sail-training for future sea-going officers; there must surely be a moral in this!

One of the more commendable applications of plastic materials has been the production of various moderately-priced sextants which are capable of surprisingly accurate working. As there are several uses for a sextant which are entirely practical in coastal navigation, there can be no doubt that the sooner one starts to familiarise oneself with the instrument the easier its use will become and will thus encourage the owner to progress to astro navigation . . . ? Now for two final thoughts I would leave with the reader. The first is in connection with the financial aspect of sailing – always a very daunting subject! A well-designed and well-built boat which has been

properly looked after will, in normal circumstances, retain its value for a very long time; it will certainly keep pace with inflation and may even show a paper profit when you sell it.

The second sounds a note of caution. It is all too easy to buy hurriedly a small out-board speed boat, take it down to the sea, then launch it and drive away. All very simple . . . but possibly highly dangerous to the novice. *My advice is don't*: find out more about the subject first! Even rowing a dinghy in strong tidal waters can be an illuminating experience for a beginner . . .

A Short Glossary of Sailing Terms

Aback A sail is backed or aback when the clew is hauled to weather, i.e. to the windward side of the ship as when hove-to. A vessel is 'taken aback' when an unexpected wind shift causes this to happen.

About To change tack, i.e. to so alter course that the wind direction changes from one side of the boat to the other and, during and after the change, continues to come from a forward direction.

A'hull Lying a'hull: in severe weather conditions a sailing vessel with no sail set which has been allowed to take up her own position in the sea.

Apparent Wind The strength and direction of the wind on a sailing boat that is caused by the set of the sails and the motion through the water and which is thus different to the true wind, i.e. the unaffected wind. The boat's burgee shows the apparent wind.

Aspect Ratio The ratio between the height and width of a sail, rudder or keel etc., e.g. high-aspect ratio rig is one that is tall and narrow.

Ballast Displacement Ratio The ratio between the ballast weight and displacement expressed as a percentage. A high ratio, greater than say 40%, would indicate a 'stiff' boat which would not heel easily.

Bear away To alter course away from the wind.

Broach To round up sharply when sailing downwind so that the boat comes at right-angles to the wind and sea.

Broad Reach Sailing with the wind on the quarter.

By the Lee Sailing downwind with wind coming over that side on which the boom lies – and thus approaching the angle at which a gybe can take place.

Centre of Effort – (C.E.) The combined centre of power of the sails.

Centre of Lateral Resistance The centre point of the sideways resistance of a hull as determined by her profile.

Close Hauled Sailing as close to the wind as possible.

Close Reach Not as close to the wind as when 'close hauled'.

Collision Course When the relative angle of approach between two vessels does not alter, they will collide if both maintain their respective courses.

Dead Beat A course line directly into the wind which involves alternate tacks at an equal angle to the wind.

Dead Reckoning Calculation of a vessel's position from a previously-known position using only course and speed.

Gybe When running before the wind and a change of course, or a change in wind direction from one quarter of the boat to the other round the stern, causes the mainsail to swing rapidly across to the opposite side. The term applies to any fore-and-aft sail. An unpremeditated gybe in strong winds can cause damage to the gear.

Hard Over Putting the helm fully across to one side or the other.

Leeway The sideways drift of a vessel due to the pressure of wind on her sails and hull.

Hove-to A vessel is 'hove-to' when her foresail is hauled to the weather side of the deck and tiller put slightly to leeward. The vessel will then make forward way slowly at about 90° to the wind.

Luff up To alter course towards the wind.

Pinch To sail too close to the wind thereby reducing the efficiency of the sails, and thus the vessel's speed as well.

Point A sailing boat 'points' well when it sails close to the wind in an efficient manner.

Weather Helm A boat is 'carrying weather helm' when it is necessary to keep the tiller up to the windward side of the boat. Generally speaking the term is only used when the pressure required to keep the tiller up is excessive. Conversely 'lee helm' occurs when it is necessary to keep the tiller to leeward to stay on course.

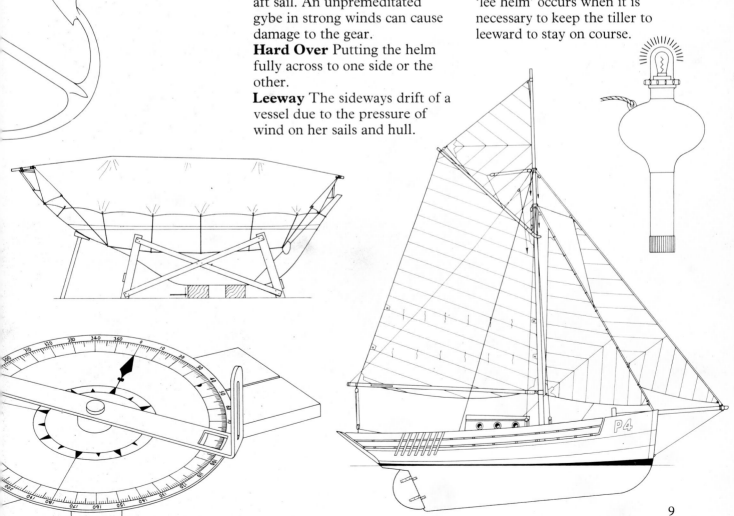

Ch.1 Choosing Your Boat

The best advice you can offer to the beginner who is thinking of buying a boat is – sail in as many types as possible before committing yourself to a particular line of action. In the event of a scarcity of friends with boats of their own, there are many clubs which welcome newcomers wishing to sail and who are prepared to crew for a start. There are also a number of sailing schools where instruction is given in the handling of different sorts of boat, but remember that it is desirable to select a school which is recognized by the national yachting authority of the country concerned. In short there is no necessity for anyone to embark upon the serious project of buying a boat without some basic knowledge at least.

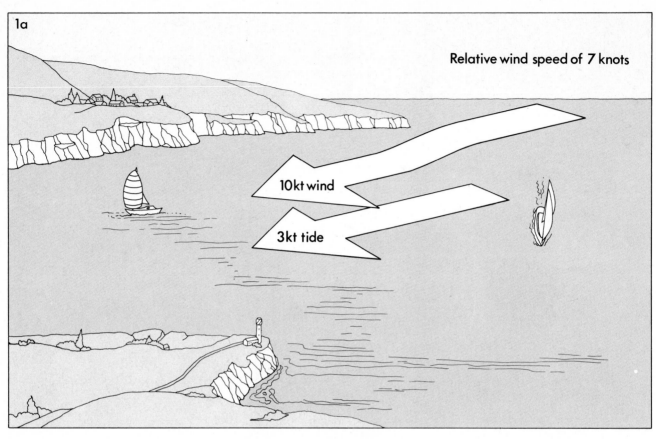

Relative wind speed of 7 knots

10kt wind

3kt tide

1 (a) Wind and tide together. (b) Wind and tide opposed.

Once a certain amount of experience has been gained it is naturally much easier to decide what type of craft is suitable and safe for the area in which you propose to sail. You sometimes hear the question posed 'is a certain boat a safe one?' The question should really be rephrased to 'can I safely handle that type of boat?' There is no such creature as the ideal boat for all men and all places; the location where you intend to sail is an important factor in making the decision regarding the type of boat to buy. It must, however, be admitted, referring back to the original query, that there are boats (but fortunately few) whose safety in bad conditions would be questionable in *anyone's hands*. . . . With a little experience and some knowledgeable friends, you should have no difficulty in avoiding these craft.

In the matter of safety it is important to allow for the local conditions in the area you will be sailing most of the time. For example, the man who intends to start his sailing career on an inland reservoir, always assuming he can swim, is hardly likely to come to any harm. Therefore his selection of a boat is less critical than that of the man who will be learning on a tidal estuary. For the latter, the variety of boats to choose is considerable – bewilderingly so – but they must have one thing in common: seaworthiness. One way out of the difficulty is first to decide the type of boat, i.e. dinghy or cruiser; secondly the area of operations. Then fix a financial limit and – finally – consult a knowledgeable friend.

The sailing area is important because, until you have built up a little experience, appearances in tidal waters can be very deceptive; the combination of

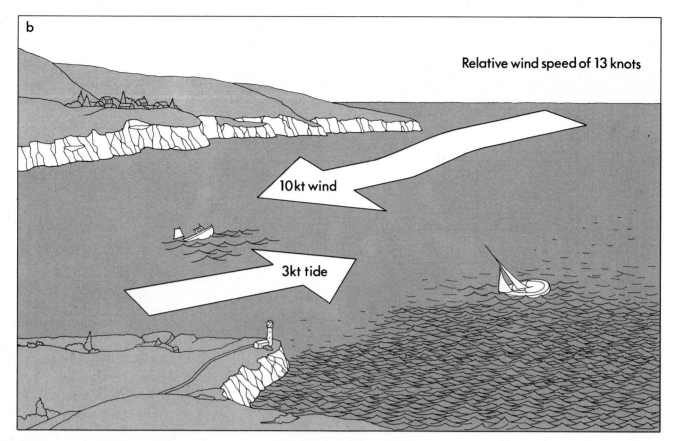

b

Relative wind speed of 13 knots

10 kt wind

3 kt tide

wind and tide can on occasion produce some surprising results. For example, imagine a pleasant summer day with the tide flooding into a small estuary in a westerly direction with the wind, a moderate breeze from the east, blowing in the same direction as the tide. Conditions may be ideal for some exhilarating sailing in a small dinghy and the unwary may be tempted to sail farther from the land than is prudent. Then the tide begins to ebb, which under the given conditions means that it will now flow in an easterly direction against the wind, thus causing an apparent hardening in wind speed relative to the tide allied to a consequent increase in the disturbance of the surface. In Fig. 1 (a) the tide is flowing at 3 knots and the wind 10 knots in the same direction giving a relative wind speed of 7 knots. However, when the tide changes direction as in (b), the relative

wind speed is 13 knots – force 4 – which in some circumstances would make sailing in a small dinghy uncomfortable at the very least. . . .

The situation also applies to the small high-speed outboard runabout which, in similar circumstances, might find itself in serious difficulties should it be unable to get back to shelter before the sea builds up. The principal involved is one which applies to all sizes of boats to greater or lesser degree. For example, a 10 ton sloop enjoying fast sailing in a Force 5 wind, with comparatively smooth water, will find the situation uncomfortable when a tidal stream change may push the effective wind strength up to Force 6 or even Force 7. In the chapters on navigation (see pages 106–145), we shall see that tides play an extremely important part in sailing and that they cannot be ignored.

Right: Pupils at the Cowes Sailing school being towed out for a day's tuition.
Above: The very popular *Mirror* dinghy.

Selecting the craft

Whereas it is difficult to recommend any particular type or class of boat, it is fairly safe to say that any boat of a well-known class or make in good condition will be a 'safe buy' – assuming of course that it is suited to your circumstances and local conditions. The first-time purchaser of a second-hand dinghy, for example, could do worse than to buy one of a national class that has passed the peak of its racing prime. The price should be reasonable and the buyer will have the comforting knowledge that his boat is well designed and that it should provide a satisfying way of learning to sail. One of the best-known types for a beginner is the *Mirror* dinghy designed by Jack Holt, of which over fifty thousand examples have been built in various parts of the world. It is available in kit form and is easily assembled with the collection of tools to be found in the average D.I.Y. home-workshop. Whereas it is perhaps invidious to mention any class by name, as there are so many of them in the dinghy world, the National Firefly, Fireball, Hornet, and the slightly longer Wayfarer will all provide excellent sailing and an opportunity to race in club events. Although the cruising yachtsman may consider racing a dedicated specialist's pastime, there is no doubt that a modicum of racing is excellent practice in that it tunes up your sailing abilities in a way that ordinary cruising will never do.

The point must also be made that it is not obligatory to start sailing in a dinghy – particularly if you have reached the age when regular immersions in cold salt water does not evoke any true enthusiasm . . .!

Cruising Yachts: general

The choise of a cruising yacht as your first purchase requires a different approach to the purchase of a dinghy. Whereas a dinghy 'good buy' would very probably be one of the many excellent classes used in racing, this principle would not necessarily be right in the case of a 5 to 7 metre (16–24 ft approx.) boat for family cruising. There are many small off-shore racers capable of keeping at sea in bad weather while at the same time maintaining high speeds. To the comparative novice this may seem an excellent reason for purchasing such a boat, but let us consider the way in which this performance is achieved.

The boat will undoubtedly be light in construction and beamy, with a very short keel and a hung rudder (fig 1a). Because of her beam she will have great initial stability and consequently will be able to carry a large sail area. She will therefore be extremely efficient to windward *but* she will be ultra lively and, due to her very short keel, difficult to sail on a constant course. The helmsman, therefore, has to give his whole attention *all the time* to the matter of steering – and not just

Below : The yacht *Stella Lyra* is a good example of a traditionally built small cruiser-racer. The *Stella Class* was originally designed as an English answer to the *Folkboat*, and is a compact, fast boat ideal for the sailing family. The picture clearly shows her classic deep keel lines.

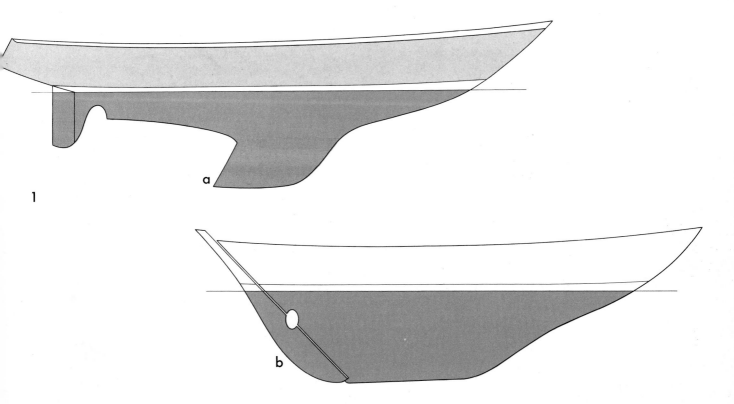

1

when he is trying to get the best out of the boat. For the family man with, say, two children, this is not at all acceptable. He must be able to leave the helm to cope with minor domestic emergencies without possibly disastrous consequences. Quite apart from this the younger members of the family will rightly expect to take their 'watch' on the tiller and, if the vessel is not well mannered and easy on the helm, a good crew member may become disenchanted for life.

Now examine the other extreme of hull form (fig 1b). In this boat the keel is long in the traditional manner and the vessel has the ability to maintain course without constant attention to the helm. In fact the helmsman can safely leave the cockpit for a few moments, to find on his return that the vessel has only moved a few degrees off course. Indeed with the helm lashed and sails correctly trimmed she would probably sail herself almost

indefinitely until the weather conditions changed. This type of hull will inevitably be slower than a comparable size of fin-and-skeg design (fig. 32), due to the greater wetted surface (the under-water body) and the heavier hull form.

Between these two extremes of hull design lie an infinite variety of profiles, each with their own special traits. If, however, you bear in mind the main characteristics of each of these two hull forms, you are less likely to make a disastrous choice when looking at a hull or a set of plans. Inevitably any design of cruising yacht is a compromise, because the cruising man wants to voyage in comfort with good accommodation and make fast passages in safety. These requirements are not necessarily compatible and the one which should have the lowest priority is speed. On the other hand, do avoid the boat which really consists of a hull built around over-lavish accommodation. . . .

Above: The authors boat *Saremja*, a *Westerly 33*, reaching off the coast of Belgium.

Opposite: Chay Blyth's all-steel ketch *British Steel*. Built by Philip's Yard, Dartmouth, to an overall length of 59 ft. (17.98 m.), she circumnavigated the world non-stop against the prevailing winds, leaving Hamble on October 18th 1970 and returning to the same port on August 6th 1971.

Left: A gaff-rigged ketch with a Bermudan mizzen sail.

Cruising Yachts – Rigs

Bermudan Sloop This rig is the simplest, the most effective and the conventional rig for the average-size of cruising yacht. With a single mast, mainsail and foresail the rig is easy to control and handle, and it is not until large genoas and spinnakers are added to the sail wardrobe that more expertise and muscle-power is needed to handle the increases in sail area. It has great advantages for the newcomer in ease of handling and is deservedly the most popular rig for cruising and racing. With a well-designed hull form it has good windward performance and will handle under either foresail or main alone, which is an advantage when picking up moorings. Understandably it is the rig most commonly seen afloat.

Bermudan Cutter In this rig the foretriangle (the space before the mast) carries two sails instead of the single one of the sloop rig thus giving, among other advantages, rather greater controllability of the sail area. When reefing, for example, the foremost sail or jib can be dropped as the first stage, leaving the foresail alone and thus effectively reducing sail area without the difficulties of

changing headsails. With cutter rig it is customary to have a bowsprit, though it is not absolutely necessary. Modern developments have got rid of the bowsprit of the past, which was a heavy and lengthy spar sticking out from the stem-head and fitted with a bobstay and shrouds. The modern equivalent is an extremely strong, much shorter plank-type platform or grid, with the guard rails carried out to its end thus giving a useful extension to the working deck space. A short rod-type bobstay takes the place of the long chain bobstay of the past.

The second sail requires an additional pair of cross trees at

the point on the mast where the inner forestay (supporting the second sail) is attached, together with a second pair of shrouds. Cutter rig has another advantage in that it enables the same spread of canvas to be set on a lower mast than would be necessary in the more normal sloop rig.

Ketch Rig The term 'ketch rig' is on occasions somewhat loosely used today. Technically a ketch is a vessel with the aftermast stepped forward of the rudder and shorter than the mainmast, whilst a yawl has the mizzen or smaller mast stepped aft of the rudder. Some vessels

1 Sloop rig, a single mast with mainsail and one foresail. (a) The *Hustler 30* with masthead rig. (b) The three-quarter rig of the *Folkboat*.
2 Cutter rig, either gaff or Bermudan, can carry two sails forward of the mast.
3 (a) Traditional bowsprit with traveller for outer jib. (b) Modern plank-type bowsprit.

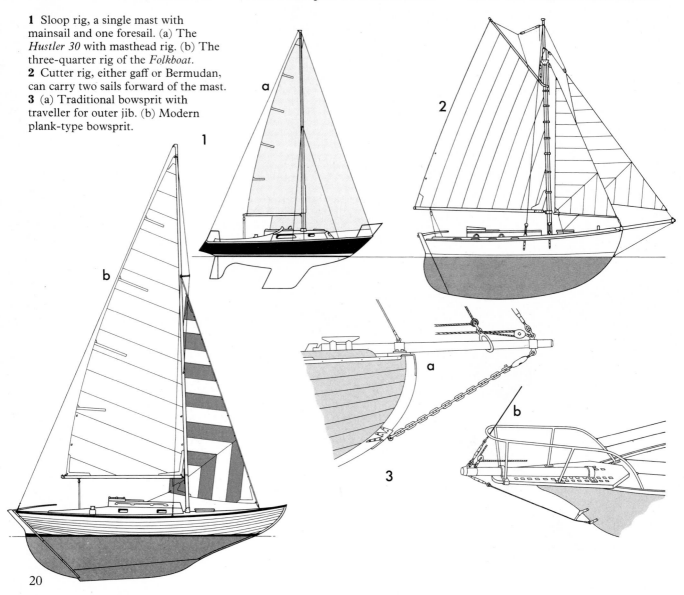

which are really yawls are described as ketches, the term 'yawl' having almost fallen into disuse. A ketch has the advantage that the addition of the mizzen sail splits the rig as a whole into more manageable proportions, which is a distinct advantage with a small crew. When it becomes necessary to reef the furling of the mizzen is a first step which is easily carried out. Alternatively, and an attractive course of action from the point of view of the short-handed family cruising man, the mainsail can be dropped leaving the vessel under mizzen and foresail – a very snug and balanced rig. There

are, however, disadvantages to ketch rig, the first one being the additional cost of the extra mast, and standing and running rigging, for a given sail area. Secondly, the rig is not so efficient to windward as the sloop rig and the mizzen may tend to give heavier weather helm. When running, the mizzen will tend to blanket the main and on this point of sailing it will therefore be of little use. The best point of sailing for a ketch is undoubtedly on a reach when a mizzen staysail can be set. This sail is set between the main and mizzen masts as shown in the diagram and gives a considerable increase in sail

4 The ketch-rigged *Trintella III*. The aft, or mizzen, mast is the shorter of the two on a ketch. The addition of the second mast enables a staysail to be set between the two (a).
5 A *Bowman 46* rigged as a yawl.
6 Variations of sail area on a ketch: (a) under mainsail and genoa, (b) under mizzen and genoa, and (c) under jib only.

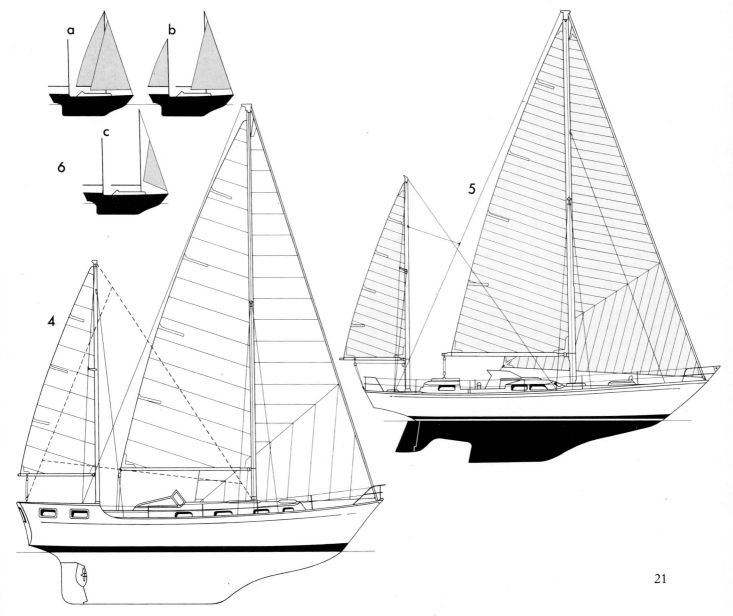

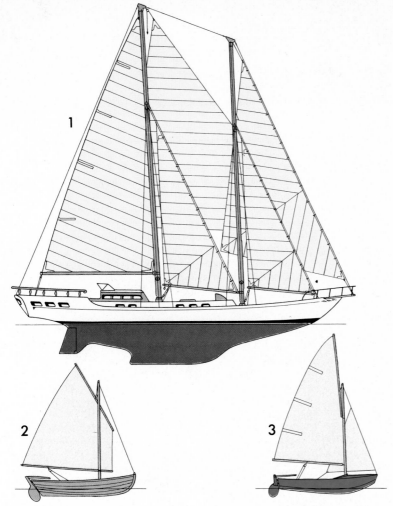

1 Schooner rig, the aft mast being the taller of the two.
2 Dipping lug.
3 Gunter rig.

Opposite: Galway Blazer Commander Bill King's junk-rigged schooner. Her jury-rig mast can be clearly seen on the foredeck as can the absence of any stays or shrouds.

area. The mizzen staysail is perhaps something of a light weather sail but it is also a good driving sail in the right conditions.

In general the ketch rig does not come into its own until the hull length is of the order of 10 m (about 30 ft) or more but, even at 10 m, the ratio of sail areas between mains and mizzen is important. A mizzen of 60 sq.ft (5.5 m^2) on a boat of this size is not really worth having; a minimum of 90 sq.ft (8.3 m^2) would be more practicable.

Yawl The difference between the yawl and ketch has already been explained and little more needs to be said other than that the remarks about over-small mizzens is even more pertinent in the yawl rig where the mizzen is of necessity positioned further aft.

Schooner In the schooner rig the aftermast is taller than the foremast and carries the mainsail. The rig is essentially for sailing vessels much larger than those we are generally considering in this book. It is most attractive in appearance and perhaps more than any other rig conjures up visions of the romantic past of sailing vessels.

Dipping Lug One of the traditional rigs, used commonly by fishermen and small coasters in the nineteenth century.

Although it is a reasonably efficient sail to windward it never really entered the yachting scene until recent years, its reappearance being due no doubt to the revival of interest in traditional boats. Some small firms now market this rig on little day boats. The true dipping lug requires the sail to be moved from one side of the mast to the other when tacking.

Gunter Rig Gunter is somewhat similar to the gaff rig (see page 30) except that the spar or gaff hoists nearly parallel to the mast. In the sliding gunter rig the spar extends vertically above the mast, producing, in effect, a Bermudan rig. Although less efficient than the Bermudan rig, it is useful in small day boats in which it is desired to keep the mast short when the sail is stowed.

The Junk Rig The history of the Chinese junk rig is almost as old as the history of sailing, but it has only been accepted in the Western World in comparatively recent years. Although unquestionably a seaworthy and very easily handled rig, it has never become popular in the western hemisphere for a variety of reasons. There is no doubt about its seaworthiness which has been proved by the frequent and successful transatlantic passages of Col. 'Blondie' Hasler's junk-rigged Folkboat, *Jester*, and also the circumnavigation of the world by Bill King in *Galway Blazer*. To the Western eyes in general however it looks unconventional – and indeed unsafe – with a single unstayed mast setting one sail only. The single sail, however, takes the place of the entire wardrobe of sails on a conventional cruising yacht and the halyards and sheets can all

appears to produce a somewhat complicated set of running rigging as the sail concertinas on to the boom between, in effect, topping lifts or lazy jacks. Despite this apparent complexity, however, users of junk rig regard it as infinitely more controllable than conventional Western rigs. The one apparent disadvantage is its poor performance to windward in very light airs compared to a high-aspect ratio Bermudian rig. A further advantage of the rig is the lack of unpleasant consequences in the event of a gybe, due to the absence of any standing rigging. With these manifest advantages to the cruising man (including the complete absence of a wardrobe of sails to be stowed below decks) one may well ask why there are so few production-line boats with junk rig. So far as the writer is aware there is only one firm in the United Kingdom producing a small cruiser with junk rig as an option to the conventional ones. Unfortunately you cannot expect any firm producing boats for a mass market to embark on a product for which there is not as yet a proven market.

Wishbone Rig An unconventional rig in which the mainsail of a ketch is extended at the top between a double spar (fig. 3) thus allowing the sail to take up an aerofoil section, which theoretically produces a very efficient sail. Together with mizzen staysail (see page 21), this fills the area between main and mizzen masts in a more efficient manner than does the conventional Bermudan ketch rig. However, the sail appears to be difficult to control and, due to its complete lack of popularity, is of little more than academic interest.

1 *Jester* possibly the most well-known and successful example of a junk rig used on a conventional hull platform. Colonel 'Blondie' Hasler designed the coachroof, interior and rig specifically for singlehanded sailing. Hasler's design was based on the well-tried Folkboat hull form and in 1953 she was built of carvel construction by Harry Feltham. Although her original rig was different it was under the junk rig that she competed in the first Singlehanded Transatlantic Race of 1960. Since then she has made many further crossings with no serious trouble from the rig.

be controlled from a central point: the cockpit. The idea of a single sail which can be reefed to any extent without leaving the cockpit and then reset again from the same position, is an extremely attractive proposition when one has spent an uncomfortable trip changing headsails on a plunging foredeck. Incidentally the rig is not always confined to a single mast and in fact *Galway Blazer* was rigged as a schooner. The method of reefing the sail

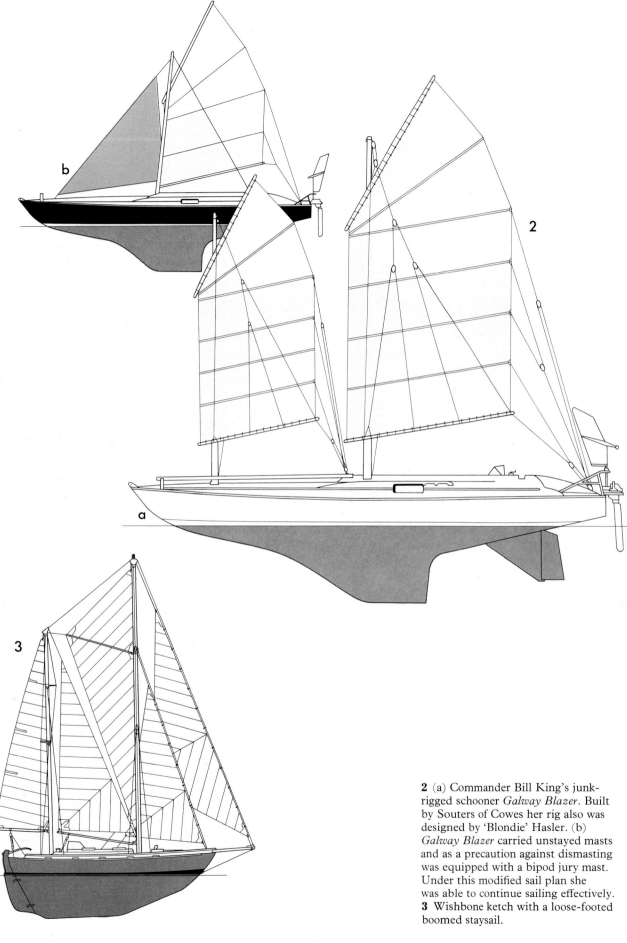

2 (a) Commander Bill King's junk-rigged schooner *Galway Blazer*. Built by Souters of Cowes her rig also was designed by 'Blondie' Hasler. (b) *Galway Blazer* carried unstayed masts and as a precaution against dismasting was equipped with a bipod jury mast. Under this modified sail plan she was able to continue sailing effectively. **3** Wishbone ketch with a loose-footed boomed staysail.

Catamarans and Trimarans
These two hull forms are grouped together as their construction and performance are totally different to any of the conventional monohulls. Although very much recent additions to the yachting scene their ancestry stretches back to the catamarans of the ancient Polynesians, who can deservedly rank among the world's great seamen and navigators. The catamaran basically consists of two long and narrow hulls joined by a frame or deck which in the case of the larger 'cats' embodies part of the accommodation. The trimaran consists of a main central hull with two outriggers, one on each side. The outriggers are relatively small and thus offer little space for accommodation which in general must be provided in the main hull. For the average cruising man, therefore, a trimaran has little advantage over a monohull or catamaran. Small catamarans of up to, say, 5m (16ft) in length are regularly raced in various classes, and due to their effective waterline length are extremely fast in the right conditions but, if capsized, they cannot be righted as easily as a conventional centre-board dinghy. The larger cruising catamarans possess far more accommodation than a monohull of the same length, having full standing headroom in the two hulls, together with considerable cabin space on the frame between them – admittedly with some restricted headroom. Its accommodation, together with a cockpit of truly impressive proportions, makes the catamaran a most attractive proposition to the family cruising man. The hull form gives great initial stability which is a very worthwhile quality when cooking and navigating at sea are being considered. However, this stability, so attractive at sea, can lead the unwary into trouble as, unlike

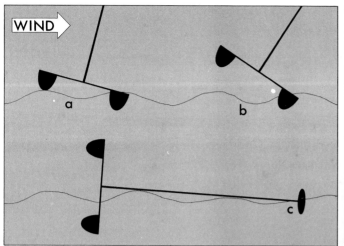

When hard pressed by a strong wind (a), a catamaran cannot heel over as a monohull does. Under severe conditions, the windward hull can lift as the leeward hull digs into the sea (b). For this reason many cruising catamarans are fitted with a masthead float (c) which prevents a total capsize.

Above: A *Telstar 35* trimaran. Note the windward hull is out of the water making the stability dependent on the leeward hull.
Left: A Prout *Snowgoose 37* catamaran in the English Channel. Note spacious accommodation with double aft cabins and large protected cockpit.
Overleaf: All the speed and exhilaration of a fast catamaran is summed up in this picture. In the distance can be seen a sedate monohull race.

the monohull which will give ample warning when hard pressed and over canvassed, the catamaran needs more careful watching in strong winds. Catamarans and trimarans have capsized at sea in conditions in which a monohull would probably have survived. A deep-keeled monohull can be pitch poled, that is rolled end over end, or rolled over sideways and, providing the hull and deck are not severely damaged, she will probably finish floating the right way up although she may have lost her mast in the process. The protagonists of multihulls will however point to various epic voyages as proof that they are sound sea-going craft. Rosie Swale, in her book *Children of the Horn* (Elek, 1974) paints a convincing picture of the safe performance of a small cruising catamaran in experienced hands.

Gaff Rig – General The gaff rig is the old traditional rig of fore-and-aft sailing vessels which has largely disappeared since the advent of the jib-headed or Bermudan mainsail. Nevertheless, due to the interest of traditionalists, there are signs of its returning to popularity in some quarters. The main disadvantages are the complexity of standing and running rigging and its relatively poor performance to windward, compared to the modern Bermudan rig. Due to the gaff, i.e. the spar at the head of the main, it is necessary to have two halyards, the peak and the throat, the latter hauling up the mainsail at the luff and the peak halyard hauling up the gaff. In general it is necessary to haul both these halyards together until the luff is set up taut after which the peak is finally set up. Together with the necessity for having running backstays, this makes the rig more complex to operate than the modern Bermudan sail. The running backstays are, in effect, adjustable mast stays, the weather one being set up taut and the lee one slacked off. Although they are controlled by purchases or Highfield levers, it will be appreciated that the operation of the backstays adds to the work in tacking, and especially in gybing when there is less time to set up the weather one.

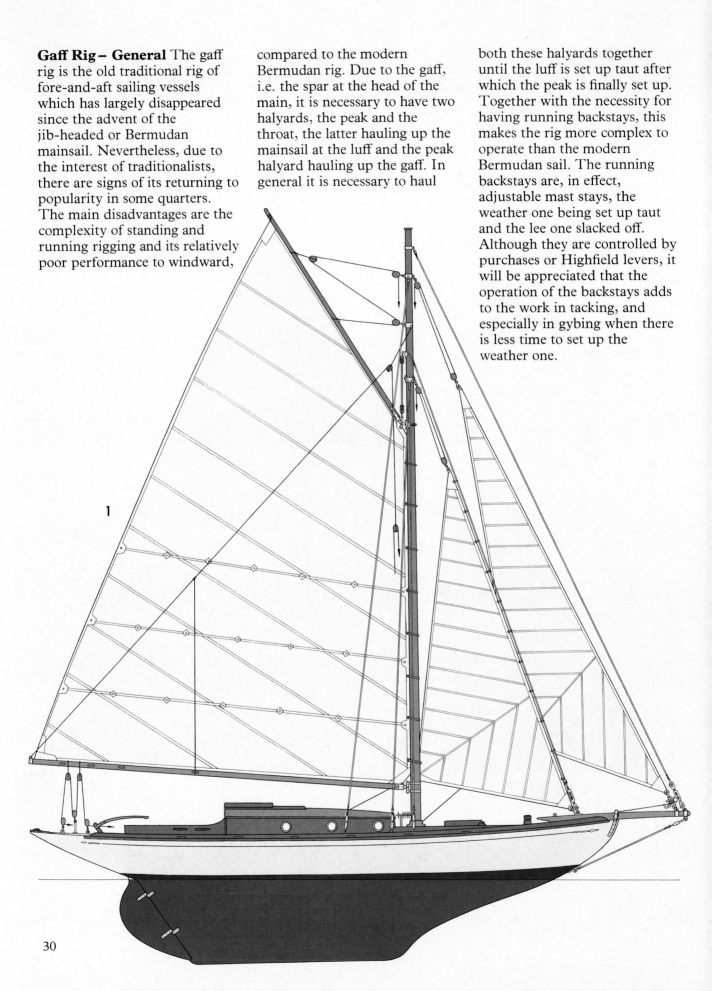

1

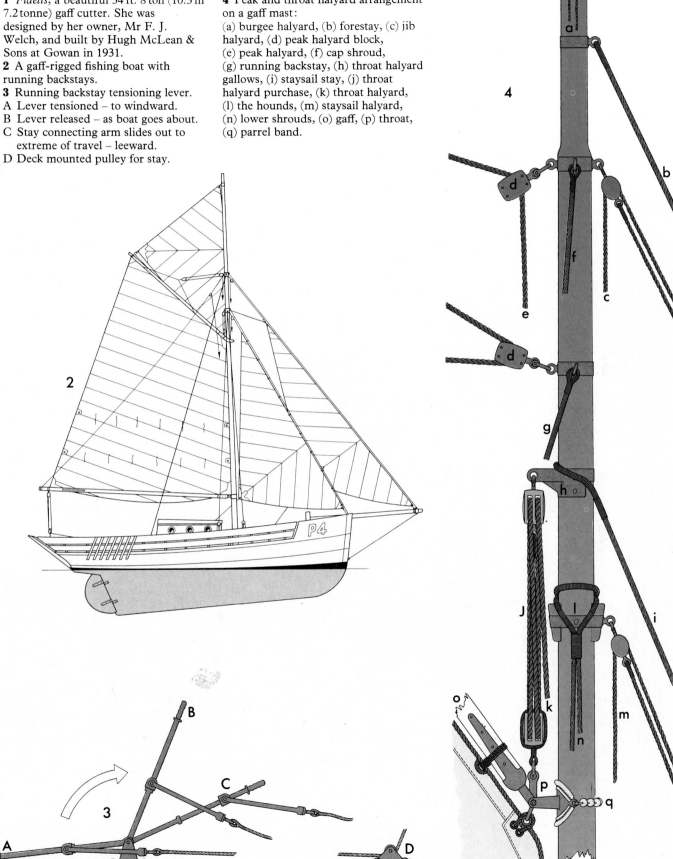

1 *Fidelis*, a beautiful 34 ft. 8 ton (10.3 m 7.2 tonne) gaff cutter. She was designed by her owner, Mr F. J. Welch, and built by Hugh McLean & Sons at Gowan in 1931.

2 A gaff-rigged fishing boat with running backstays.

3 Running backstay tensioning lever.
A Lever tensioned – to windward.
B Lever released – as boat goes about.
C Stay connecting arm slides out to extreme of travel – leeward.
D Deck mounted pulley for stay.

4 Peak and throat halyard arrangement on a gaff mast:
(a) burgee halyard, (b) forestay, (c) jib halyard, (d) peak halyard block, (e) peak halyard, (f) cap shroud, (g) running backstay, (h) throat halyard gallows, (i) staysail stay, (j) throat halyard purchase, (k) throat halyard, (l) the hounds, (m) staysail halyard, (n) lower shrouds, (o) gaff, (p) throat, (q) parrel band.

Hulls – Types and Construction

Long Keel This type has already been mentioned earlier in the chapter. It is a traditional type of hull and its main characteristic is its ability to maintain course with a minimum of rudder movement. The hull form is 'sea kindly' and easy to sail but has little to offer the off-shore racing man. The large underwater body or 'wetted surface' means that it will inevitably be a little slower than a smaller size of boat with fin-and-skeg profile.

Fin-and-Skeg The fin-and-skeg design has developed over the years due to the quest for speed and the extreme design is now strongly represented in the racing world. As we have seen, the design does not necessarily represent the ideal for cruising as it demands constant attention to keep it sailing. The less extreme examples of this type of design, however, form a good basis for a cruising yacht being handy, easy on the helm and well-mannered.

Bilge Keel The bilge keel is a most practical development of hull design for regions where shallow draft is important and where it may be necessary on occasions to take the ground. The design obviates the necessity for the legs or props which would be required in these circumstances with a single keel vessel and, in the unfortunate event of an unpremeditated grounding, a lot of the discomfort and worry are removed from the incident. The performance at sea is generally a little slower than the equivalent single keel and it will not point so high when going to windward. In a really well-designed bilge

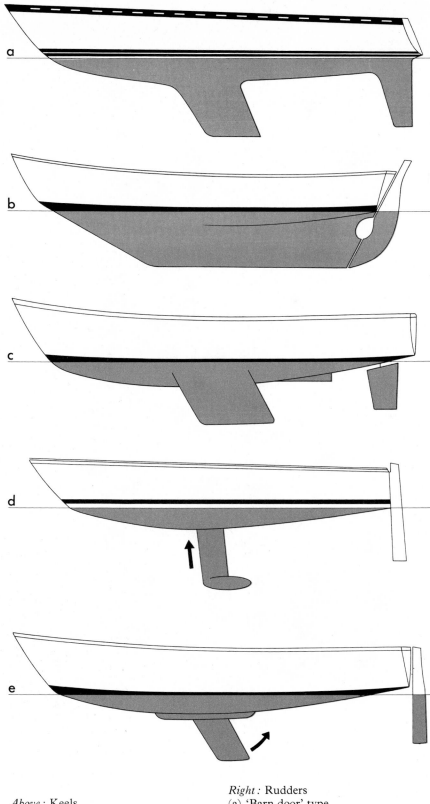

Above: Keels
(a) Fin and skeg
(b) Long Keel
(c) Bilge Keel
(d) Lifting Keel
(e) Centre-plate

Right: Rudders
(a) 'Barn door' type
(b) 'Folkboat' type
(c) 'Motor sailor' type
(d) Lifting
(e) Transom hung with skeg
(f) Balanced

keeler, however, its performance as a cruising yacht leaves little to be desired.

Centre Boards The centre board or centre plate hull design normally has an even shallower draft with her keel up than the equivalent size of bilge keeler, but when it is down has a deeper draft, thus giving her a better performance to windward. Many centre boarders have a small fixed keel which results in an uncomfortable angle of heel if it is necessary to take the ground which, coupled with the danger of stones jamming in the centre board housing, make it undesirable to go aground if it can be avoided. The basic design of a centre board is a plate accommodated in a housing above the keel, pivoted at the forward end and lowered out of this housing by means of a wire rope or chain attached to the after end. It will be appreciated that the design and construction of the housing and equipment must be good if it is to work effectively and not be a source of leaks, or too much of an intrusion into the cabin lay-out.

Lifting Keel The lifting keel is similar to the centre board in principle but the plate, instead

of being pivoted at one end, drops vertically rather in the manner of a dagger plate in a dinghy. The main advantage of the design is that the housing tends to take up less room in the cabin and the profile tends to be more akin to a fin-and-skeg design. The latter advantage varies of course from one particular design to another.

Rudders
The basic requirement of a rudder is to produce the maximum turning effect on the hull for a minimum of effort required on the tiller with the least possible drag on the hull. Without going into design details, it will be appreciated that a rudder with a high-aspect ratio will require less power to operate it than, say, a square one of the same area – which is the first point to be borne in mind when considering a rudder's shape. Secondly, as the rudder angle is increased it reaches a point at which it starts to stall – that is to say turbulence occurs and the rudder begins to act as a brake rather than a steering device. Then the vessel slows down to below the stalling speed and the rudder becomes effective again. Therefore, turbulence should be reduced

to a minimum and the first step is to streamline the rudder shape, as turbulence starts at the leading edge of the rudder. The streamlining is further improved by fitting a skeg immediately in front of the rudder with a minimum gap between the two. The skeg streamlines the water-flow over the rudder and therefore improves its efficiency. Various types of rudder and their characteristics are as follows:

The traditional basic rudder: somewhat inefficient and hard on the helm, but matches the traditional hull design it will be found upon.
A lifting rudder: probably will be used in conjunction with a centre plate boat for shoal draft work. High aspect ratio and reasonably efficient.
The deep-keel boats traditional transom-hung rudder: with the dead wood of the keel acting as a skeg and streamlining the water flow. This is an efficient rudder.
The modern skeg design: efficient and requiring little effort to operate.
The balanced rudder: it will be seen that the leading edge, back to the stock or pivoting point, is acted upon by the water-flow so that it assists the movement of the helm rather than resisting it, as does that part of the rudder behind the stock – the trailing part. Depending on the position of the pivoting point the servo effect of the leading edge can (in extreme cases) assist the rudder so much that there is very little pressure on the helm which feels quite dead.
The intermediate type: the skeg of the hull itself ensures a fair flow over the rudder, although it will be disturbed by the aperture for the propeller.

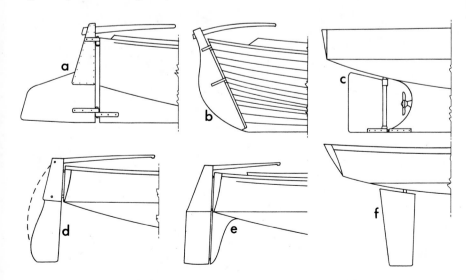

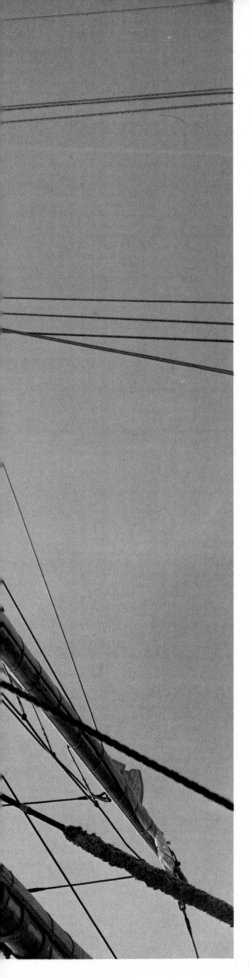

Standing Rigging The modern sailing cruiser usually has its standing rigging made of stranded stainless-steel wire, but in some vessels galvanized-steel wire is used and it does have its advantages – apart from the obvious one of being less expensive – in that it doesn't fail unpredictably as have some grades of stainless steel been known to do. Properly maintained galvanized steel wire has a good useful life. However, modern practice in large off-shore racing yachts is to use stainless-steel rod rigging in certain applications but in general it is considerably more expensive than stranded-steel wire. The metal rod is smaller in diameter and smoother than the comparable wire stay and the basic reason for using it is its reduced stretch under load. Wire rigging of spiral construction must inevitably stretch under load, which is to be avoided if possible in a well-tuned racing yacht. . . .

Standing rigging ends should all terminate in toggles to ensure that no twisting strain can take place at the mast or deck fittings (see page 42). The latter will consist of a rigging screw, or turnbuckle, attached to a chain plate on the deck and it is used to set up the stay to its correct tension.

Running Rigging Halyards used to hoist the sails are made of rope, flexible stainless-steel wire, or, in some boats, a flexible steel wire with a rope tail spliced to it to save the hands of the crew. The normal material used for rope halyards is pre-stressed terylene, which will not stretch under load like normal terylene or nylon rope. It is important that the luff of a sail should remain taut after it is set up and not gradually slacken. Modern practice is to lead the halyards down inside the mast, thus providing a cleaner air flow across the sail.

Sheets used to control the foot of the sail are generally made of braided terylene, or a similar material, to facilitate handling. Unlike halyards, for which the main criterion is the *strength* of the rope, sheets must be selected on the basis of strength plus ease of handling. The braided or plaited rope is much easier to grip than the hard, smooth, laid rope.

Rigging terminals: (a) traditional dead-eye, (b) galvanised steel, (c) bronze, (d) stainless steel, and (e) toggle.

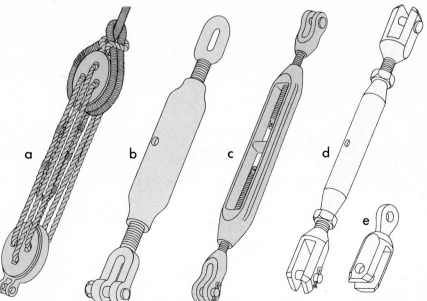

a   b   c   d   e

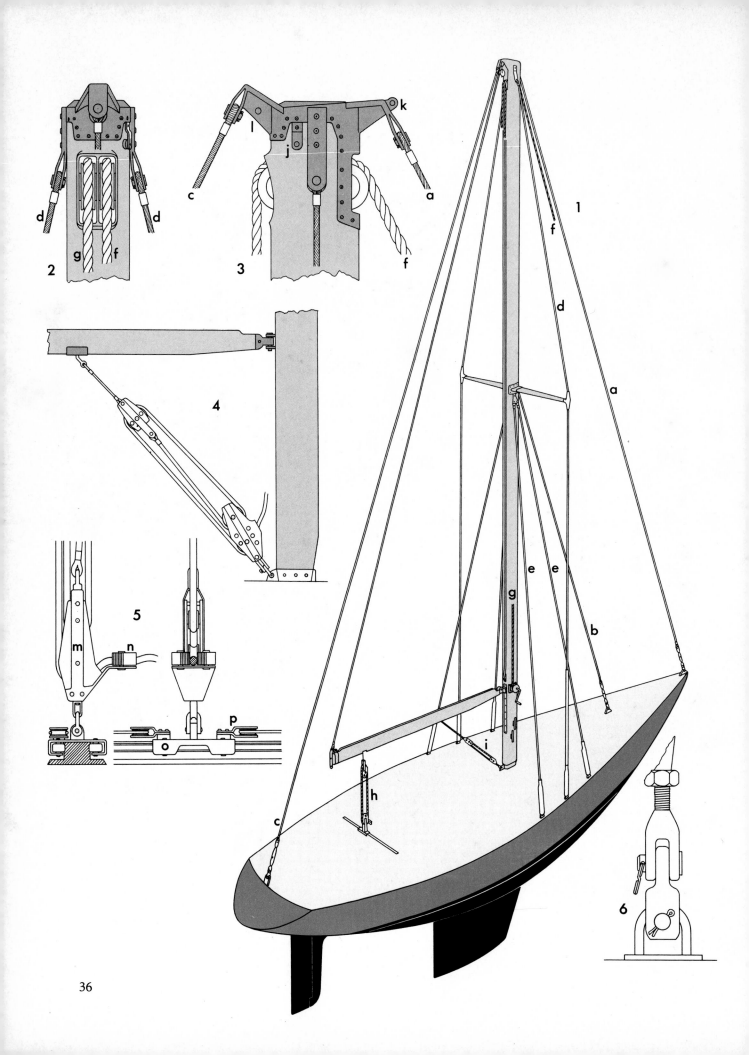

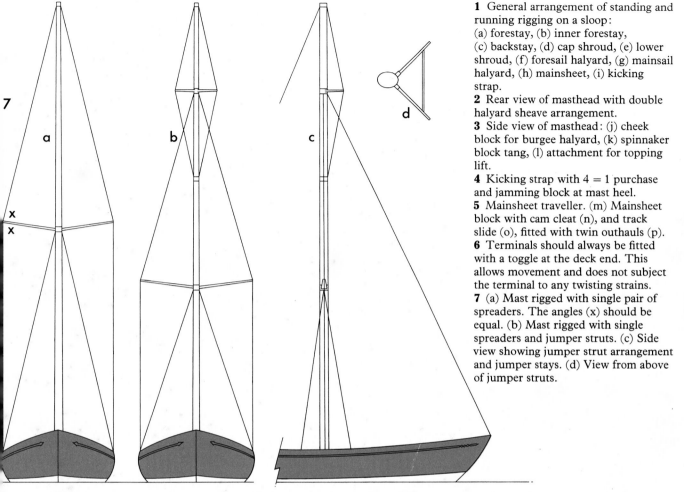

1 General arrangement of standing and running rigging on a sloop:
(a) forestay, (b) inner forestay, (c) backstay, (d) cap shroud, (e) lower shroud, (f) foresail halyard, (g) mainsail halyard, (h) mainsheet, (i) kicking strap.
2 Rear view of masthead with double halyard sheave arrangement.
3 Side view of masthead: (j) cheek block for burgee halyard, (k) spinnaker block tang, (l) attachment for topping lift.
4 Kicking strap with 4 = 1 purchase and jamming block at mast heel.
5 Mainsheet traveller. (m) Mainsheet block with cam cleat (n), and track slide (o), fitted with twin outhauls (p).
6 Terminals should always be fitted with a toggle at the deck end. This allows movement and does not subject the terminal to any twisting strains.
7 (a) Mast rigged with single pair of spreaders. The angles (x) should be equal. (b) Mast rigged with single spreaders and jumper struts. (c) Side view showing jumper strut arrangement and jumper stays. (d) View from above of jumper struts.

Rigging – General The purposes of the various parts of rigging, both standing and running, are mostly clear from the diagrams, but the functions of the less obvious ones are listed below:

Kicking strap: a strong purchase attached to the base of the mast and then to a spot on the boom between a quarter and a third of its length away from the mast. Its primary object is to keep the boom horizontal, thus keeping the sail flat and preventing the top from twisting. The tendency for the boom to lift is accentuated when running before the wind and, in the event of an umpremeditated gybe, the absence of a kicking strap would allow the boom to kick up violently and possibly cause damage to the rigging.

Boom guy: a rope attached to the outboard end of the boom, then led forward and secured. It reduces the possibility of gybing when running before the wind with the boom squared off.

Vang: a rope attached to the peak of a gaff sail to haul it to weather in order to keep the sail as flat as possible.

Topping lift: a halyard attached to the outboard end of the boom to support it when the sail is dropped.

Jumper stays: a small pair of stays fitted to the mast when the foresail is attached to the mast at a point well below the top. The stays are braced by small jumper struts which are at the level of the point of attachment of the foresail and ensure that the mast does not bend at that point. Also used on the foreside

of the mizzen mast when it is not practicable to fit a backstay.

Running backstay: with gaff rig it is usual to position the lower shrouds further aft. However, in this position they could cause severe chafe to the mainsail and the boom when running free. The end of the shroud is therefore attached to the deck by means of a strong purchase which can be slacked off on the lee side, thus allowing the boom to swing out. When changing tack the old lee shroud can then be set up tight and the other new one slacked off. Alternatively the setting up can be carried out by a device known as the Highfield lever (see illustration on page 31), which provides the necessary mechanical effort more rapidly and easily than does a purchase.

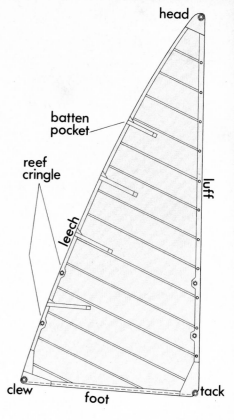

Sails

A good Bermudan rig is a very effective one, with well-designed sails working efficiently at all wind speeds and still retaining their efficiency when highly stressed under strong wind conditions. Variations in the sails' shape due to wind pressure will therefore have a disproportionate effect on performance when compared with the old-time gaff-rigged vessel with flax cotton sails. The introduction of terylene and dacron made possible a much more stable sailcloth which, unlike the old flax sailcloth, does not allow the sail to become generously curved just when sailing conditions demand that it should be as flat as possible. The next stage was the development of extremely stable, specially woven sailcloths in terylene and dacron of which 'Vectis', manufactured by Ratsey and Lapthorn of Cowes, the renowned English sailmakers, is one example.

The family cruising man may consider the design and set of sails to be rather (and literally) above his head, as it is obviously a complex subject, but the man who wishes to get the best out of his boat is strongly recommended to think about it hard and in some detail. When ordering new or replacement sails it is important to explain to the sailmaker the purpose for which the boat is to be used: cruising or racing – in order that he may decide on the most advantageous weight and cut of the sail. The sailmaker will naturally also require very

head

batten pocket

reef cringle

luff

leech

clew

foot

tack

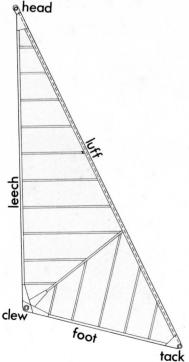

head

luff

leech

clew

foot

tack

detailed information on
dimensions of mast and boom,
apart from the actual sail size,
the desired position of reef
cringles *et al*.

Reefing A reduction of sail area
necessitated by an increase in
wind strength can be dealt with
in a number of ways, depending
on the type of boat and its gear.
In the cases of the schooner,
ketch and yawl an easy and
rapid reduction in sail area can
quickly be brought about by
simply dropping individual sails.
In the case of the sloop however
it will be necessary to reef the
mainsail and change the foresail,
or reduce the latter's area if it is
a modern furling-type foresail.
Taking the mainsail first, there
are two basic methods of
shortening sail: the old-style

Above left: The ocean racer *Red
Rock III* from Buenos Aires beats up
towards Cowes under a perfectly set
suit of sails.
Above centre: The *Minisail* planing
along with her single mainsail sleeved
onto the unstayed mast.
Above: A beautifully set spinnaker on
the ocean racing yacht *Willawaw*.

reefing points with their
modern equivalent of 'slab' or
'jiffy' reefing, and second the
roller reefing system by which
the mainsail is wound round the
boom thus reducing the area
exposed to the wind.
  When you are 'jiffy reefing',
for each reef there are two
cringles, or eyelets – one in the
luff and one in the leech of the
sail – with a row of intermediate
eyelets between the two of them.

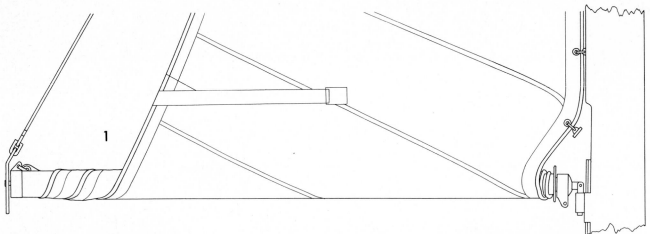

To reef the sail, the weight of the boom is taken on the topping lift, mainsheet is eased and the main halyard is lowered until the luff cringle can be either hooked to the boom end fitting or alternatively lashed to it. The reefing pendant (the line which is already rove through the leech cringle) is tightened down, thus bringing the leech cringle down to the boom where it is made fast. The main halyard is then tightened, the topping lift freed and the mainsheet hauled. A length of light line can then be passed round the boom and threaded through the intermediate eyelets to tidy up the foot of the sail. Alternatively, a length of 'shock cord' can be permanently rove through the eyelets and then pulled down on to lacing hooks fixed on alternate sides of the boom. The latter is obviously a much quicker method as it does away with having to pass a lacing line round the boom when conditions may be a little fraught.

Again, roller reefing consists of rotating the boom and winding the mainsail round it. There are three methods in general use: (a) a worm-drive mechanism on the fore-end of the boom; (b) a ratchet and pawl system and (c) 'through mast' reefing in which the reefing handle operates through the mast and on to the end of the boom. A fourth type, which the author tried out on a boat some years ago and found extremely effective, consisted of a drum on the inboard end of the boom with a small flexible-steel wire rope wound round it and its end then secured. The other end of the wire rope was shackled to a purchase which in turn was attached to the mast just below

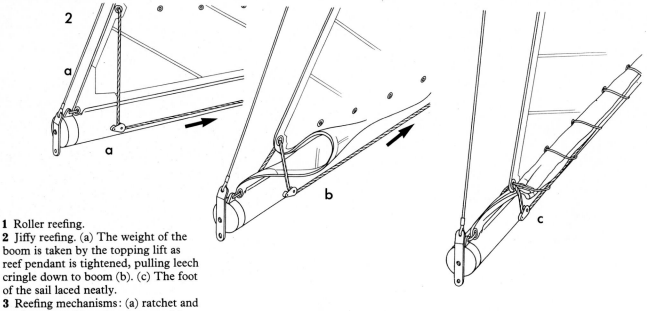

1 Roller reefing.
2 Jiffy reefing. (a) The weight of the boom is taken by the topping lift as reef pendant is tightened, pulling leech cringle down to boom (b). (c) The foot of the sail laced neatly.
3 Reefing mechanisms: (a) ratchet and pawl system, (b) enclosed worm drive system, and (c) through-the-mast system.
4 Headsail furling and reefing gear.

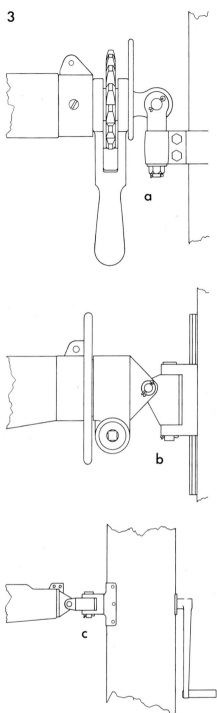

3

roller reefing system is 'boom droop'. This comes about by the increase in effective diameter of the inboard end of the boom as the luff of the sail winds round it, thus causing the outboard end to droop and, consequently, a badly-setting sail. There are two methods of overcoming this problem. The first is to fix tapered splines to the outboard end of the boom and thus increase its diameter as the leech of the sail winds round the boom; this system was understandably popular with wooden booms. The second solution, a common one with metal booms, is to form a narrow neck at the end of the boom which allows the luff rope of the sail to build up several turns before it increases the boom's diameter.

Headsails The average small family cruiser will normally change headsails to reduce the area of the foretriangle. Modern practice, however, is reviving an interest in the furling of headsails and developments in this field, based on the original Wykeham Martin roller jib, offer great relief to the short-handed family cruising man. The Wykeham Martin gear used to rely on the rotation of a steel wire rope which inevitably twisted slightly, thus producing uneven rolling. Modern practice, which utilizes a tubular component, is more effective – but is also naturally more expensive.

If the owner of the small cruiser does not think the expense of modern reefing gear is justified, he may well decide to employ the old-fashioned but well-proven method of reefing headsails by means of reef points. The procedure is similar to that employed on a mainsail, with leech and luff cringles and

a row of eyelets in between. Shortening sail is carried out in exactly the same way. This routine is worthwhile too, if you wish to make economies, but do remember to consult the sailmaker as to the suitability of the sailcloth for taking the increased loading which will be put upon it when the reefing has been carried out.

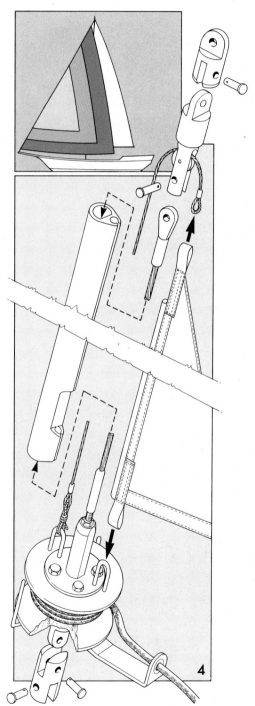

4

the cross trees. To rotate the boom it was only necessary to haul on the purchase, thus rotating the drum. It was simple, highly effective and easily made-up and fitted. It could well have originated on the old Morecambe Bay prawners on the north-west Lancashire coast of England. The major problem with any

Deck Equipment

The functions of most deck fittings are obvious and in general need little explanation. However a few comments may assist the newcomer to a better understanding of some gear and its uses.

Anchors Every cruising yacht, motor or sail, should carry two anchors: (1) a main or bower anchor of suitable weight and (2) a lighter one as a kedge anchor.

Principal types of anchors used are: the Fisherman, the Danforth and the C.Q.R. (the stockless anchor, being of little use to craft under 20–30m (60–100ft) long as it relies for its holding power largely on its weight).

There is also a new anchor, named the Bruce, which is of completely different design to those old favourites we have already mentioned. It has been developed for use in offshore oil rig applications and has a very high power/weight ratio with a very short scope capability. Although compact in design it is not particularly easy to stow on the foredeck of a small yacht but its light weight is a great advantage. Its makers claim that a 10kg (22lb) Bruce anchor has holding power equivalent to a 35–40lb plough type. In addition, they say that it can be used with much less scope than the standard 'plough' anchor. The Fisherman anchor relies mainly on its weight to penetrate the ground and consequently it has disadvantages for the smaller craft where it is necessary for an anchor to be light in weight. The digging type of anchor, e.g. the C.Q.R., once it has penetrated the ground, continues to plough its way in as the horizontal pull increases and it is thus an effective anchor for use in small craft. If the

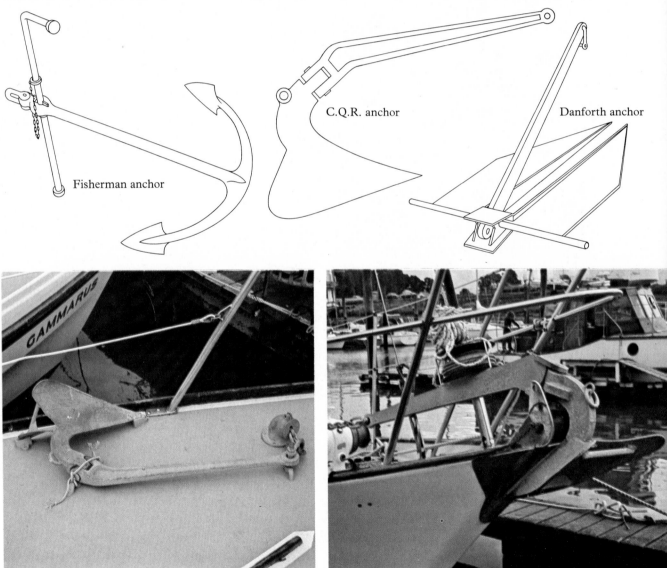

Fisherman anchor

C.Q.R. anchor

Danforth anchor

ground is very hard the C.Q.R. may have difficulty in penetrating it initially but this is a failing common to all light-weight anchors. The Danforth anchor is an effective digging anchor but it does not plough its way in as well as the C.Q.R. does. However, it has the great advantage of stowing neatly – which is very useful in small craft.

As a basic rule a vessel should carry the largest anchor it can conveniently accommodate, and when you are anchored in difficult conditions it contributes wonderfully to one's peace of

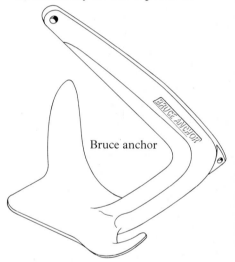

Bruce anchor

mind to know that the ground tackle is adequate! The following suggested sizes should be regarded as *minimum* ones and due allowances must always be made for the type of hull, the conditions under which the vessel may be anchored, good or bad holding ground and so on.

8m.	Fisherman	30–35 lb
(26 ft)	C.Q.R.	25–30 lb
craft	Danforth	25–30 lb
	Bruce	16 lb
10 m.	Fisherman	35–45 lb
(32 ft)	C.Q.R.	35 lb
craft	Danforth	30–35 lb
	Bruce	22 lb

Right: The upper fluke of this badly stowed Fisherman type anchor could inflict serious damage on both crew and flapping headsail alike.
Above: A Danforth anchor mounted on the foredeck of a small cruiser.
Opposite left: A C.Q.R. anchor neatly stowed on specially designed blocks screwed to the deck.
Opposite right: C.Q.R. anchor mounted in a bow sheath.

Winches These are some of the most expensive items of deck equipment and merit careful attention before purchase. The purpose of the sheet winch is to produce sufficient mechanical power to handle foresail sheets when the sails are of such a size that they can no longer be sheeted home with hand-power alone. Naturally a dinghy does not require sheet winches and moving on to, say, the small 7 m (23 ft) cruiser, the winches could be of the direct acting or ungeared type. These consist of a simple drum barrel with a winding handle; as the length of the handle is increased in relation to the diameter of the drum so the power increases. There are, however, obvious practical limitations to the length of handle that can be used.

As the size of craft, and consequently the size of its sails, get bigger, so will the power required of its winches increase. This is where geared winches enter the picture.

In a typical 8–9 m (25–30 ft) cruising yacht two-speed winches should be fitted. In this

A Lewmar self-tailing top-action sheet winch.

type of winch the rotation of the handle one way gives a direct drive, thus enabling the first few feet of the sheet to be wound in rapidly. As soon as the strain comes on, the rotation of the handle is reversed and the gearing comes into play,

Using a mainsail halyard winch.

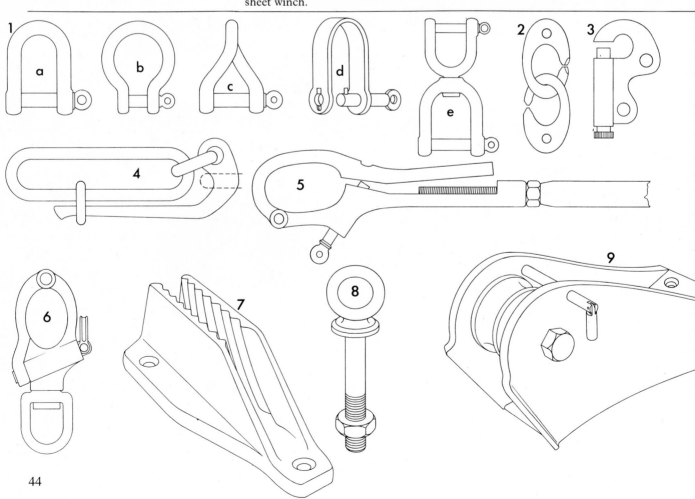

decreasing the speed of rotation of the drum but considerably increasing the power available. A typical sheet winch fitted on a boat of this size would be a 1:25, in which the power ratio on gearing would be twenty-five to one. Generally speaking geared winches are necessary to control any sail exceeding, say, 150 sq.ft (14 m²), and with a comparatively weak family crew the larger the gear ratio the better – in other words: buy the best winches you can afford! Halyard winches on the other hand do not have to deal with the greater strains of sheet winches. Smaller ungeared winches mounted on the sides of the mast can be used for this purpose.

Cleats The function of the cleat is to enable a rope to be secured quickly under strain and, equally important, to enable the rope to be freed quickly too. There are two main kinds in use: the traditional one which should always be of adequate size to permit sufficient turns to be put on for the rope to grip the cleat, and the modern type of 'jam cleat' which grips the rope as soon as the cleat is allowed to take the strain. It is essential with the latter cleat that it should be so constructed and positioned that the rope may be released immediately it becomes necessary.

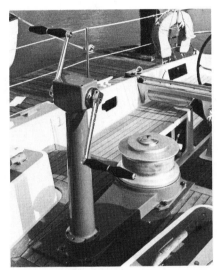

An efficient anchor windlass installed on the foredeck of a *Westerly 33*.

A Lewmar automatic three-speed 'coffee-grinder' winch.

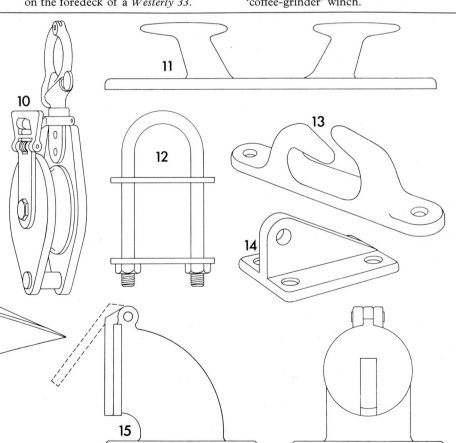

Shackles, sail hanks, rigging screws etc

1 (a) D shackle, (b) Bow shackle, (c) Twist shackle, (d) Captive-pin shackle, (e) Swivel shackle.
2 Inglefield clip
3 Piston hank.
4 Senhouse slip.
5 Adjustable pelican hook.
6 Swivel snap-shackle.
7 Jam cleat.
8 Eye bolt.
9 Stemhead fitting with double roller and drop-head pin.
10 Snatch block.
11 Bow mooring cleat.
12 Chainplate.
13 Fairlead.
14 Deck plate.
15 Chain pipe, (side and front view).

Ch.2
Principles
of Sailing

The newcomer to sailing might imagine that running before the wind, that is with the wind coming from dead astern, is both the fastest and easiest way of sailing. In point of fact neither is true. When running before the wind the boom will be squared off to present as much sail area as possible to the wind and the vessel will probably be carrying a spinnaker as well. On this point of sailing it will be obvious, bearing in mind the friction of the hull through the water, that the vessel cannot travel as fast as the wind. The wind will therefore spill from the edges of the sails, thereby causing turbulence and thus reducing their efficiency and the speed of the vessel.

The fastest point of sailing for a fore-and-aft rigged vessel is when she is reaching – when the apparent wind (the wind actually reaching the sails) is between 45° of the bow and 45° of the stern. When reaching the apparent wind passes from the leading edge of the sail, across its surface and leaves at the leech with minimum turbulence. The wind on the leeward side of the sail has to travel farther than that on the weather side and therefore increases its speed, thus reducing its pressure and causing a vacuum effect on the lee side. The result of the vacuum is to suck the sail forward, thus moving the boat against the wind. This is an over-simplification of the subject but illustrates the principle of

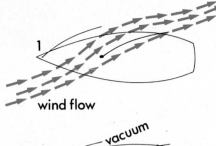

wind flow

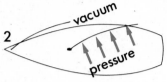

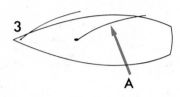

vacuum

pressure

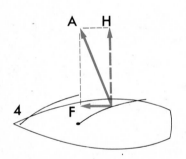

A

A   H

F

3 Vacuum and pressure vectors (forces) reduced to one force A at right angles to the centre of the sail.
4 Force A resolved into two forces; H – the heeling force, and F – the driving force, – thus moving the boat forward.

the sail's driving force. The following diagrams illustrate how this force can be reduced to a simple parallelogram of forces.

You will see that the small forces, acting over the whole surface of the sail, can be reduced to one force acting at the centre of effort of the sail. This central effort is then resolved into the two main forces: the heeling force, causing the boat to heel and make leeway, and the smaller component which is the driving force moving the boat forward.

The foresail, in addition to producing its own driving power, combines with the mainsail to form a 'slot' which materially increases the wind speed on the lee side of the mainsail. This is known as the venturi effect and, with the two sails properly sheeted, produces a substantially greater driving force than the simple sum of the two individual sails.

The necessity for reducing turbulence around the sails becomes more obvious when you consider the manner in which the sail works. The importance of a taut luff – the leading edge of the sail – need not, therefore, be emphasized. A

very slack luff gives a concertina-like appearance to the sail which will break up the smooth air flow across its surface and thereby materially reduce its driving power. It is equally important to set up the luff of the mainsail tightly, although it does not have such a good 'entry' into the air stream due to the presence of the mast on its leading edge. Incidentally, one of the reasons for the use of internal halyards within the mast is to reduce turbulence at this point.

The average sailing man is unlikely to wish to pursue the theoretical aspects of sail design but he will be more concerned with the practical matters of sail setting and trimming.

Sail Trimming

Reaching The fundamental necessity for taut luffs has already been explained and we can now assume that the main and foresail have been correctly set up and that the vessel is reaching to windward, that is with wind coming from slightly for'ard of the beam.

The basic rule for sail

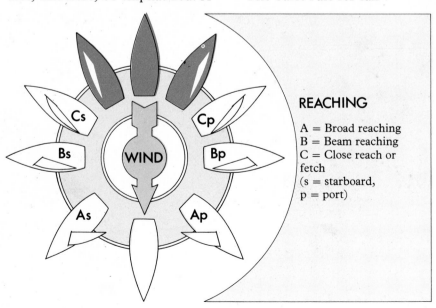

REACHING

A = Broad reaching
B = Beam reaching
C = Close reach or fetch
(s = starboard, p = port)

trimming is 'watch the luff'. If the foresail sheet is slacked away a stage is reached when the luff starts to flutter. This is the point when the driving power of the sail falls off considerably. If the sheet is now tightened the flutter will stop and the sail is again drawing well. It is just after the point at which the flutter ceases that the sail is operating efficiently. If the sheet is hardened in too much, then power is lost again. As a general rule the inexperienced helmsman usually has sheets hardened in too much, rather than having them too slack. Modern sailing practice has introduced wool or nylon tufts or ribbons in the luffs of sails to indicate when the sail is 'drawing' correctly. In the case of the foresail there will probably be three tufts about one tenth of the width of the sail back from the luff and disposed vertically in the lower part of the sail. These tufts pass through the sail with an equal length of say 9 inches hanging on each side. Due to their lightness the tufts indicate perfectly the direction of air flow across the surface of the sail, and if the sail is setting

correctly the tufts will stream out horizontally. However, if the sail is incorrectly adjusted turbulence will occur and then the tufts will start to flick around in all directions, indicating the broken air flow. Disturbance normally starts on the leeward side of the luff and therefore the leeward tufts are the most important ones to watch, although from the helmsman's angle of view they may not be too easily visible. Let us now assume that the foresail is drawing well and both the windward and leeward tufts are flowing back smoothly and horizontally – indicating a clean air-flow over the sail. Then a slight wind shift occurs and the windward tufts start to flutter – indicating that the wind has drawn ahead slightly. The angle of the apparent wind to the sail is now too slight and the sheet requires tightening in, or the boat paid off to leeward a little to increase the wind angle. If, on the other hand, the leeward tufts start to flutter first it indicates that the angle to the apparent wind is too great and either the sheet can be eased or the vessel pointed higher into the wind.

In the case of the mainsail the bulk of the mast forward of the luff inevitably produces turbulence close to the luff, even on a perfect point of sailing. For this reason the tufts should be positioned rather farther aft, say, one third of the width of the sail; the leeward tufts will probably give a more immediate indication of incorrect air flow than the windward ones.

Beating to windward
Close-hauled windward sailing is probably one of the most searching tests of a helmsman's ability to get the best out of his boat and undoubtedly calls for more skill than a broad reach – 'the soldiers' wind'. However, if the basic rule of 'watch the luff' is borne in mind, the newcomer will soon develop the 'feel' which is necessary to get the best out of his boat. Beating to windward requires the course 'made good' to be directly into the wind. Therefore alternate tacks must be made at equal angles to the wind. In these circumstances each tack must be made as close to the wind as possible consistent with sailing fast and it will be found that the boat with well-trimmed sails and a watchful helmsman will prove her worth over the carelessly-sailed boat.

When starting to beat to windward the sheets will be hauled in until the sails are in the close-hauled position: that is to say 10°–12° from the centre line of the boat (the mainsheet traveller, if one is fitted, will have been hauled up to weather). The vessel will then be turned up towards the wind (luffed up) until the luff of the mainsail begins to quiver or the tufts indicate unstable air flow. The vessel is then 'paid off' – that is she bears away from the wind – until the fluttering ceases

BEATING

D = Close-hauled or beating
E = In 'irons', in the eye of the wind. When tacking it is necessary to go through the eye of the wind, e.g. from Ds to Dp or vice versa.
(s = starboard,
p = port).

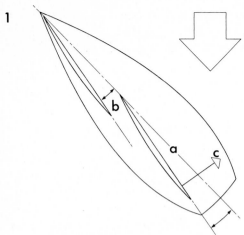

1 Close-hauled sail trim. (a) Centre line of boat, (b) sails trimmed at 10 degrees to centre-line, and (c) mainsheet traveller hauled to windward.

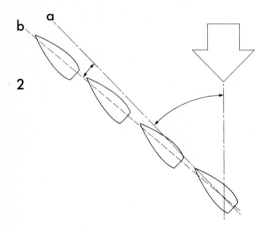

2 The effect of leeway on a course: (a) course steered at 45 degrees off the wind, (b) actual course made good with 5 degrees of leeway.

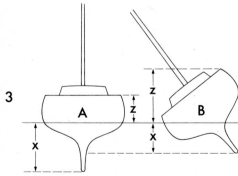

3 The effect of heeling on leeway. Boat A sailing upright gives the maximum resistance to leeway, (x), and the least windage, (z). Boat B by heeling gives the least lateral resistance to leeway, (x), but increases the amount of windage, (z).

and the sails are drawing fully again. This will be the best point of sailing and will indicate how well the boat 'points', i.e. how close to the wind she will sail and maintain optimum speed. Normally this will be in the region of 30° to the apparent wind but the angle to the true wind will be of the order of 45° in the case of the average family sailing cruiser. When working to windward, however, the actual track angle will be over 45° as the leeway angle must be added to the tacking angle. Thus the track angle, or the angle actually made good, will probably be more in the region of 47° to 50°. . . .

Reverting to the parallelogram of forces (fig. 4), you will note that the force pushing the boat to leeward is much greater than the component driving it forward and, therefore, it is important to consider how best to overcome this sideways or adverse force. The hull profile obviously has a large bearing on the problem for the greater the windage on the hull, the larger is the force driving it to leeward. If the major portion of the hull is below the water then the windage is less and, therefore, the sideways thrust is also reduced. Nevertheless, the deeper hull has a greater 'wetted surface' with a consequent increase in friction and it therefore requires more power to drive it through the water. As with so many problems in life the solution is one of compromise – either in hull design or the type of hull, i.e. a dropped keel or centre plate. A further point to consider in this connection is angle of heel. If the boat stays absolutely upright in the water it will be apparent that its underwater profile offers maximum opposition to

sideways thrust. Assuming now that the boat heels to an angle of 45°, the projected image of the profile will be reduced and it will therefore present less resistance to the sideways thrust, with a corresponding increase in leeway. For this reason the aim should always be to sail the boat as near to the vertical plane as possible – which is comparatively easy to achieve in a small dinghy or day boat where the crew act as mobile ballast.

To sum up, the good helmsman, beating to windward, will concentrate on being as one with his boat. He will develop a *rapport* that will tell him when to luff up and so make that little extra ground to windward in the puffs, or, conversely, when to pay off a little when there is a temporary wind shift. He will watch the luffs of the sails (or the tufts) and will ensure that the sail is kept flat by tightening down on the kicking strap (see page 36) as wind strength increases.

Running With a boat running before the wind a completely different set of conditions arise. The boat no longer heels and the apparent wind speed is considerably less as boat and wind are travelling in the same direction. For this reason a greater area of sail can be carried than when beating to windward in the same force wind. The increased sail area normally takes the form of the spinnaker, that large balloon-shaped sail which has so much driving power in the right conditions, and looks so impressive, when it is doing its job properly.

Imagine now that the boat is on a broad reach and a course alteration is planned which will bring the wind right astern. The main and foresail sheets are

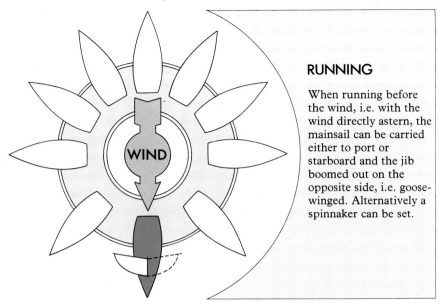

RUNNING

When running before the wind, i.e. with the wind directly astern, the mainsail can be carried either to port or starboard and the jib boomed out on the opposite side, i.e. goose-winged. Alternatively a spinnaker can be set.

eased away, the helm is brought up and the boat moves off the wind bringing the wind round on to her stern. Sheets are trimmed, squaring off the sails to catch the maximum amount of wind and . . . it then becomes obvious that the driving power of the foresail is considerably reduced as it is now blanketed by the main. Taking the mainsail first, the kicking strap should be 'bowsed down', or tightened, to flatten the sail as much as possible and reduce the 'twist' which will occur between the head and the foot. In the case of cruising yachts which may be on a running course for some considerable time, the boom guy should be set up to steady the boom. The guy should be attached to the outboard end of the boom (this should preferably be done before squaring off), led forward and secured. At this stage let us think about one of the problems of running which beset the helmsman and which may prove disconcerting to the newcomer.

With the wind light and steady the hull is driven smoothly, and little, if any, heeling is experienced. But as the wind increases in force the boat starts to show a tendency to roll from side to side and the helmsman's natural efforts to counteract the motion may only accentuate it. Unless this rolling is decreased the vessel may eventually broach to, that is swing broadside on to the wind and sea, and thus risk capsizing. Sail must be reduced. If a spinnaker is being carried it should be taken in and, if the vessel is still overpressed, the main must be reefed. The possible dangers associated with an unpremeditated gybe in these conditions are dealt with under 'Tacking and Gybing'.

Let us now see what the sail drill is on a small family cruiser which does not carry a spinnaker and which is starting a long run down wind. The foresail will be blanketed by the main and will be doing very little. If, however, the foresail sheet is hauled to the weather side the foresail can be made to draw on the opposite side to the main, and, being in reasonably clear air, will do some useful work. This operation is known as 'goose-winging' and, if a boom or 'whisker' pole is fitted to the clew of the sail and the other end secured inboard at the mast,

a stable balance can be achieved. An alternative, which may be tried on a long run before the wind, is the use of twin headsails, instead of main and one headsail, in the manner favoured by Trade Wind sailors. If twin forestays are fitted it is a simple matter to hoist one foresail on each stay and boom them out, one on either side. More likely in the type of craft we are considering only one forestay will be fitted but the same method can be used, albeit in a slightly cumbersome way. The foresails are hanked alternately onto the single stay and both sails are then hauled up together. The result is a pair of 'twins' which will pull well and at the same time reduce the tendency to roll.

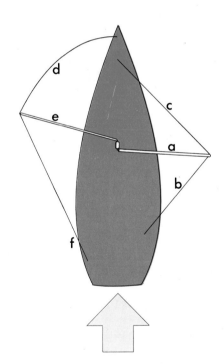

Above: Running goose-winged before the wind: (a) main boom out to starboard, (b) mainsheet fully out and the kicking strap bowsed down tightly, (c) boom foreguy, (d) foresail boomed out to port on whisker pole, (e). The foresail sheet can be led right aft for running, (f).

Getting under way under sail

This is a good point at which to discuss the use of the outboard or auxiliary engine which many newcomers will regard as essential for leaving and picking-up moorings or for anchoring. In crowded moorings or anchorages it would be foolhardy for the inexperienced owner to leave and pick up moorings under sail alone; a sudden shift of wind, before the boat has picked up sufficient speed to be manoeuvrable, can lead to a difficult situation. However, if there is sufficient room available to make the operation possible then every opportunity should be taken to try it – but with the auxiliary ticking over and ready for action if necessary. Now that auxiliaries are universal in small cruising boats many otherwise experienced people never attempt this operation, forgetting that one day an auxiliary may fail at the critical moment and difficult

manoeuvres may then have to be carried out under sail. If the operation has been successfully attempted before under varying conditions of wind and tide, a degree of confidence will have been built up that will enable the emergency to be dealt with instead of it developing into a last minute panic. Imagine the boat lying to her mooring, pointing into the tide with a light breeze blowing on the beam. The first step is to ensure that the vessel, in the time-honoured Naval phrase 'being in all respects ready for sea', is properly prepared. The dinghy should be well secured astern or to the buoy if it is being left on the mooring and any loose equipment on deck, such as boat-hooks, must also be properly secured. It is equally important to ensure that equipment and articles below decks are also adequately stowed and secured. This may sound very obvious but it is easily overlooked and a

devastating clatter from below decks is a little disconcerting in the middle of a critical tack. It is wise to develop a standard drill before sailing, both above and below decks.

The first decision to be made is which sail to hoist first. The first consideration is the direction and strength of the wind in relation to the way the vessel is pointing. Assuming that the breeze is light and coming on to the beam, either the main or foresail can be hoisted but in general it is preferable to hoist the main, if this is practicable, as it leaves the foredeck clear for dropping the buoy or recovering the anchor. Having decided that the main can be used it should be hoisted with the sheet freed and the topping lift supporting the boom. The sail will then fill and blow out to leeward, thus spilling the wind, whilst at the same time the boat will tend to turn up into the wind, spilling further wind. When the mooring is ready to be dropped

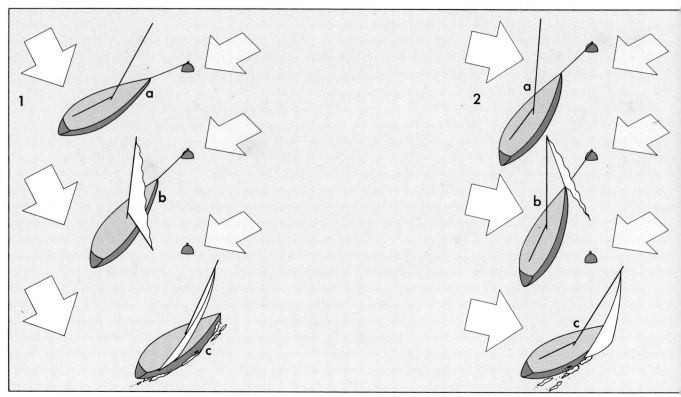

the foredeck crewman can slack away on the topping lift, the main sheet can be hauled in and the mooring dropped as the vessel gathers way ahead. Assuming there is a clear run ahead, the foresail can now be set and with it pulling well the boat is under complete control. Alternatively, the foresail can be left until the moorings are cleared when the boat can be rounded up into the wind and the sail set at leisure.

If the wind is coming from astern of the beam the picture is a little different, however, as it will be apparent that, no matter how much the mainsheet is slacked away, the mainsail will invariably fill with wind whilst it is being hoisted and cause the boat to sheer about on the mooring. In addition the sail would be pressed against the shrouds and the head of the sail, and possibly the battens, would jam under the cross trees. In this situation the foresail can be set up with sheets free and then

sheeted in when the helmsman is ready, the buoy being dropped as steerage way is picked up. The boat is then sailed on until a convenient place is reached to luff up into the wind and set the main. Incidentally, with a new boat it is worth finding out as soon as possible how she handles under either main or foresail alone. Most boats will tack to windward, albeit rather slowly, under either, but some may be rather unhandy under foresail alone. Reverting to the question of which sail to hoist first, the salient point to remember is that the foresail can be hoisted (with sheets freed) whatever the wind direction, whereas the main can only be hoisted, in safety, with the wind forward of the beam. Ideally the boat should point up into the wind to hoist any sail but this is not always possible in tidal waters and this fact must be accepted. With wind and tide together this situation will obtain and then both main and foresail can be set up easily

before the mooring is dropped. It is important to stress, however, that if the moorings are close together and some tight turns are necessary to clear them then sails should not be set until the vessel has reasonable manoeuvring space.

Now let us examine getting under way with the vessel at anchor. The general comments above regarding sailing from a mooring apply, but with two differences. Firstly, if it is at all possible, avoid hoisting the foresail, as the crewman recovering the anchor requires adequate space to work in without a foresail flapping round his ears, and when the anchor is recovered it will probably bring with it some mud onto the foredeck. If this happens and some of it gets onto the foresail it usually turns out to have some peculiar staining properties. The second point to remember is that, instead of dropping a mooring, one has to move the vessel up to the

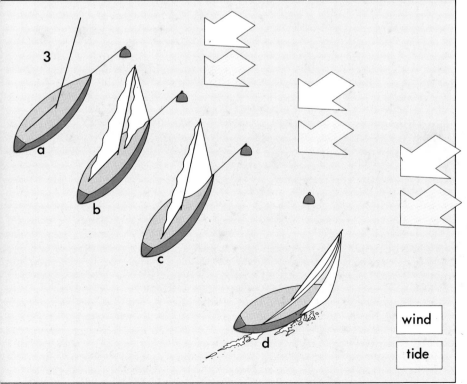

1 Leaving a mooring under mainsail only.
(a) Boat lying head to tide with a light breeze on the beam. (b) Mainsail hoisted with the mainsheet free. (c) As the mooring is dropped the mainsheet is hardened in, the sail draws and the boat makes headway.
2 Leaving a mooring under headsail only.
(a) Boat lying head to tide with a light breeze just abaft the beam. (b) The foresail is hoisted with the sheets free. (c) The foresail sheet is hardened in and as the boat draws forward the mooring can be dropped.
3 Leaving a mooring with both main and headsail set.
(a) Boat lying head to wind and tide. (b) Mainsail and foresail can both be hoisted with all sheets free. (c) The foresail sheet is hardened in to the windward side of mast, backing the jib: the boat's head pays off to leeward. (d) The mooring line is dropped, the mainsheet hardened in as the jib sheet is freed and hardened in to leeward.

The end of a perfect day's sailing with the boat snugly moored in a peaceful anchorage.

anchor. If the boat is heavy and the tide is strong the foredeck crewman will not be able to haul in the anchor cable without assistance, i.e. power to move the boat forward, either by sailing it forward or by using the auxiliary. Unless the wind is from dead ahead it should be possible to sail up to the anchor to enable it to be broken out. If the wind *is* dead ahead then tacking up to the anchor is the only solution. This is not recommended for the novice

to tackle as it requires considerable judgement or else the foredeck crewman is faced with a very difficult task which should not be attempted, unless it is really essential.

Picking up moorings
One of the satisfying moments in sailing comes when, after a pleasant day's sail, one approaches one's mooring and quietly, without any fuss, stop with the stem just nudging the mooring buoy, pick up the buoy

direction of the element having the strongest effect upon them. As in many situations, however, the picture is seldom clear cut – with a strong tide and wind the boats will probably be pointing somewhere halfway between wind and tide. Whilst this may sound somewhat complicated it is in fact quite simple to appraise the position rapidly and take the necessary action. It is worth mentioning that the most common mistake, and a very understandable one, is to attempt to carry out manoeuvres with too little sail rather than too much. If the boat has a reasonable sail area set and is obviously not over-pressed, then the helmsman will have effective control and if, perchance, the mooring is missed he can sail on, round up and have another try. If insufficient sail is being carried there is always the danger of the helmsman losing control if the buoy is missed, or, even worse, on the run up to the buoy. When this happens it may take some little while to set more sail and pick up speed again and in the meantime you may have drifted into a difficult situation and possibly fouled another boat. The important thing to remember is to maintain manoeuvrability. Some boats manoeuvre well under main alone, and some under foresail alone, but in general (and in light airs anyway) when in doubt carry both sails until the last possible moment. Assume now that the actual mooring operation will be wind against tide and it is known that the boat will be tide rode, i.e. she will point up into the tide when moored. The classical approach in these conditions is to get up-wind of the buoy, drop the main and run back under foresail alone, free foresail sheets by the buoy and pick up the

rope and secure the ship. Naturally it takes much practice to achieve perfection and conditions are rarely alike on two consecutive occasions. The first and more important lesson to remember is that a boat under sail has no brakes, but the wind and tide used properly are a very effective way of stopping a vessel. When entering the moorings under sail it is of paramount importance to visualize the stages involved, including the all-important final

one when the vessel has to be stopped and the mooring picked up. It is obvious that the vessel must arrive at the buoy heading into the tide (or if the effect of the wind is stronger, then heading into the wind), in order to halt her at the right moment. Judging the relative strength of wind and tide is comparatively easy if the helmsman looks closely at comparable craft to his own lying on the moorings. The moored boats (of similar type) will be pointing in the

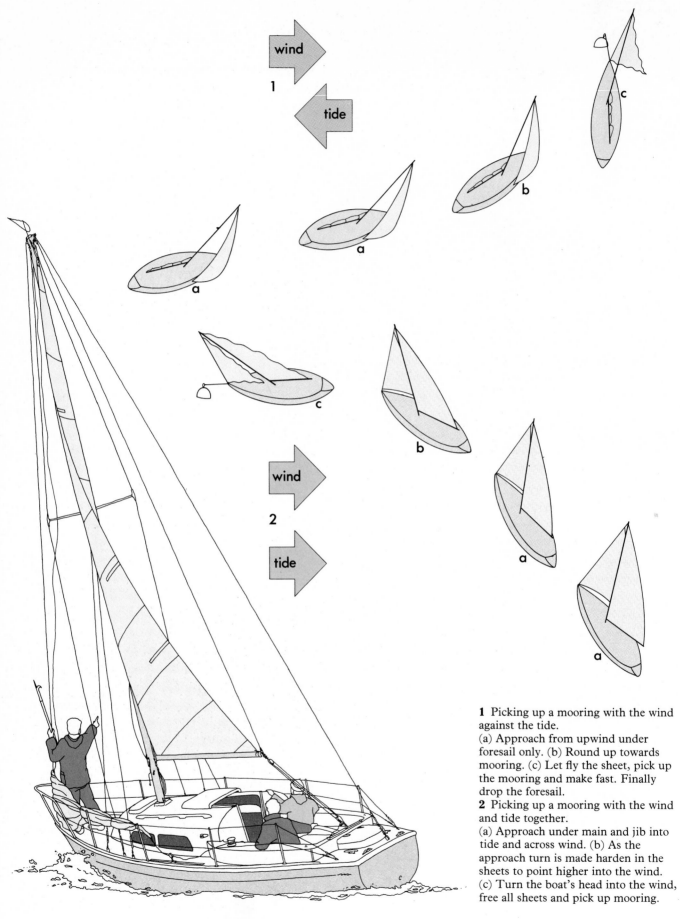

1 Picking up a mooring with the wind against the tide.
(a) Approach from upwind under foresail only. (b) Round up towards mooring. (c) Let fly the sheet, pick up the mooring and make fast. Finally drop the foresail.
2 Picking up a mooring with the wind and tide together.
(a) Approach under main and jib into tide and across wind. (b) As the approach turn is made harden in the sheets to point higher into the wind. (c) Turn the boat's head into the wind, free all sheets and pick up mooring.

56

mooring, dropping the jib at leisure. If the mooring is missed sheet in the foresail, turn round, run downwind, set the main at a convenient position and tack back for another attempt. It will be appreciated that, with wind against tide, the wind will be blowing from astern when you arrive at the buoy and the mainsail will therefore be difficult to drop, and will probably cause the vessel to sheer about unduly. The mainsail must therefore be dropped at a convenient point on the approach when the vessel can quickly be rounded up into the wind. The foresail can be left drawing until near the buoy and the sheet let fly when you reckon that the vessel is carrying sufficient way to reach the buoy. The foresail is thus readily available if the operation has been slightly misjudged and more power is required at the last moment. If the helmsman is really confident he can order the foresail to be dropped before reaching the buoy. On the other hand, if it is known that the wind and tide will be together then, with an approach against both of them, the main and foresail can both be carried up to the last moment when the buoy is picked up. When the mooring has been picked up both sails will lie quietly until they can be dropped and will not cause the boat to sheer about. With a short-handed family crew the aim should always be for a properly controlled approach to the buoy, with an adequate amount of sail set, in order to give everyone on board plenty of time to think out their next move and anticipate possible difficulties.

There will be occasions when the wind is abeam or from astern at the mooring buoy but,

for various reasons, the helmsman would prefer to arrive under main only with the foresail out of the way. In the old days, when gaff rig was common and auxiliaries were rare, one would often see an approach to a mooring or quayside under a 'scandalized' main. The peak of the main was lowered (after the topping lift had been set up) with the result that the sail lost most of its driving power – in fact the drive of the main could be adjusted by the amount the peak was dropped as the quayside was approached. Although it is not often seen today the same basic technique may be used with a Bermudan sail. Imagine that the vessel is approaching the mooring with the wind aft and you wish to reduce speed. Round up into the wind and drop foresail, take the weight of the boom on the topping lift, then slack away the peak until it has dropped by, say, one-third. The foot of the sail is quickly bundled up with tiers or shock cord thus leaving a much smaller mainsail with a slack luff and consequently little driving power. This method

Scandalised mainsail on a Bermudan sloop.

is simple and effective. It can be used in many situations with advantage, for example when picking up the mooring or dropping the anchor it is the work of a moment to drop the peak and 'kill' the sail completely. From the single-hander's point of view it can be particularly useful for, as he moves forward to pick up the mooring or drop the anchor, he only has to cast off the peak halyard from its cleat in passing.

When you are learning to handle your boat one of the important things to discover quickly is how long it will carry its way through the water when the driving power has been removed? A light shallow draft craft will stop very quickly indeed whilst the heavy displacement vessel with fine lines will carry way in calm conditions for several boat's lengths. Every opportunity should be taken to learn the characteristics and limitations of your craft under varying conditions as soon as you can. It is not necessary to carry out these experiments for the first time in crowded moorings. A quiet part of the harbour or estuary should be chosen where a small anchor, with a fender as its buoy, can be dropped and then practice runs may be made up to the fender from all angles – the seamanship that will be learnt in an afternoon of practice in this way is quite surprising! Lastly, when you are sailing in restricted waters always be thinking ahead. If the buoy is missed for example, what is the escape route . . .? Sailing up to a particular spot to anchor requires the same fundamental approach as does sailing up to a mooring but there are a few differences. These are dealt with in the chapter on Seamanship (see page 62).

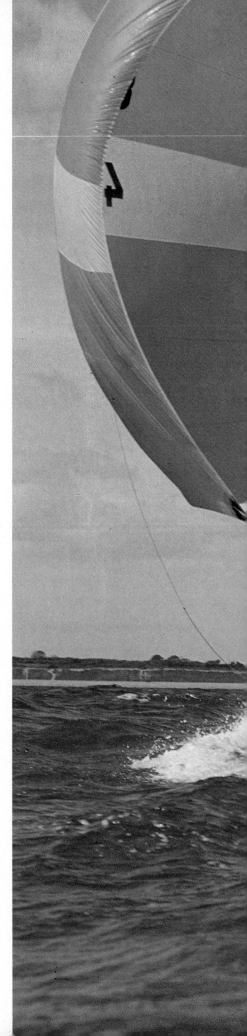

Right: The International *Dragon* Class. Designed in 1929 by the Norwegian Johan Anker as a fast two-man, one-design racing cruiser with a fixed keel. Her beautiful lines and superb performance have made her exceptionally popular and in 1948 she was accepted as an Olympic Class. She remained so until 1972 when her place was taken by the three-man keelboat *Soling* class. She is seen here competing in the 1974 European Cup.

Elementary Principles of Racing Some beginners are understandably a little reluctant to involve themselves in the racing scene, unless of course they have been specifically drawn to sailing by its attractions. It may appear to uninformed spectators to be a hurly-burly of cut-and-thrust with no quarter given – an exciting and rather professional affair – and it is this impression which induces their diffidence. Once you are attracted to it and, have decided to give it a try, the first hurdle to be overcome is the rule book – the International Yacht Racing Union Rules, an impressive document which may well daunt the novice with its apparently complicated rules. There are, however, a few basic ones which are easily understood and these will enable the newcomer to participate and learn the game without incurring the wrath of the fleet. Once the basic 'seamanship' rules have been applied in practice and some experience has been built up,

the 'tactical' rules will soon begin to fall into place and, slowly but surely, a climb into the placings begins. It is not necessary to give the complete racing rules here – there are many excellent books which do this in great detail – but a short summary of the basic seamanship rules will enable the beginner to get started. Incidentally it will be seen that the rules in open water, i.e. away from marks or obstructions, comply with the International Regulations for Preventing Collisions at Sea (known everywhere as the Collision Regulations), with the exception of the overtaking rule (no. 36).

Basic Racing Rules

1. A boat must not touch another boat or a mark (Rules 51 and 57).
2. Boats on opposite tacks: port boat gives way (Rule 36).
3. When two boats are on the same tack the windward boat shall keep clear (Rule 37).
4. When two boats are on the same tack the overtaking boat

must keep clear (Rule 37), but if the overtaking boat is starboard tack and the 'ahead' boat is port tack then the port tack must give way (Rule 36).

5. Before reaching a mark or obstruction an inside overlapping boat can ask for room. This does not apply on the starting line (Rules 40 and 42).

6. In open water a boat overtaking to windward can be luffed (Rule 38).

While this brief summary does not represent anything like the whole corpus – there are 78 rules in all – it will enable the novice to make a start in racing and avoid him spoiling a race for more knowledgeable entrants.

Racing may be broadly divided into two classes: class racing and handicap racing. The former normally applies to the smaller types of boats in which each one is identical in design and construction, the boats competing together around a course and the first boat home obviously being the winner. This type of racing has many attractions, not the least of which is that the expenditure is reasonably foreseeable (apart from such disasters as blowing out a spinnaker of course) and added to this, a properly maintained boat should have a long racing career. However, if a variety of yachts of different sizes are to race successfully against each other, there must obviously be a soundly-based handicapping system which may be seen by all to be fair in its application. To the average cruising man the system that is of most interest is the Portsmouth Yardstick Scheme. The normal yacht club – which consists largely of cruising yachts of great variety of type and size – would find it very difficult to arrange any racing

events at all without the use of the 'Portsmouth Yardsticks', unless of course it was prepared to go to considerable trouble to devise a handicapping system of its own.

The Portsmouth Yardstick Scheme is an internationally recognized scheme for handicapping yachts of different sizes and capabilities and in the United Kingdom it is administered by the Royal Yachting Association. The measure of performance of a yacht is defined as the time it takes to sail over a common but unspecified distance. For example, two yachts rated at 100 and 120 would take 100 and 120 minutes respectively to cover the same ground, in the same race. On another day and under different conditions the distance covered in the rated times might be very different but the ratio between the two boats would remain the same. Yardstick numbers are divided into four groups – briefly:

a. 'Yardstick Numbers' are Portsmouth numbers of one design or standard production cruisers which clubs and the R.Y.A. agree should serve as a basis for rating other yachts of

dissimilar characteristics.

b. 'Primary Yardstick Numbers' are numbers agreed by many clubs as a result of racing experience.

c. 'Secondary Yardstick Numbers' are not as well proven as 'Primary Yardsticks' but are in fact in process of being built up.

d. 'Provisional Portsmouth Numbers' are based on very limited information. They are usually used as trial ratings until the club handicapper has built up sufficient information, based on firm results, to report his conclusions to the R.Y.A. Naturally these Numbers should not be used as a basis for rating other yachts.

The system depends for its success on club secretaries returning information to the R.Y.A. (or its equivalent body outside the United Kingdom) at the end of each racing season, in order that fresh Yardsticks may be built up and the old ones modified if necessary. All the same this system, useful though it is for club cruiser races which after all constitute a major part of the sailing scene, is not precise enough for the dedicated

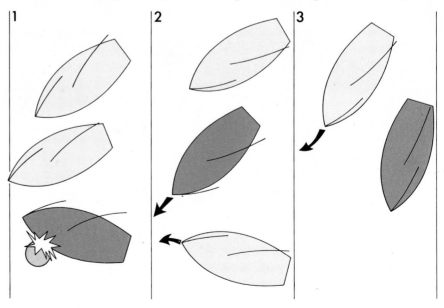

off-shore racing man. The International Offshore Rule (I.O.R. Mark III), produced as a result of international discussions, enables the rating and hence the handicap, of any particular yacht to be measured and calculated. It also gives the yacht designer scope for pitting his design ability against the rating rule. Thus from the family cruising man's point of view the I.O.R. Rating rule is of somewhat academic interest and is not likely to affect his very pleasant, enjoyable and hard-fought club cruiser races.

The skipper who has fallen for the attractions of racing and who has decided to try his luck must start his preparations well before the race if he wishes to acquit himself well. We may assume that his craft is in good trim and prepared for racing, and thus the first step is to study the sailing instructions carefully and to make sure that the course is thoroughly understood, in particular the sides on which marks should be passed and the positions of the starting and finishing lines – with their transits. If it appears at all complicated he should make a copy plan of the course

and keep it in a transparent plastic envelope for quick reference during the event. (This suggestion is sparked by the optimistic assumption that the vessel will, at some time, be leading the fleet!) Always get to the starting line in plenty of time to enable some practice starts to be tried and to find out which end of the line offers the most favourable conditions, bearing in mind the position of the first mark out on the course. It is particularly important to cross the line on the starboard tack to ensure right of way in close quarter situations.

Starting signals are clear and ensure adequate notice of the beginning of the race. At precisely ten minutes before the start the appropriate code flag of the class which is racing will be hoisted, and an audible signal will be sounded. At five minutes before the 'off' the Blue Peter will be hoisted up and an audible signal sounded. At this point all entrants come under starter's orders and are subject to the racing rules. If it is a cruiser race it is possible that late arrivals may have been using their auxiliaries to manoeuvre. This must stop

immediately the five minute gun is sounded or preferably before. The start is signalled by dropping both flags together, with an audible signal. The dropping of the flags is the true start signal while the audible signal is merely to call attention to the flags being dropped. Having crossed the line remember that it is important to sail in clear air as much as possible – sailing in the wind shadow of other boats inevitably slows you down, and in this position it is worthwhile sacrificing time by putting in a tack to get into clear air. Also, when you are approaching the first mark there will be a concentration of boats in a small area, so do not forget the advantage of the starboard tack and the inside position for rounding it. Remember that races are won by boats sailing the course in the shortest time – which may not necessarily mean sailing the shortest distance! Concentration and anticipation are the keynotes of successful racing and can place a good helmsman ahead of the field even if his boat is marginally slower. . . .

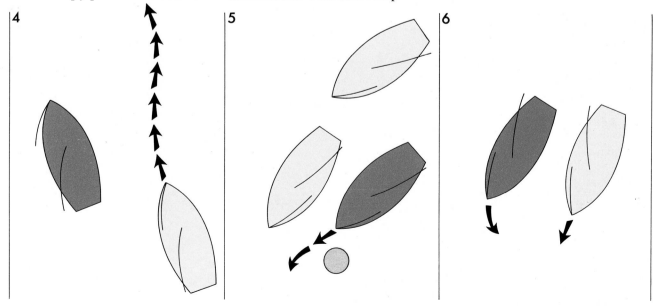

Ch.3 Seamanship Pt.1

Cadets manning the bowsprit on the 1,727 ton German Sail Training ship *Gorch Foch*.

Ropes

Coiling and handling One of the ways in which an experienced seaman may be spotted is by how he picks up, coils and secures a rope. This may sound an exaggeration but it is important to develop a professional approach to rope handling. Securing a rope may look easy – and it is, but it is equally important that you should be able to release it just as quickly. There are certain simple rules which should be followed to ensure that a rope will always handle properly. New rope may occasionally have a tendency to kink, although this is not so noticeable with modern synthetic ropes as it was with natural-fibre cordage, such as hemp and manila. Natural-fibre ropes are rarely used in yachts today and thus there is no reason to examine their various characteristics here. The main types of synthetic rope of use to yachtsmen are: terylene or dacron, nylon, polythene and polypropolene. Terylene or dacron line is considerably stronger than the natural-fibre equivalent, it has great resistance to wear and, if properly looked after, it has a much longer life. Terylene can be obtained in two stranded forms: normal and prestretched – the latter must be used for halyards where it is essential that no stretch occurs once the hoist has been set up. Plaited terylene may be obtained which looks and feels like a cotton rope and it is consequently easy on the hands when used for sheets. Nylon rope is immensely strong but it also has great elasticity and thus it is not used for sheets or halyards, but this property is invaluable in applications where it is necessary to absorb shock loads – for example, an anchor

1

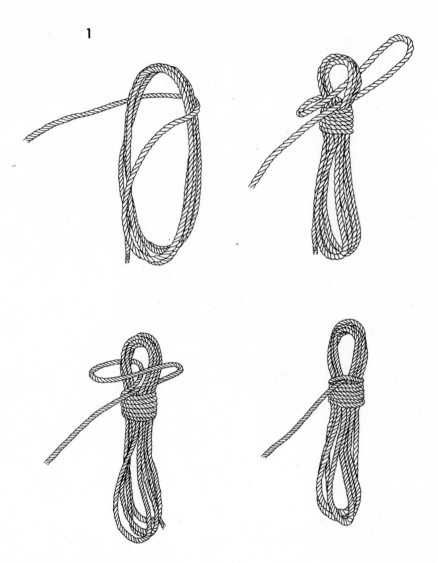

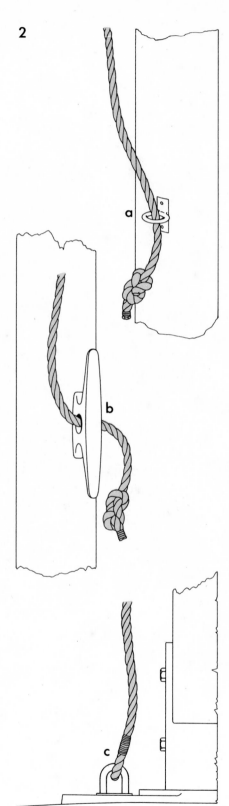

2

warp. Other plastics, e.g. polythene and polypropolene, are used for ropes which have the ability to float. When compared with terylene and nylon they are comparatively cheap to produce, and are normally used for such purposes as mooring ropes. Nearly all ropes are laid up right-handed and they should therefore be coiled up clockwise or right-handed to avoid kinks or twists being formed in the coil.

Imagine now for a moment the everyday job of cleating and coiling down a halyard. Once the halyard has been hauled down tightly a complete turn round the cleat should be made, followed by a figure of eight turn, and then a hitch on one of the horns of the cleat. It is important to make these turns round the cleat before putting on the hitch otherwise the strain will come directly on to the hitch and probably jam it. The hitch is put on to prevent the halyard coming adrift – not to take the strain. Having made the securing hitch the surplus rope is then coiled-up, working away from the standing part or cleat towards the free end of the rope; never coil from the free end or fall, to the cleat. Doing it in the correct way ensures that any twists in the rope are thrown out. Many owners very sensibly have the free end, or fall, of the halyard secured at deck level to

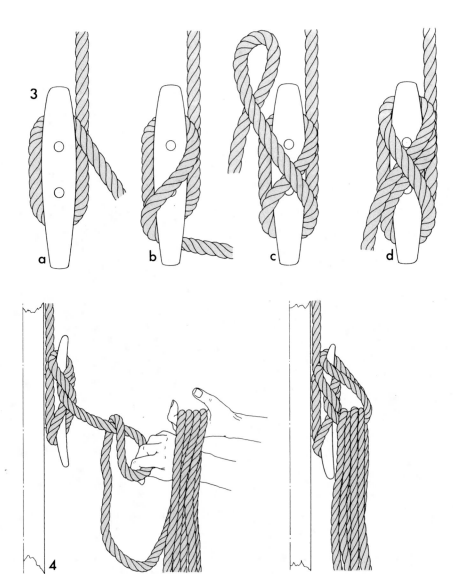

1 Capsizing a coil of rope.
2 Securing the tail of a halyard with:
(a) a mast ring and figure-of-eight knot,
(b) a hole through the halyard cleat,
and (c) a ring bolt fitted at deck level.
3 Cleating off a halyard.
4 Securing a halyard fall.

avoid embarrassment in a strong wind when the end flies out beyond reach – or even worse, shoots up to the mast head! The end should be passed through a ring bolt and finished with a figure of eight knot. By this method any twists can work themselves out. But of course if there is a hole in the body of the cleat this can be used in the same way as a ringbolt.

We have coiled the fall of the rope and it now has to be hung on the cleat in such a way that it will not fall off and yet it can be readily released. The best method is quickly and easily done (fig. 4). The coil is held by the left hand close to the cleat so that not more than, say,

15 inches of rope is left 'free' between the coil and the cleat. The right hand is then passed through the centre of the coil to grasp the 'free' length which is pulled back, twisted, passed over the top of the coil and then looped over the horn of the cleat. This will hold the coil very securely but it can also be released immediately. As a general comment ropes should never be left lying about on deck but should always be neatly coiled and secured – apart from looking untidy and somewhat unseaman-like, a loose rope lying about on deck can be a danger to life and limb. It is easy to trip and fall – possibly over the side, a subject which is

discussed at length in 'Safety at Sea' (see page 110).

Spare warps, which need to be stored below deck, must be coiled and secured in such a manner that they may be used again immediately. The most satisfactory method of storage is to coil up the rope in the normal manner leaving sufficient for, say, 7 or 8 turns round the middle of the coil, before the last few turns are put on, push a loop through the top half of the coil and bring it back over the top of the coil (known as capsizing it) and then pull the end tight. With this method the coil will not get into a muddle and the capsized turn may be released quickly.

Splicing

The ability to splice and whip a rope's end is a simple and satisfying skill to have. The whipping of a rope's end in this day of synthetic cordage may appear to be old-fashioned when today the rope's end may be sealed by heating it, but there are still plenty of opportunities for splicing. The most commonly-needed splice on a yacht is the eye-splice and the procedure is simple:

Eye Splice – three stranded rope

1. Unlay the strands at the end of the rope so that there is enough to put at least three tucks in (this will be about six times the diameter of the rope) and then form the eye by laying the three strands on top of the standing part of the rope. If the object is merely to form a loop in the end of the rope the starting position is not particularly important. If, however, you want to make an eye splice round a thimble then some care is needed to ensure that the splice fits tightly round the thimble with the first tucks.
2. Tuck the middle strand underneath the nearest strand of the standing part from *right* to *left*.
3. Tuck the left hand strand under the strand in the standing part to the left of the one which was used for the first tuck (again from right to left).
4. Now turn the whole splice over, take the third end and lead it over to the right of the remaining strand in the standing part, tuck it underneath, again from right to left.

There should now be one strand coming out from between each strand and its neighbour. If there are two coming out together from under one strand you have made a mistake and the splice must be started again.
5. Pull each end tight to ensure a neat start to the splice and a tight fit round the thimble.
6. For the next round of tucks take each end over one strand

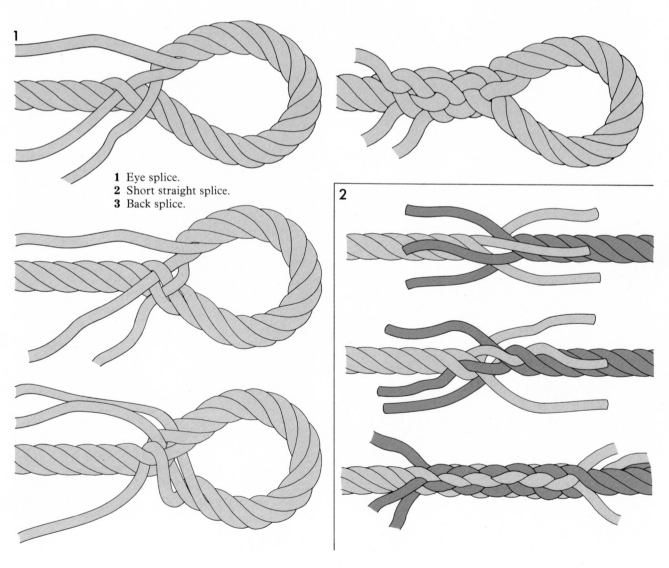

1 Eye splice.
2 Short straight splice.
3 Back splice.

and under the next, pull each end tight and then make the third round of tucks which will complete the splice.

7. To make a really neat, tapered splice each end can now be halved and then tucked under as before, continuing with one more round of tucks after halving again.

Short Straight Splice for joining two ends of similar size rope.

1. Unlay the strands of the two ropes for a sufficient length to allow three tucks each way.

2. Place the ends together so that each strand lies between two strands of the adjacent rope.

3. Hold firmly and pass each end over one strand and under the next, as in the eye splice, repeat for the other end of the splice.

4. Complete at least three tucks each way and then taper as described in the eye splice.

Back Splice When a rope is not required to run through a block a back splice makes a neat end to the rope.

1. Unlay a sufficient length of strands and form a crown by interlacing the ends so that each end comes out between two strands.

2. Pull lightly and then continue back along the standing part in the same manner as a straight splice.

3

Below: Halyards neatly arranged at the mainmast tabernacle on the *Gorch Foch.*

Knotting

There are many kinds of knots which have been developed over the years for a multitude of purposes and, not unnaturally, the majority have their origins at sea. For the average cruising man, however, a few knots will more than suffice but it is important that they are well known and can be made rapidly and correctly (and in the the dark!). The word 'knot' is often incorrectly used – a 'bend' is used to join two lengths of rope together and a 'hitch' secures a rope to some object such as a cleat or spar.

1. **Round turn and two half hitches:** a very simple and quickly made hitch generally used for securing a dinghy painter to a ring bolt.

2. **Clove hitch:** a hitch to be used with caution, preferably not to secure the end of a rope which may be subjected to strain as it may jam and prove difficult to release. Useful for securing a rope at intermediate points.

3. **Sheet bend:** an extremely useful bend which can be used for securing the ends of two ropes together or to secure one rope to a thimble, for example, a sheet to the clew of a sail. In the double sheet bend the working part is passed round twice for extra security.

4. **Rolling hitch:** a useful hitch which can be used for a variety of purposes. Start as for a clove hitch and put an additional turn between this and the standing part. Then finish off with another turn away from the standing part. Used for such purposes as securing the tail of a purchase to a mooring rope to take the strain off the latter temporarily.

5. **Figure of eight knot:** used at the end of a rope to prevent it running through a block.

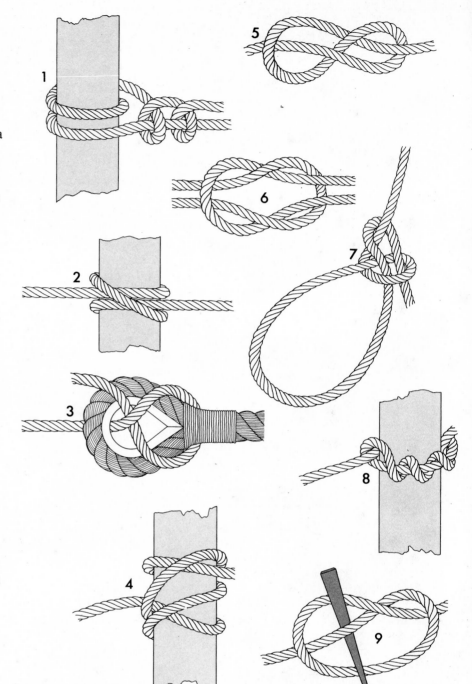

6. **Reef knot:** useful for joining together small ropes, e.g. reef points on a sail. It should not be used for joining the ends of large ropes, or ropes of different sizes or materials, as it may capsize under strain.

7. **Bowline:** an essential knot for use at sea whenever it is desired to put a loop at the end of a rope. It can be made quickly and easily and will never jam, no matter how much strain is put on the rope. Even after tension it is quite easy to release.

8. **Timber hitch:** used for lifting a spar or plank, easily made, grips the spar under tension but is easily cast off when tension is released.

9. **Marlin spike hitch:** a little-used hitch but very useful on occasions. As will be seen from above it is easily and

quickly made either at the end of a rope or in the bight. A marlin spike or shaft of wood is slipped through the loop and can be used for applying tension to the rope.

10. **Whipping:** The usual method of 'whipping' the end of a synthetic rope is to heat-seal it, which melts all the fibres into a solid mass, thereby preventing the rope from unravelling. There may, however, be occasions when you want to put a traditional whipping on a rope's end and the quickest and easiest of these, the Common whipping, is illustrated below.

(a) Cut off a suitable length of twine and lay one end D along the end of the rope.
(b) Take half a dozen turns around the rope and the twine, then pull each one tight working towards the end of the rope and against the lay.
(c) Now lay the other end of the twine BC along the rope and over the first turns. Resulting in loop E.
(d) With part A make turns over part B and when the loop at E becomes too small, pull tight on C and cut off the end. Similarly cut off any end of D still showing.

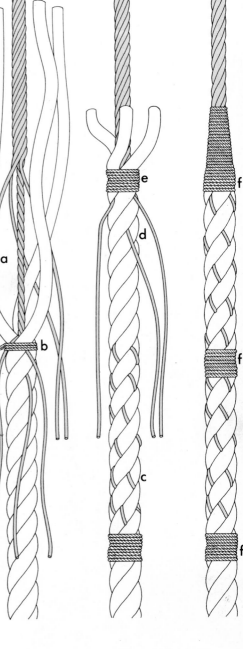

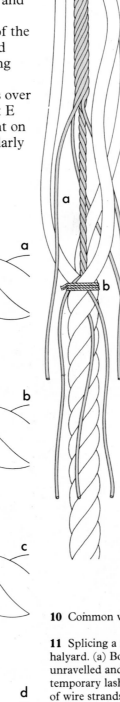

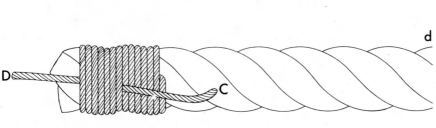

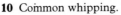

10 Common whipping.

11 Splicing a rope tail to a wire halyard. (a) Both rope and wire are unravelled and held together with a temporary lashing, (b). The first set of wire strands are rove through the rope, (c). The rope is then re-twisted round the remaining wire core, (d), and another temporary lashing made at (e). Finally, the rope end is thinned down and permanent whippings made, (f).

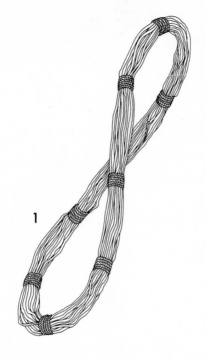

1

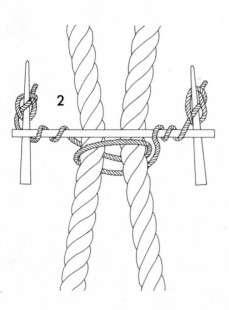

2

Use of strops A strop is a short length of rope, preferably plaited rather than laid, which may be in the form of a loop. It is used for securing a block or purchase to a spar or to another rope under tension in order to transfer the strain. A selvagee strop is a loop formed of yarn or twine made up on a board between pins, turns of yarn are made and then seized at intervals. This produces a soft but strong strop which has great holding power on a smooth surface such as a spar. It would only be used on very infrequent occasions on a cruising yacht but, if really needed in a hurry, its presence on board would be very welcome indeed.

Spanish Windlass This is a useful but very little-used method of applying tension to a rope. As in the case of the selvagee strop you may go a life time without using it but an occasion may arise when the ability quickly to use a spanish windlass may prove invaluable. As will be seen from fig. 2 a short piece of timber (broom stick) and a spike or another piece of wood as the handle are all that is required in the way of material. In the case of A the windlass is applied to any section of a rope and as it tightens in both directions it does not need to be supported, the strain in each direction being equal. The uses of a spanish windlass on a small craft may appear to be rather limited but there is one occasion which may arise when it really comes into its own: a riding turn on a winch.

Riding turn on a winch A riding turn can occur on a halyard winch but is more likely to occur on a sheet winch. This is fortunate because a jammed halyard resulting in

complete inability to lower a sail could be extremely serious. Once it has happened there is usually no easy way out and if it is necessary to make another tack quickly the situation could become somewhat awkward.

Before sorting out the riding turn let us first understand how it gets there. When the foresail is to be sheeted in, the sheet is quickly laid round the drum of the winch and about three extra turns are laid on, above the standing part of the sheet, to enable it to grip the drum barrel. Thus we have the standing part on the bottom of the winch barrel with three turns above it and the tail leading off from the top. The winchman now winches in the sheet whilst maintaining tension on the tail. Now if the winchman decides to 'surge' the sheet (i.e. slacken the tension) the direction of rotation of the turns on the drum will reverse. This results in the bottom turn, the standing part, moving down on to the skirt of the drum which tends to throw the turn back towards the centre of the drum. Should this occur it will jump up and overlay one of the other turns. If the winchman does not spot this and attempts to regain control by winding in again, then the over-riding turn will lock up solid and we have the classic over-riding turn situation.

The only effective action that can now be taken is to release the tension on the standing part in order to sort out the turns on the drum with a spike. The real problem now becomes very apparent – the sail is sheeted hard in, cannot be released and in all probability it will shortly be necessary to put the vessel over on to the other tack. Under these circumstances the prudent skipper will put the vessel aback, heave to and give himself

1 A selvagee strop.
2 Spanish windlass.
3 Riding turn on a winch.
The first turn of a sheet (a) is anchored with two extra turns above it (b). If the tension is slackened the sheet will reverse into the drum which can cause the sheet to ride over the extra turns (c) and results in a locked up winch (d).

a

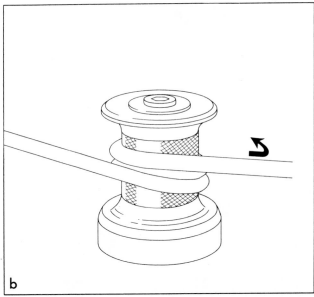

b

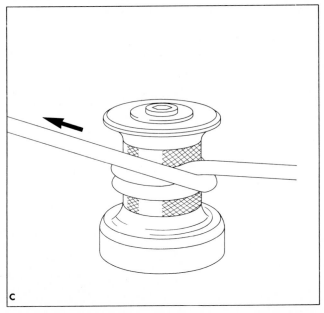

c

d

time to sort out the trouble. In these circumstances the spanish windlass may prove to be the only possible solution. The problem divides simply into two halves, firstly attaching a line to the sheet and secondly applying sufficient power to it to relieve the tension on the winch drum.

Dealing first with the problem of securing a rope to the sheet, it may be possible to attach it to the clew of the sail and then lead it via a snatch block to a convenient position. Assuming that this is not possible, as

would be the case with a jammed halyard, a method must be found whereby a line can be secured to the sheet under tension in such a manner that it will not slip. A soft rope stopper made up of four or five feet of plaited terylene rope is the best answer and is used in the following manner. The two ends are knotted together to form a loop and laid on the sheet. Each end of the loop is then passed through the other, pulling the turns tight, until the stopper is wound

round the sheet and a line is attached to the final turn. When tension is applied it compresses the sheet and grips it in the same manner as does the wire stocking which is used for pulling cable into a pipe.

A spanish windlass is then rigged up, tension applied and the riding turn on the winch sorted out with the aid of a large spike. The whole procedure may sound rather complicated but, provided it has been thought out before, it can be carried out quickly and effectively.

Anchoring Basically anchoring is a simple procedure but, like all simple procedures, it needs thinking about before putting it into action. There are two points to attend to before any anchoring is carried out on a new yacht. Firstly, check that the inboard end of the chain is secured with a heavy lashing and not shackled; it may be necessary at some time to slip the cable quickly. Secondly, it is extremely useful if the cable is marked at regular intervals, say five, ten, fifteen fathoms and so on. This can be done by either painting several links or better still by putting a small lashing on a link which can be felt in the dark. It may sound obvious but it is most important to know how much chain is out. The amount of anchor cable that is veered out must always be equivalent to at least three times the maximum depth of water which will occur whilst the vessel is anchored. This will ensure the nearly horizontal pull on the anchor which is essential to maintain good holding power. If nylon warp is being used then at least five times the depth is necessary. Also with nylon warp it is important to have, say, two fathoms of chain shackled to the anchor with the warp secured to its end. This has a two-fold effect: it helps to keep the nylon down, so providing a horizontal pull, and also avoids chafe on the nylon in contact with the ground. Before anchoring there

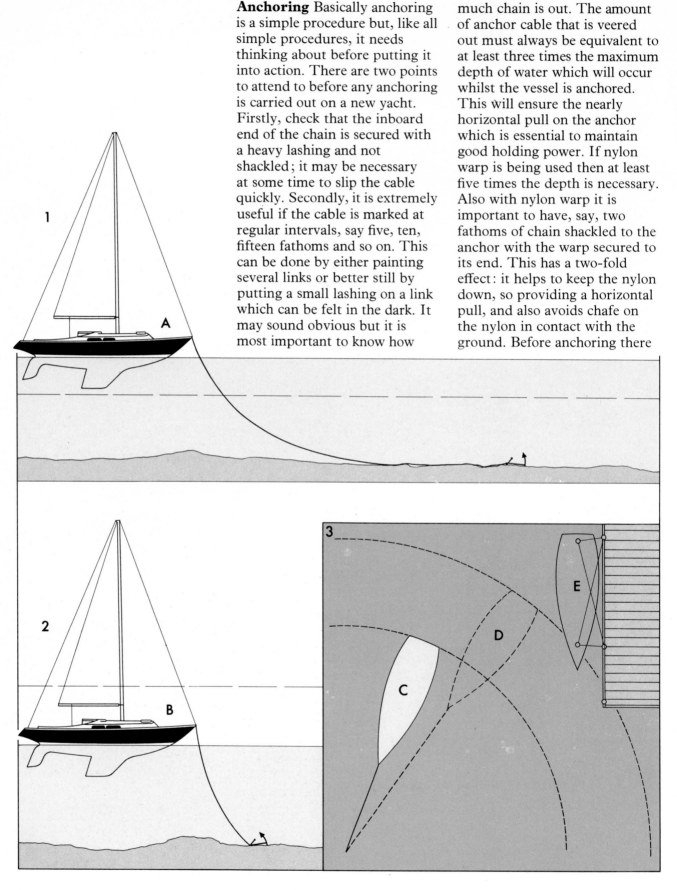

are several factors to consider. Firstly, is the boat to stay for several tides? If so it is obvious that there must be sufficient depth of water at L.W. to keep the craft afloat (it is assumed in this case that it is not a bilge keel vessel which will happily take the ground). Secondly, in view of the amount of chain that will be out, is there sufficient swinging room at low water to avoid other craft? A further point is whether or not the craft is to be left unattended for several tides? If it is lying to one anchor, this will trip on each tide and then rebury itself, which could lead to considerable movement over a few tides, with of course the possibility of it fouling itself and dragging. In these circumstances it is desirable to lay out a kedge anchor as described later.

When the position in which you wish to anchor is known, the anchor should be prepared for dropping: suspended from the stemhead roller, and the chain already checked for free running. The approach should be up into the tide until the boat is just past the selected spot, the vessel is stopped, anchor is dropped and as she drifts back on the tide, chain is veered out. Do not shoot out all the chain the moment the anchor touches ground or it will probably pile up on the anchor and foul it. When the correct amount of chain has been paid out the vessel should be in the desired

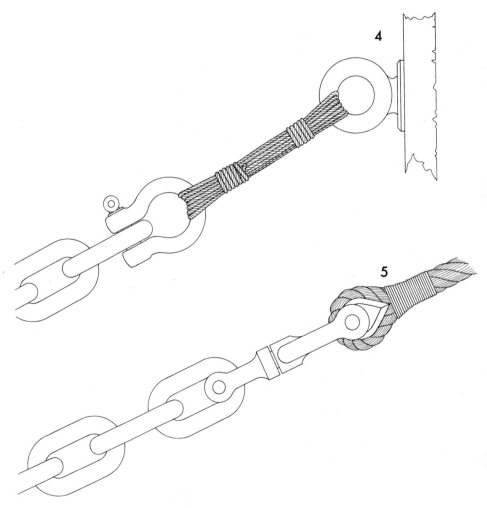

1 Boat A is anchored at high tide with chain paid out to at least three times the maximum depth of water. The dotted line indicates the low water mark.
2 Boat B is anchored at low water with a very short scope of chain. As the tide rises she will break out her anchor and drift away. The dotted line indicates the high water mark.
3 Boat C has anchored at high water in a seemingly safe position. However, as the tide drops her swinging circle will increase to position D, where she would be in danger of collision with boat E. For this reason it is always advisable to shorten the anchor cable relative to the tidal drop.
4 The inboard end of the anchor cable should be secured with a lashing which can be cut in an emergency.
5 A length of chain between anchor and warp helps to make the anchor settle well. It can be connected with a strong swivel shackle.

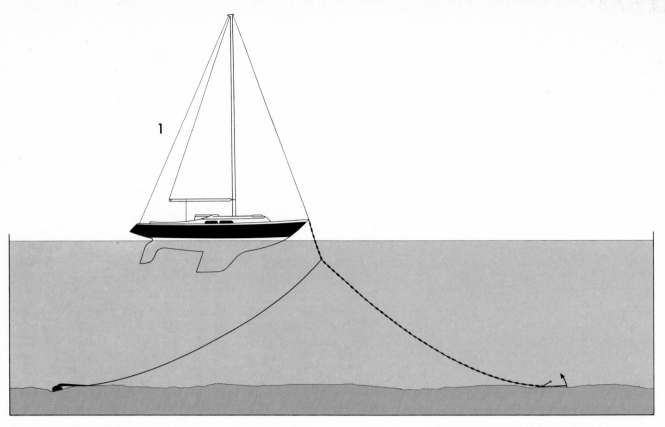

1 A boat riding to a bow anchor with chain cable and a kedge anchor on a nylon warp. The kedge warp should be at a depth which is safe not only for passing craft, but also so that it does not foul her own keel.
2 When anchored at night a riding light should be shown in this position.

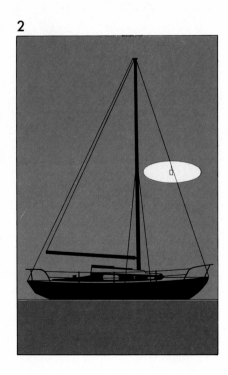

position. If you now intend to leave the vessel and lay out a kedge anchor, this is the procedure for doing so.

The kedge anchor should be prepared with an appropriate length of strong warp, taken out in the dinghy and dropped as far astern as possible in the line of tide. The end of the warp should then be shackled to the bower anchor cable just above water level and sufficient cable then veered to sink the warp below the propellers of passing craft. When anchored in this way it will be appreciated that the vessel lies to each anchor in turn and thus there is no danger of her shifting position due to tripping an anchor. If a dinghy is not readily available the operation can be carried out quite simply as follows: as the anchoring position is approached the kedge anchor is dropped and the vessel then sails on to the advanced position where the bower anchor must be dropped. When the vessel has drifted back on the tide to the desired anchorage the kedge warp is

hauled tight and shackled to the bower cable as explained above.

When you are finally anchored, it is important to take a bearing on some fixed object ashore, or to get two objects in transit, so that a periodic check may be made on the vessel's position to make sure that she is not dragging. It is also important to remember that, when at anchor at night an all-round white light must be displayed forward, and a black ball of adequate size by day, also forward of the mast.

Clearing a fouled anchor
When anchoring somewhere where the 'hook' might be likely to foul an underwater obstruction, it is sound practice to buoy it. A length of strong line, equal to the maximum depth of water, is attached to the crown of the anchor with a small buoy at the other end. In the event of the anchor being fouled – quite possibly under an old mooring chain – the vessel should move up to the anchor under auxiliary power, then the

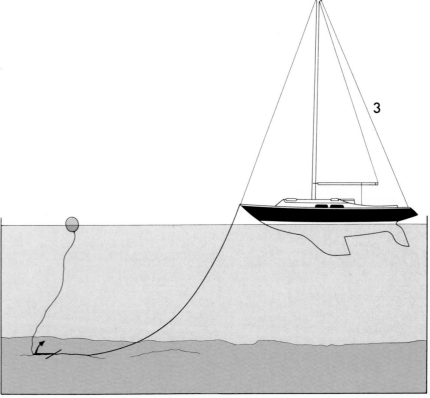

3 At anchor with a buoyed tripping line.
4 Using a grapnel to clear a fouled anchor.
5 A chain sling worked down the anchor cable can clear an obstruction if purchase is applied from a favourable direction.

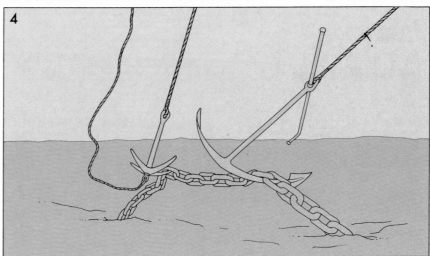

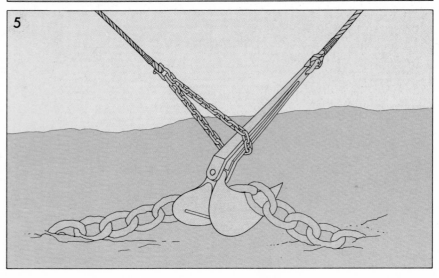

anchor buoy rope is hauled in, and in all probability the anchor will clear itself. If the anchor has not been buoyed the problem may become a little more difficult. The first step is to lift it as far as is practicable after which it may be possible to get a rope under the obstruction, which can then take the strain, allowing the anchor to drop free. Alternatively a grapnel (with a recovery rope on the crown!) may be tried to lift the obstruction. Other measures include sliding a small chain sling, attached to a warp, down the anchor cable so that tension can be applied to the anchor to pull it out from under the obstruction.

It is worthwhile securing a weight halfway down the tripping line in order to prevent it ranging about too much and possibly fouling passing propellers. If the anchor buoy is marked as such it will stop some innocent visitor picking it up under the happy impression that it is a vacant mooring buoy with perhaps expensive results.

Auxiliary Yachts – manoeuvring under power

The importance of learning to handle one's craft in confined spaces under sail, and thereby acquiring a good knowledge of its capabilities, has already been stressed but it is also wise to familiarize oneself, as soon as possible, with the manner in which the craft handles under power. This is particularly important in the case of sailing yachts with auxiliary power. A sailing yacht is, quite naturally, designed to operate at maximum efficiency under sail, and its performance under power is therefore a secondary consideration – for example when going astern its behaviour will be less predictable than that of a similar size of motor-cruiser.

In a sailing vessel with auxiliary power you must understand that the propeller exerts side thrust as well as forward and reverse motion and that this thrust occurs at right-angles to the fore-and-aft line of the vessel. When viewed from astern a right-handed propeller – that is to say one turning in a clockwise direction when going ahead – will tend to push the boat to starboard when going ahead. The reason for this is that the lower half of the propeller is operating in water of higher density than the top half and it therefore exerts more force.

An easy way to remember this fact is to assume that the propeller is a wheel resting on the bottom, as it turns to the right it will move the boat to the right. When going astern the reverse action takes place, that is a right-handed propeller will thrust towards the port side and a left-handed propeller towards starboard.

This knowledge of the boat's characteristics is very useful when manoeuvring it in restricted spaces. For example, if the stern kicks to starboard when going ahead then, obviously, a much tighter turn can be made to port than is possible to starboard. If it should be necessary to make a tight turn to starboard it would probably pay you to give a short burst of throttle astern, thus swinging the stern to port before making the starboard turn. It should be noted that this sideways thrust is most pronounced *before* the vessel gathers steerage way ahead or astern. Thus a sharp burst of throttle before the vessel picks up steerage way has much more effect than opening the throttle slowly. For this reason the most effective way of manoeuvring an auxiliary yacht in confined spaces is with short, sharp bursts of throttle with full helm on.

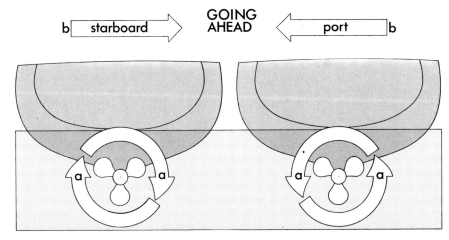

b starboard → ← port b

Opposite page: A folding propeller on the left and a feathering propeller on the right.

Right: The diagram illustrates the particular directional bias to expect from the rotation of the propeller: (a) = direction of revolution, (b) = direction of resultant thrust.

Below: Conditions such as these render any attempt to use sail foolhardy. The Angus Primrose designed *Warrior* prudently noses into her berth under power only. With so many other craft around her the skipper must exercise both skill and judgement in the control of her speed and direction.

Ch.4 Seamanship Pt.2

Preparing for sea During a normal season the average small cruising yacht undergoes some rough treatment and it is surprising the amount of wear that can take place. Any preparation for an off-shore passage, therefore, should include a thorough check of all gear which is subject to wear or deterioration. In a well-maintained vessel this should be a comparatively simple matter and the following points are suggested as a simple checklist.

1. Check standing rigging – are all bottle screws correctly adjusted and locknuts tight? Are there any suspicious looking strands sticking out of the rigging adjacent to ferrules etc?
2. Running rigging – check for chafe at any points subject to wear, are shackles properly moused where necessary?
3. Reefing gear – check that all is in order if a detachable roller reefing handle is used. Is there a spare one on board?
4. Sails – will normally have been checked by the sailmaker at the beginning of the season and should therefore be in good order. Have you a good strong storm jib on board?
5. Bilge Pumps – are bilges clean and free from any material that may clog the pumps?
6. Safety equipment – personal buoyancy and safety harnesses for all crew members. Rocket flares, hand-held flares, life raft or inflatable dinghy.
7. Auxiliary Engine – check water filter, lubricating oil and fuel supply.

In addition of course there should be adequate navigation equipment. This does not necessarily mean sophisticated electronic gear but the basic essentials of up-to-date charts, tidal stream atlases, *Reed's Nautical Almanac*, and chart

instruments. Are there spare batteries for the echo sounder and radio, and a spare line for the Walker log (if one is carried)? Most important of all on the navigation side is a compass complete with deviation card. The preparations for navigation are dealt with fully in the appropriate chapter (see page 106). The above points form the basis of a checklist which any owner can work out for himself and thus make the task more simple.

Yacht handling at sea Yacht handling at sea really means handling the boat under difficult conditions. The carefree sail on a beautiful afternoon, wind F3, presents no problems. It is when the weather deteriorates and things look difficult that seamanship in handling the vessel becomes important. If the owner has practised the manoeuvres already suggested under both power and sail he will be well on the way to becoming a proficient seaman able to cope with the awkward situations which will, sooner or later, inevitably arise at sea.

Difficult circumstances at sea can be roughly divided into – bad weather, bad navigation and gear failure. The case of man overboard is a potential disaster which is considered more fully in the section on emergency procedures (page 91). As a general rule, with the possible exception of navigational problems, all tricky situations ultimately require good seamanship to resolve them, hence it should be the aim of every yachtsman to become a good seaman as soon as possible.

Preparations for heavy weather The prudent seaman on passage will normally listen regularly to weather-forecasts,

Opposite: Any trip for'ard is made a safer proposition if a sound set of stanchions and guard rails are fitted. The arrangement shown is a first-class example. Firstly, the height of the stanchions is about mid-thigh; a lower rail could flip a person over the side by catching them behind the knees. Secondly, the stanchions are upright with an angled base to offset the camber of the deck; all the bases are through-bolted for strength and bracing has been added where most needed. Lastly, two sets of lifelines are rigged; the lower of the two prevents the likelihood of slipping under the top rail when the deck is awash.

watch his barometer and the local portents in the sky, in order to have an adequate warning of impending bad weather which will enable him to take the correct action before it starts. In the case of a coastal passage it will probably be possible to make for a port of refuge in good time, although if it is one on a lee shore, and perhaps with a bar, it should be avoided at all costs, unless the skipper is confident that he will arrive there before the bad weather does. However one day it may be that bad weather will have to be faced at sea and it is sound practice to know what steps are necessary well in advance of the actual event.

When it is obvious that heavy weather is on its way the first step, apart from reefing, is to ensure that all loose equipment is really well secured. If a dinghy is carried on deck additional lashings should be put on, adequately secured to strong points – which raises the question, are the eyebolts fitted for this purpose really strong enough? Hatches should be properly secured and tightened down. If foresails are normally changed and handed down the forehatch, it would probably be a good idea to have the storm jib readily available from the cabin, rather than risk opening a forehatch under rough weather conditions. Every effort must be made towards minimising discomfort for the crew, and in this context it is surprising the amount of water that will find its way down an anchor chain hawsepipe under extreme conditions and it should therefore be blocked up with rag. Life lines should of course always be rigged so that any crew member can go forward from the cockpit without having to unclip his safety harness.

Below decks all gear should be properly stowed and secured, for, apart from other considerations, miscellaneous gear being thrown about in the cabin is not conducive to peace of mind. In the average family cruiser under bad conditions it is unlikely that normal cooking will be carried out. Even if the crew's stomachs are strong enough, boiling water can be potentially dangerous in these conditions. It is good practice to heat water beforehand and store it in thermos flasks for producing hot Bovril, instant soups, coffee and so on when things become uncomfortable. This aspect of the preparations is dealt with more fully in the section on cooking at sea (see page 225). Sea-sickness pills should be available and issued to any crew member who may need them.

Whilst these preparations are in hand the skipper will have ensured that his plot on the chart is up-to-date and will have been considering the various options open to him. These usually resolve themselves into three possibilities. The first one is to stand on and continue to make for his destination, assuming of course that there will be no difficulties en route such as overfalls or tidal races which would be rendered dangerous by the impending weather, and also that the proposed destination is such that it may be entered in the conditions to be expected on arrival there. The second alternative is to run for another destination where conditions will be safe for entry, while the third is to stand out from the coast and make a good offing, thus obtaining plenty of sea room in case it should be necessary to heave to. It is always tempting to run for

shelter and very understandable, but it is most important to appraise the situation carefully before deciding to do so.

Finally it is worth remembering that the well-found little ship can take far more punishment than her crew, and also that the deeper the water the safer is the situation.

At Sea

Reefing The first problem that normally confronts the inexperienced yachtsman is the necessity to reef the vessel on the approach of bad weather. As

the wind force increases and the boat becomes hard pressed the difficulties of reefing become very apparent and thus there is a great temptation to put it off in the hope that the weather will improve. This is a very natural reaction for the inexperienced seaman – the foredeck suddenly looks a most uninviting place, but the postponement of shortening sail must be resisted at all costs. It is far better and more seamanlike to put a reef in the main and change down to a smaller headsail *before* it is really necessary than to leave it until it becomes essential – and difficult.

The ship will be far more comfortable, easier to handle and will travel as fast or even faster than if she is over-pressed.

The various systems of reefing have already been described in the section on sails (page 40) and it is assumed that the owner is fully familiar with the gear and how to operate it. The prudent seaman will already have tried it all out on a calm day, initially no doubt on his mooring, and so will be familiar with the steps to be taken, which it may, after all, be necessary to carry out in the dark.

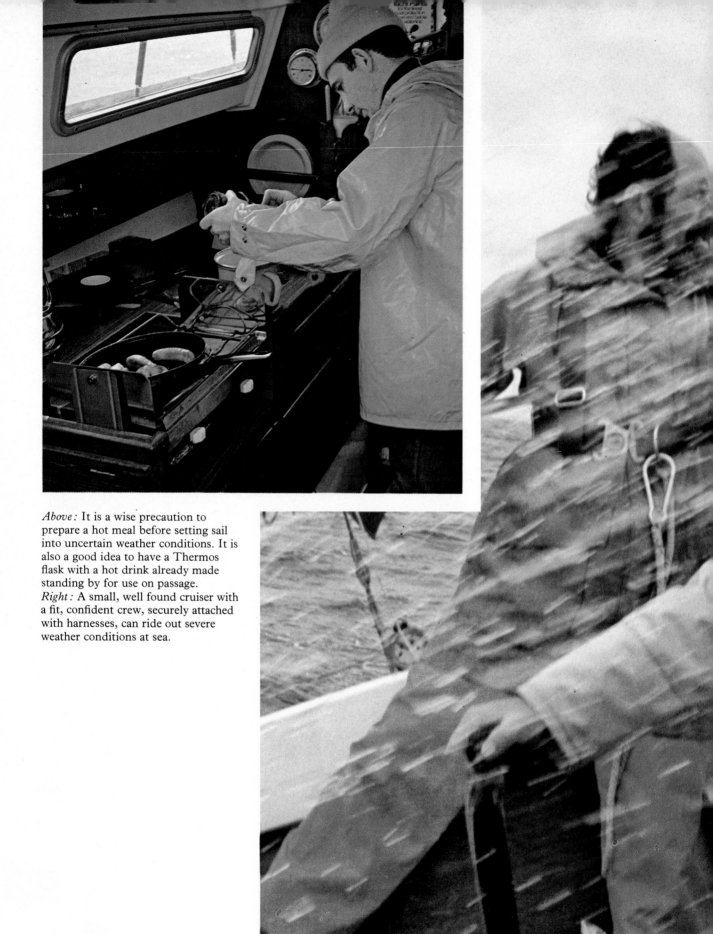

Above: It is a wise precaution to prepare a hot meal before setting sail into uncertain weather conditions. It is also a good idea to have a Thermos flask with a hot drink already made standing by for use on passage.

Right: A small, well found cruiser with a fit, confident crew, securely attached with harnesses, can ride out severe weather conditions at sea.

There are certain points in connection with sail handling in strong winds which are worth remembering and practising at all times. Dealing with foresails first, remember that the most slippery thing on a foredeck (short of a patch of ice) is a wet terylene sail – never tread on one if it can be avoided. Having released the foresail halyard do not just drop it and move forward, if possible ease it up as the sail comes down, looking aloft to make sure that the slack halyard is not tying itself in a knot round the crosstrees. There may be a sense of urgency in the sail change but efforts should be made to maintain some tension in the halyard to keep it out of trouble until the sail is on the foredeck. As soon as the sail is down secure the halyard to the pulpit with a quick hitch to keep the halyard and the head of the sail under control. Remember that a sail billowing out on the foredeck can be a powerful adversary in strong winds and should be approached with due care. Tackle the sail from the luff, bundling it up and working back to the clew putting on stoppers as you go. Ideally these stoppers should already be in position. They are short lengths of line clove-hitched to the top life line with the two ends hanging down of sufficient length to pass round a bundled genoa. When this job is completed the hanks can be taken off the forestay and the new headsail hanked on, the halyard attached, the sheets changed over – and the new sail is ready for hoisting. On the other hand the replacement foresail may be hanked on to the forestay whilst the original one is still up, by hanking it on between the bottom hank and the foot of the one which is set.

Thereafter all that is necessary is to drop the sail, unhank, transfer halyard and sheets and hoist the replacement. In normal cruising, with plenty of time to spare, it is probably better to remove one sail completely before bringing the second one on deck, in order to keep the foredeck as uncluttered as possible. This operation will be rendered much easier if the headsail is folded (*not* rolled) in its bag so that the hanks may be attached to the forestay whilst the main bulk of the sail is still held inside the bag. Different owners develop their own methods for these operations but the important thing is to avoid having the sail flapping about on deck whilst efforts are still being made to hank it on to the forestay. Always remember, if the foredeck is jumping about, *sit down* to carry out the hanking operation – it's much safer! When the new foresail is to be hoisted always remember to look aloft, when hauling on

the halyard, to ensure that it is running free of obstructions. A jammed halyard at sea in bad weather can turn a difficult situation into a dangerous one.

The procedure for reefing the mainsail should be clearly understood and if it is carried out methodically it should present no difficulties. Two points to watch are as follows. Firstly, where roller reefing gear is fitted disconnect the kicking strap and put on the 'wind-in tape' (a wide nylon tape several feet long which is wound in with the mainsail and attached to the kicking strap). Secondly, always remember to take the weight of the boom on the topping lift before lowering the main halyard. Lastly, open the gate at the base of the mast track to allow the luff to wind round the boom. Before attempting to reef the main it will help matters to stop it drawing, which renders it more tractable. This is normally done by freeing the sheet or perhaps

1 Foresail hanked to forestay and retained in sailbag. Note the sailbag lashed to pulpit; it is often the case that an owner only remembers to do this as he sees his sailbag whisked over the side in a stiff breeze.
2 Wind-in tape used to replace the kicking strap when reefed.

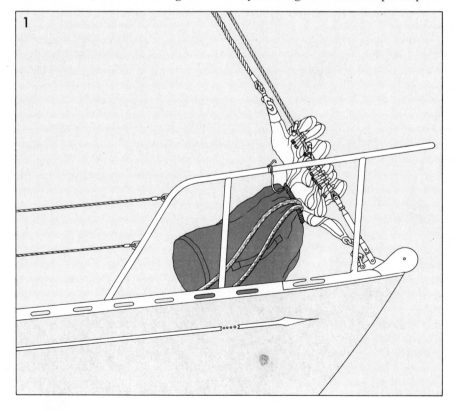

even heaving to, remembering that with roller reefing some weight is required on the sail to make it roll neatly. Ideally with roller reefing the halyard should be slacked away as the boom is rotated, thus ensuring a tight roll. This calls for the use of both hands and it is therefore a job which should be done sitting down if possible. If the roller reefing handle can be used from either side of the boom, choose the weather side as this will help you considerably in keeping your balance.

As the reef is rolled in, the after end of the boom will tend to sag down due to the build up at the luff; a tapered batten rolled in by the leech will help to overcome this. Some mainsails do not roll properly unless the leech is pulled out as the boom is rotated. If this can be done by someone in the cockpit, it results in a sail which sets better when the reef is completed.

Every yachtsman will agree that the wind force appears suddenly to increase when altering course from running to reaching, and it is particularly important to remember this point. On a run, reefing might be delayed to the point where the vessel could broach to and be struck by a heavy sea broadside on. Therefore, when running, be particularly careful to watch for any signs that reefing is needed. It will be necessary to round up into the wind to reef the main, and care is needed in watching the sea for a suitable 'smooth' during which to do this and thus avoid broaching to.

Finally, summing up on reefing procedures in general, always remember:
1. Reef in good time, before it is really necessary.
2. Always wear a safety harness.
3. Avoid treading on wet sails.
4. Always look aloft when dealing with halyards.

Heaving to The words conjure up pictures of old-time square-riggers but the operation is equally useful in the modern fore-and-aft-rigged family cruising yacht. It is a manoeuvre which can be extremely useful in a variety of circumstances, and not only when it is blowing a gale and sailing is impossible. The short-handed cruising man may want to go below to do a little gentle chart work or make a cup of tea without disturbing the watch below – or even to minister to a seasick member of the crew. This means that he must be able to leave the vessel to look after herself, possibly for an appreciable period of time and a prerequisite under these circumstances is that speed should be as low as possible and that the motion should be comfortable.

In the old days of gaff rig and long keels it was a comparatively simple matter to heave to – the mainsail was eased slightly, the foresail was backed and the tiller was lashed slightly to leeward, the vessel would remain almost in the same spot, rising and falling with the seas at a very comfortable angle of heel. The main and foresail worked against each other with the result that the vessel fore-reached very slowly, probably at less than a knot, and at an angle of around 60° off the wind. In fact she would lie almost in the normal close-hauled position and then the angle of heel would be very small. This ability to heave-to easily and comfortably was of considerable importance to vessels such as pilot-cutters and quay-punts which might remain on station for days at a time, very often in bad weather and with a very small crew. Their normal drill was to heave to on the starboard tack thus giving

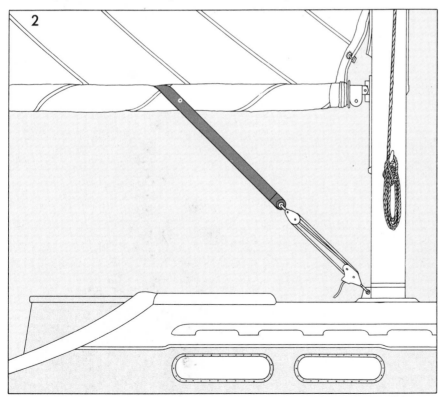

them right of way over other craft and thereby reducing the amount of work on board whilst waiting for their customers. However, with modern light displacement fin-and-skeg hulls and high-aspect ratio Bermudan rig things are rather different. The modern hull is comparatively easily driven and the problem is to so trim the sails that their drive is reduced to an absolute minimum, yet at the same time keeping the boat in a constant position in relation to the wind. The ideal is for the boat to fore reach at about one to one-and-a-half knots while remaining at a comfortable angle of heel.

A good deal of experimental work in differing wind strengths is called for before a satisfactory sail arrangement can be found for a modern fin-and-skeg design. In some extreme cases – notably out-and-out racing designs – it may not prove possible to heave-to satisfactorily without fairly constant attention to the helm. It is therefore important to find out early on how your own particular craft behaves when hove to – in fact it should be regarded as part of the 'safety first' drill which should be familiar to all crew members. After all it may be the skipper, not the crew member, who falls down the hatch and who needs first aid. . . . Initially, practice the drill in open water on a day with a reasonable breeze blowing and plenty of sea room to play with. Start by trying to heave-to in the conventional manner: mainsail fairly close-hauled, foresail to weather and helm to loo'ard. If, as may well happen, the boat continues to forge ahead at an unacceptably high speed, then further measures must be taken.

The basic problem is that the efficiency of the rig must be reduced to make the boat lie quietly and comfortably. The obvious way of reducing the driving power of any sail is to slacken the luff and this should be tried, starting with the foresail. If the halyard is slacked sufficiently to drop the sail by, say, 10% of its luff length it will have its driving power considerably reduced, which may be sufficient to achieve the object of the exercise. If this does not have sufficient effect then the luff of the main can be eased away gently to see what happens (but remember to set up the topping lift). In addition to slowing down the vessel it is also important to try and get her pointing more up into the wind, which will give a better angle of heel and therefore a more comfortable ship. The modern Bermudan rig has a tendency to lie across the wind when hove-to – which naturally produces an uncomfortable angle of heel.

After some trial and error the method most suitable to the particular boat will be discovered and the skipper will be comforted by the knowledge that he can, when the necessity arises, stop his boat and lie-to in comparative comfort. Summing up, the aim should be to reduce speed to an absolute minimum and point as high as possible, thereby ensuring a more comfortable angle of heel and at the same time reducing the wind pressure on the sails. The latter point is particularly important when the vessel is hove-to under stress of bad weather.

Lying a'hull It should never become necessary for the everyday small family cruiser to encounter survival conditions during her lifetime if her passages are planned with due regard to prevailing weather

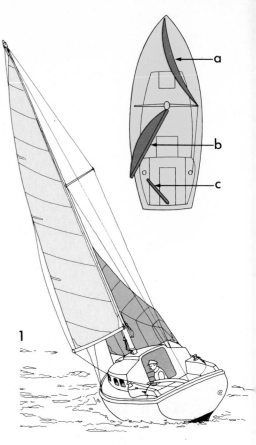

1 Heaving-to on the starboard tack. (a) Foresail backed to windward, (b) mainsheet eased and the boom out to leeward, (c) tiller lashed to leeward.

conditions. However, as his experience grows, there will be a natural tendency for the owner to extend the duration of passages and, when these begin to exceed twenty-four hours, then the possibility of encountering heavy weather obviously increases. Depending upon her hull formation and sail plan, the average small cruiser will heave-to in winds of surprising strength once the problem of sail balance has been solved. Heaving to satisfactorily does depend largely on a reasonably consistent wind pressure on the sails maintaining the boat in a constant position relative to wind direction. When the seas become so high that the vessel is completely blanketed in the troughs it is obvious that there

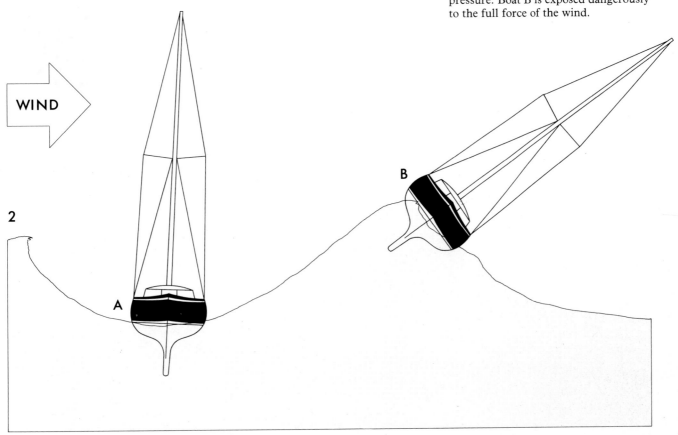

WIND

2

A

B

2 Riding under bare poles: lying a'hull. Boat A in a trough between wave crests is shielded from excessive wind pressure. Boat B is exposed dangerously to the full force of the wind.

is a real danger of her being knocked down, when she is exposed to the full blast of the storm on the crests, if any sail at all is set. Hopefully it is unlikely that the average family cruiser will have to tackle such an experience but, nevertheless, it is a wise precaution to think about it just the same. Assuming, therefore, that conditions are such that the skipper decides it is dangerous to stay hove-to – either because of the weight of the wind on the crests or because it is not possible to keep the speed through the water sufficiently low – then alternative methods of riding out the gale must be found. A fundamental point to remember is that if the hull gives way easily to the seas it is less likely to suffer damage, and

thus the light displacement hull may suffer less than the deep heavy displacement one which, being stiffer, presents more resistance to the seas. Under these circumstances, if all sail is stripped off the boat and she is left to take up her own position in the sea, she is said to be 'lying a'hull'. The boat will, however, continue to fore-reach slowly due to the pressure of the wind on the mast and rigging, the helm can be lashed down so that there will be a tendency to luff up, behaving rather as if she is hove-to but with less of the disadvantages. The unfortunate inexperienced skipper who is faced with this situation may feel that 'lying a'hull' is almost a policy of despair – that he is giving up control of his craft. The situation, however, is a

survival one – one in which he cannot fight back but can only help his ship to look after herself. A considerable weight of evidence produced by experienced ocean cruising men shows that many yachts have weathered storms by lying a'hull in circumstances where other methods might well have led to their loss. One of the real dangers in heavy weather is that of having a port smashed in by a breaking crest. Any craft likely to be caught out in this sort of weather should therefore take the precaution of having sufficient material aboard to effect repairs in the event of it happening, or better still have screens ready to fix over the ports when the weather worsens.

In some production-line boats the term 'port' is not

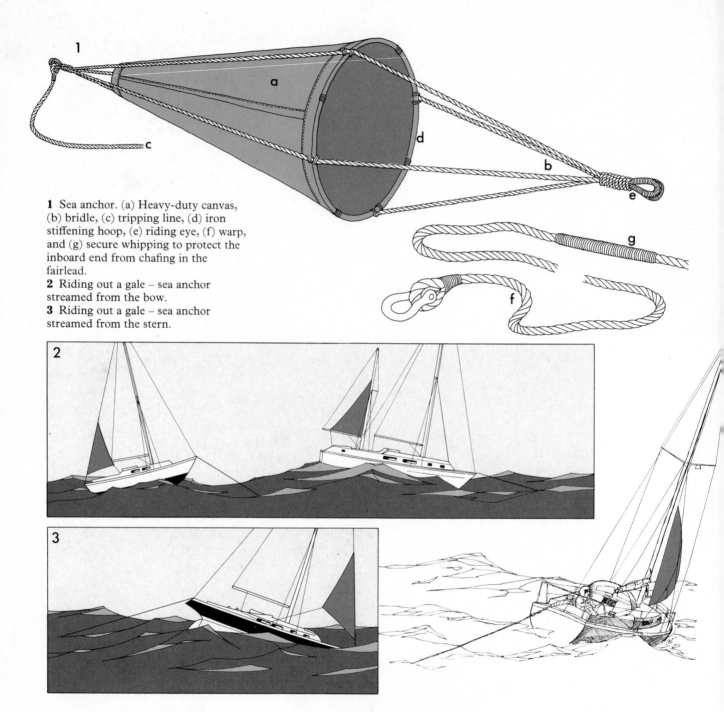

1 Sea anchor. (a) Heavy-duty canvas, (b) bridle, (c) tripping line, (d) iron stiffening hoop, (e) riding eye, (f) warp, and (g) secure whipping to protect the inboard end from chafing in the fairlead.
2 Riding out a gale – sea anchor streamed from the bow.
3 Riding out a gale – sea anchor streamed from the stern.

applicable – they are windows and special measures are needed to protect them if long-range cruises are to be made.

Sea Anchor Every student of marine literature will be familiar with the sea anchor. This piece of equipment has featured in so many epic stories of the sea, and in particular those of Captain J. C. Voss in his voyages in the canoe *Tilikum*. He showed that a small shallow-draft craft will ride out a gale in safety when lying to a sea anchor with a small riding sail right aft to keep her head to wind. There is little doubt that a really strongly-constructed sea anchor with adequate gear can play a vital part in the defences of a small boat in really bad weather. The position of the modern light displacement cruiser is, however, somewhat different to that of the *Tilikum*, which, like the average ship's life-boat, had a fairly symmetrical profile – that is to say the windage and grip on the water was roughly similar at both stem and stern. The

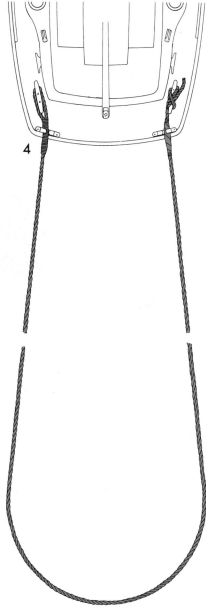

4 Trailing a warp over the stern in a large bight. The warp should be the largest, longest and strongest on board and should be very firmly secured at the inboard end.

light displacement cruiser will probably have more windage forward and a better grip on the water aft, with the result that the bow will normally tend to pay off downwind. With the anchor streamed from the bow the result will be that the vessel will tend to lie broadside on to the seas. This tendency may be overcome by setting a reefed

mizzen in the case of a yawl or ketch, or a storm jib on the backstay of a sloop. When the anchor is streamed from the bow the yacht will make sternway and this may be at such speed that there is danger of damaging the rudder. In these circumstances it is preferable to stream the sea anchor from the stern, which has the advantage that a certain amount of control can be exercised by the rudder and also that the riding sail will not be required. The disadvantage is that the most vulnerable part of the vessel, the cockpit, is presented directly to the advancing seas, but on balance that is probably preferable to lying to the anchor from the stem. It must be emphasized again that the strain on the gear will be considerable and, once it has been streamed, it is essential regularly to check the towing warp for chafe at the fairlead or alternatively shackle a short length of chain to the warp at the inboard towing end.

Trailing Warps An alternative to lying to a sea anchor is to tow warps, when running before the wind under bare poles. The principle here is different to the sea anchor technique, where the aim is to keep the ship end on to the sea and moving as slowly as possible. When trailing warps the vessel is allowed to run before the wind but at a controlled speed which will allow her to be kept end on more readily. The warp must be of large size and towed in a bight over the stern, one end being made fast to each quarter. Provided sufficient rope is carried on board the length streamed can be varied to regulate the speed to choice. In addition, it is probable that the bight of a large rope towed

astern will create a slick which results in smoother water astern. The differing methods of riding out storms in small yachts all have their advocates, but one of the most widely-travelled of cruising men, Eric Hiscock, in *Voyaging under Sail*, states that in his opinion trailing warps offers the most satisfactory method.

It is possible that the newcomer, in his early off-shore trips, may find himself embroiled in what may seem to him at the time to be survival conditions. Bearing in mind that Force 6 is sometimes described as 'a yachtsman's gale', it will be appreciated that Force 5 in a small cruiser of, say, 20 ft L.O.A. may be a chastening experience when it is encountered for the first time. Therefore, it is sound practice early in one's sailing career to assess what can happen in a blow by trying one out under controlled conditions. The word 'control' does not apply to the weather of course, but at least the circumstances can be controlled. It is suggested that a day be chosen when there is a fresh to strong wind but no gale warnings. The vessel is well prepared, reefed down and, accompanied by an experienced friend (and without children on board), a short trip is made into exposed water to find out what really happens. Naturally this experiement should not be attempted in very strong off-shore winds if any doubts existed about the ability of the vessel to beat back, or if, for example, there is a bar to be crossed which is known to be dangerous in the prevailing conditions. This sort of 'dummy run' will give the new skipper confidence in dealing with a gale of wind, while it may also give the over-confident some food for thought . . . !

Ch.5
Seamanship Pt.3

Emergency Procedures

It is a common human failing to assume that 'it won't happen to me' and it is true that dire disasters at sea overtake very few people indeed. This does not mean, however, that one should dismiss out of hand the possibility of fire or 'man overboard', for example. It can and does happen and, next time, it *may* be you – so be prepared. If a problem is thought about in advance, the various solutions pondered and, if possible, practised, in all probability the situation will not arise but, if it does, you will be off to a good start without losing time by wondering what to do first.

Running aground

This happens to everyone sooner or later, as a result of carelessness or poor navigation, and usually only results in a certain amount of embarrassment and loss of face on the part of the skipper. Nevertheless, circumstances may arise in which running aground can be the first step to a serious situation, and for this reason it is included in this chapter on emergency procedures.

Let us start with the example of running ashore on a flood tide with an on-shore wind, when the first step is to drop the sails to prevent the vessel driving further on as the tide makes. Assuming that the auxiliary is unable to pull her off, the next step is to lay out the kedge in deep water to prevent her being blown progressively further up the bank. When she has floated and swung round facing off-shore she can then be sailed or motored off, recovering the kedge on the way out. If the wind is off-shore then obviously no problem exists.

However, if the tide is ebbing when the vessel grounds then immediate action is necessary if a period of enforced inactivity is to be avoided. With an onshore wind the standard drill of dropping the sails, trying the auxiliary astern and then laying out the kedge astern must be put into operation at once. If she is a long-keeled boat the kedge should be laid out along the line the vessel took when grounding, as it is normally easier to pull her back along the groove she has cut in the bottom than to pull her round. It is important to remember that a fin keel boat can have her draft reduced by heeling her over, whereas the reverse applies with a bilge keel yacht – an attempt to heel the latter will merely exacerbate

the situation. If the vessel is a fin keel, as soon as tension can be applied to the kedge warp, she should be rocked from side to side by the crew in order to break out the keel if the bottom is of a muddy nature. If she does not move immediately then she must be heeled over by swinging out the boom, preferably with a crew member on it. A further possibility is to run a second anchor out abeam and then attach it to a halyard to help careen her. Conversely every effort must be made *not* to heel the bilge keel yacht – although it may help to rock her in the initial stages. Circumstances will vary considerably in each case, particularly with regard to wind direction, the power of which should be used to help if at all possible. For example, if the wind is abaft the beam it may be possible to gybe and so slew her round quickly, though due regard must be paid to wind strength. A violent gybe with the boat hard aground could part a back stay, with disastrous consequences to the mast.

Summing up, the chances of successfully getting off on an ebb tide depend very largely on the speed with which the necessary action is taken. Remember that with a 12 ft range of tide the level will fall approximately 3 inches in five minutes at its maximum rate of flow. Secondly, every effort should be made to lighten the vessel as much as possible. Any crew member not actively engaged should be put in the dinghy together with any heavy weights which can be moved rapidly. Alternatively – and offering much greater chances of success – any spare crew member should, if the circumstances permit, jump over

the side and push!

Lastly, remember the underwater profile if she is a fin keel boat. For instance it may be that she has deeper draft aft and sending the crew forward may be sufficient to free the after end.

If all these measures fail, and before the boat has time to settle down, a decision must be quickly made regarding the lie of the boat when she is finally high and dry. On an inclined bank, and particularly if it is a steep one, the vessel must be made to lie with her cockpit towards the higher level thus to avoid being swamped if there is any sea running when the tide makes. If she is pointing straight up the bank then she must be heeled over away from the prevailing wind for the same reason. The boat can be heeled quite easily (providing it is done before she settles) by swinging out the boom on the appropriate side, preferably with weight at the out-board end – for example a bucket of water. Doubtless the weather situation for the next few hours is already known and if you think that there may be a sea running when the tide makes, then further measures should be taken. Still considering the fin keel boat only, it is obvious that she will pound on her bilge – which is not the strongest point of construction. If possible shock-absorbing material such as fenders, mattresses, coils of rope and such should be slipped under the bilge before she settles; they can be adequately lashed in position later. In the extremely unfortunate event of a grounding among rocks it will be necessary to back up the soft fendering with some tough material, such as floor boards etc., in an endeavour to avoid rocks piercing the bilges as she pounds with the tide.

Having taken whatever precautionary measures are possible in this manner, the next operation is to lay out the bower anchor into deep water leaving the kedge in position to pull her off astern when the tide makes. If grounding took place near high water it may be advisable to dig a trench along the line of the kedge, if a spade can be obtained, in order to assist refloating; this is particularly important if the tides are taking off, that is, the range is decreasing. In the dire event of going aground at H.W., with the tides taking off, there is a strong possibility of being 'neaped' – in other words being stuck there until the next spring tides! In these circumstances it is essential to lighten the vessel as much as possible and arrange for a powerful tow to be available at the top of the tide.

Finally, if you run aground in a dangerous position, or in a situation that may become dangerous if the weather conditions deteriorate, then it is important that the necessary distress procedure is carried out immediately. If V.H.F. radio is available a short chat with the Coastguard to put them in the picture will ensure that help is available when it is required. If this is not possible then distress rockets should be used. It is much wiser to give advance warning of impending trouble than to wait until disaster has struck.

Man Overboard This is one of the most difficult and potentially dangerous emergencies that the average yachtsman is likely to encounter. It should never happen in a well-run ship because it can only be caused by carelessness or a moment's lack of concentration on someone's part. If it *does* happen, however,

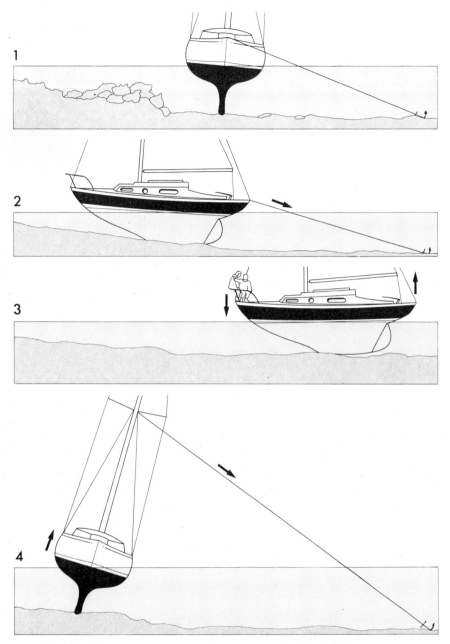

1 A kedge anchor laid out to prevent a rising tide driving the boat onto possible hidden obstructions.
2 A kedge laid out along the line of the keel to facilitate easy pulling off.
3 The crew's weight shifted to the bows can often lift the stern clear of the bottom.
4 A kedge warp shackled to a halyard and used to heel the boat, therefore reducing the draught and breaking her free.
5 A weight swung out at the end of the boom will heel the boat in the right direction when aground on a falling tide.
6 When aground on a hard bottom berth mattresses can be used to protect the bilges from damage.

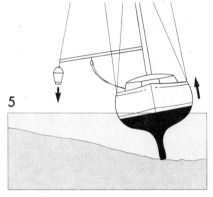

a properly-equipped yacht in which the crew have practised their drill will be able to cope with the danger much more successfully than the crew who have not worked at the problem and its various solutions. It cannot be stressed too strongly that life harnesses must be worn by all crew members on deck when conditions require them, the term 'on deck' specifically including the cockpit.

The 'man overboard' emergency divides itself into

two separate problems: firstly getting the yacht back to the man and, secondly, getting the man on board, the latter quite often being the greater one of the two.

If a crewman is seen to fall overboard the first action is to drop a lifebuoy over the stern (one should be attached to the pushpit with a quick-release mechanism) and if more than one person is left on board someone should be ordered to keep the man in sight. This is

particularly important if there is a sea running and he disappears from view periodically.

If the vessel is a sailing yacht the traditional method is to gybe immediately and work back so that the crewman can be approached from the **leeward side.** This is an important point to remember for if a yacht stops to windward the leeward drift could take her down onto the man with possibly disasterous results, especially in the case of a motor yacht with high topsides

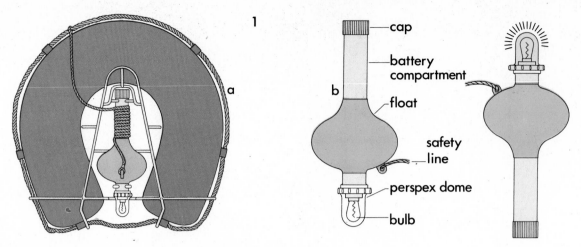

1

cap
battery compartment
float
safety line
perspex dome
bulb

and comparatively shallow draft.

Although gybing is commonly accepted as the best method it is not necessarily so in all circumstances. For example, if there was a stiff breeze blowing and a physically-weak person left alone on board a gybe would probably be inadvisable to attempt and the yacht should then be tacked round and sailed to leeward of the man in the water. If the auxiliary is easily started, this should be done at the earliest opportunity; it may not be needed but it could be very useful for

manoeuvring the vessel during the last stage of the operation. It is essential to see that it is in neutral before any ropes are thrown or the man is approached closely. With the ever-increasing number of yachts fitted with self-steering gear there is always the possibility of someone falling overboard and not being missed immediately. As soon as it is realized that someone is missing the ship's heading must be noted, the vessel put on to a reciprocal course and the log reading taken. An estimate of the time the

crewman was last seen must be made in order to fix the limit of the search area and this should be plotted on the chart. At this juncture it has to be decided whether to sail back on a straight, reciprocal course or whether to tack back, thus covering a wide area on the way. The latter method requires care, and particularly at the beginning, as the helmsman will want to know his tacking angle each side of the reciprocal course. If he puts in, say, 2 minute tacks on each leg (counting to himself up to, say,

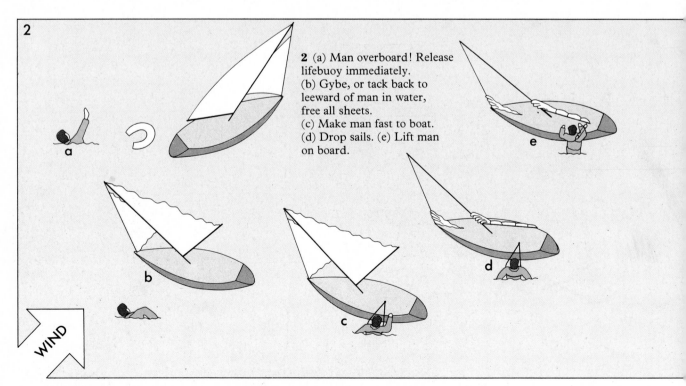

2 (a) Man overboard! Release lifebuoy immediately.
(b) Gybe, or tack back to leeward of man in water, free all sheets.
(c) Make man fast to boat.
(d) Drop sails. (e) Lift man on board.

WIND

1 (a) Lifebuoy and mounting cage for attachment to guard rail. (b) Night safety light. When the light is thrown into the sea with the lifebuoy it floats in an upright position, opposite to that in which it is stored aboard. It does not have a great range but it will help considerably to keep a position check should man-overboard occur at night.

120) at 4 knots he will cover a reasonable area each side of the track. His difficulty will be to know when he has reached the limit of the search area unless there is someone left onboard who can maintain an accurate plot. Having reached the limit of the search area the helmsman should then reverse the course and tack back downwind with the same procedure of counting on each tack. A double run like this should provide effective coverage of the area with a very good chance of success.

To sum up, the steps in the first part of the operation are:

1. If the man is seen to go overboard a life buoy should immediately be released over the stern.
2. Gybe or tack the yacht back on to a course that will bring her to leeward of the man in the water.
3. If the man has not reached the lifebuoy, sail past him and drop him another one before attempting to stop the yacht. It is a good idea to have a floating line of, say, 100 ft (30 m) attached to the yacht, with a float on the end, that can be released from the push pit; if the yacht forereaches too fast he may be able to grab it.
4. As soon as the vessel is close enough to leeward she must be stopped by freeing the sheets. As soon as a rope has been got to the man, both sails should be dropped which will have the two-fold effect of preventing her forereaching too fast and stopping any sheets from flogging and hindering the pick-up.

The Pick-up When the yacht has been positioned alongside the man in the water, he must be made fast to the boat immediately – if nothing else is handy then the end of the mainsheet will do. Next pass a line under his arms and secure it with a bowline for lifting purposes. At this stage the crew member left onboard may now feel that the most difficult part of the operation is over. If the man is still conscious and reasonably fit his recovery should present no insuperable difficulties, provided the person aboard has a clear idea of the problems involved and the necessary actions to be taken.

The first point, which must be understood, is that a man in waterlogged clothing (and probably exhausted as well) cannot be lifted aboard the average small yacht by a single person unless some sort of mechanical aid is available. This problem will be alleviated if the man himself can help by climbing up a ladder. On the subject of ladders, the rope type with round section rungs, which stows so neatly in a cockpit locker, is quite useless for this job as, when it is pressed against the ship's side the man will be unable to get his feet in it. The rope ladder with flat rungs, say four inches wide, offers a better chance provided the rungs are so roped that they cannot capsize when pressure is applied. Any sort of rope ladder, however, that is compact enough to stow in a small yacht will of necessity be light in construction and, although strong enough, will be of somewhat dubious value – particularly if there is a heavy sea running. The best type of portable boarding ladder will be rigid in construction and sufficiently long to enable a man to get his foot on the lowest rung when he is in the water. It is no use at all having a bottom rung which is on a level with the sea. There are many ladders of this type available and, although stowage may be more difficult, its presence on board in an emergency could be very useful indeed.

Other possibilities are: a transom ladder permanently mounted, preferably with the bottom half hinged up so that it can be quickly dropped down when required; or small folding steps on the transom. This arrangement is only practicable if the transom is deep enough to permit the lowest step to be easily reached by a man in the sea.

3 (a) The possible result of a pick-up approach made from the windward side. (b) A safe approach from the leeward side.

1 Recovering a man overboard by: (a) the use of the mainsheet and a sheet winch, (b) by using the main halyard or the topping lift rigged to a purchase, (c) unhanking the foresail and using it as a scoop.
2(a) Using a lightweight portable ladder hooked over the side to assist man in the water.
(b) Impossibility of one man lifting the dead weight of a man on-board without aid.

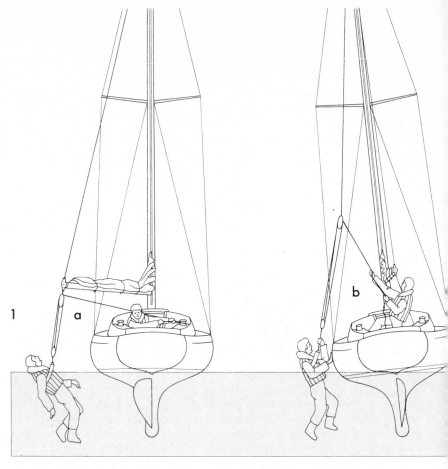

Before going into the actual technique for getting the man aboard, it is important to look at the guard rails. On the average yacht they are fairly low and, if they are of conventional design, the bottom life line will be too close to the deck to permit a man to scramble under it. The bottom line, at least, should be secured with a senhouse slip (pelican hook) or seized with a lashing at one end so that it can be quickly released or cut in an emergency. Turning now to the methods of getting the man aboard it must be stressed that some of the ideas may not be practicable on some boats. It is therefore important to work out some method of dealing with this situation before it happens (don't forget to explain it to any new crew members). Bearing in mind that the man in the sea will probably be exhausted (or

even unconscious) it is essential to have some form of mechanical aid to get him aboard, which leads immediately to consideration of the sheet and halyard winches. If the halyard winch is to be used unclip the halyard from the sail and hitch it to the loop round the man's chest. This will assist him aboard if he can use a ladder but it is most unlikely that he could be lifted aboard if he was completely incapable as it is only a single purchase, and it would not have sufficient power. If, as is highly probable, more power is required it might be possible quickly to detach the mainsheet from the boom end and hitch it to the halyard fall. The power available will be dependent on the type of purchase but in any case will be more effective than one person using a halyard

winch. It is possible that the mainsheet alone might be used if it is detached from the cockpit track slide, swung out over the boat's side and hooked directly onto the man. This would naturally be dependent on whether the topping lift is strong enough to take the man's weight.

Sheet winches are normally in a position where more effective force can be exerted on them but unfortunately the lead from them may be more difficult to adapt. If, however, the yacht is fortunate enough to have two speed winches then every effort should be made to utilize the additional power available. The pull has to be converted from a horizontal one to a vertical one and this is done best by hitching a block on to the mast or other strong point, passing a rope through it, hitching it to the man

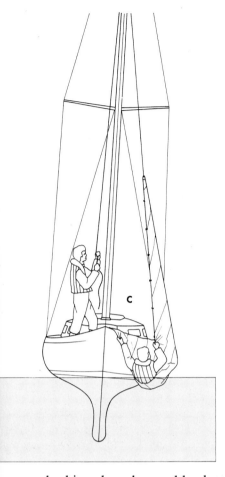

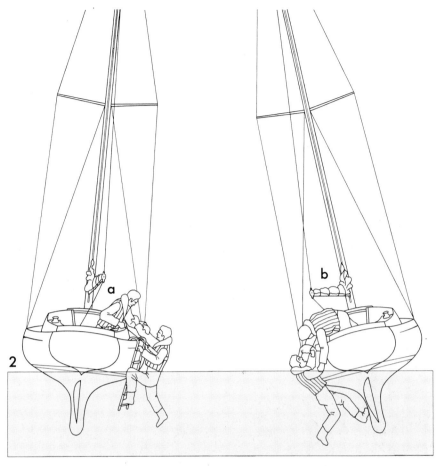

and taking the other end back to the sheet winch. It may not be possible to get a lift high enough to pull him aboard but once his shoulders are above deck level he can be secured, his feet lifted aboard and then he may be rolled in under the guard rail. If the man is completely exhausted and unable to help himself, other lines of approach may be necessary. If the foresail is unhanked from the forestay, leaving the tack, halyard and sheet still secured, the sail can be dropped over the side and the man dragged into it. The sheet should then be lightened up and the halyard hauled up, thus lifting the man in the bunt of the sail. Again considerable power is needed and it will be necessary to utilize the mainsheet hitched to the halyard, or else the two speed winch as has already been

explained. This will only be necessary after the bulk of the sail has been lifted manually on the halyard and the point is reached when the man's deadweight has to be lifted from the water. The mainsail could be utilized in a similar manner by running all the slides out of the mast track but this would not normally offer any advantage over the foresail, except for the lower free board amidships.

Many small yachts normally carry a half inflated dinghy on deck and this could be very useful as an intermediate step with an exhausted man. Dropped over the side it would be possible to drag him into it and thus provide a platform on which he could stand whilst he was being helped aboard.

While the average sailing yacht is well equipped with

running rigging, which can be utilized for the recovery operation, the conventional motor cruiser is certainly not. In these circumstances consideration should be given to carrying a strong purchase onboard and perhaps even installing a powerful winch at some convenient point.

As 'man overboard' is probably one of the most difficult situations that may occur in the life of any yachtsman, it is therefore a sensible precaution for all crew members to have a clear idea of the action necessary particularly bearing in mind that, if it should ever happen, there may be only one crew member on board to deal with the problem. A practice run one summer day with a warm sea would be a very salutary experience. . . .

Fire Precautions

Fire has always been regarded as one of the worst hazards at sea but provided sensible precautions are taken onboard it need never happen.

Engines Small vessels will normally have petrol or diesel auxiliary engines which if they are properly installed and used should not constitute a real fire risk. Naturally petrol, with its much lower flash point, is a greater potential hazard than diesel fuel and must therefore be treated with great respect. The engine installation must be beyond criticism in so far as the fuel and exhaust systems are concerned and these should be checked regularly for leaks, cracked pipes and loose connections. Most countries have strict regulations or codes of practice regarding installations of this nature in boats, but it is worthwhile when buying a boat to check that the engine has been installed in accordance with sound engineering principles. It is even more important when buying a second-hand boat, in case a previous owner has carried out some 'modifications'. Basically, the fuel tank should be situated as far from the engine and exhaust pipe as possible, all fuel lines should be of the proper grade of copper pipe, regularly clipped up at intervals to prevent there being any long unsupported length, flexible connections should be made with the correct armoured flexible pipe and all carburettors should be equipped with flame traps. Exhaust pipes should be properly lagged in those cases where the exhaust system is not water-cooled and should be properly fixed to avoid undue vibration, with the consequent possibility of fracture. Reserves of petrol should not be carried in plastic containers, for, apart from the obvious dangers of their falling against a hot exhaust pipe, if they are stored in lockers there is always the possibility of mechanical damage and subsequent leakage.

Spillage of petrol can have two possible results: a fire due to it coming into contact with a naked flame, cigarette, hot exhaust pipe, or secondly, an explosive gas collecting in the

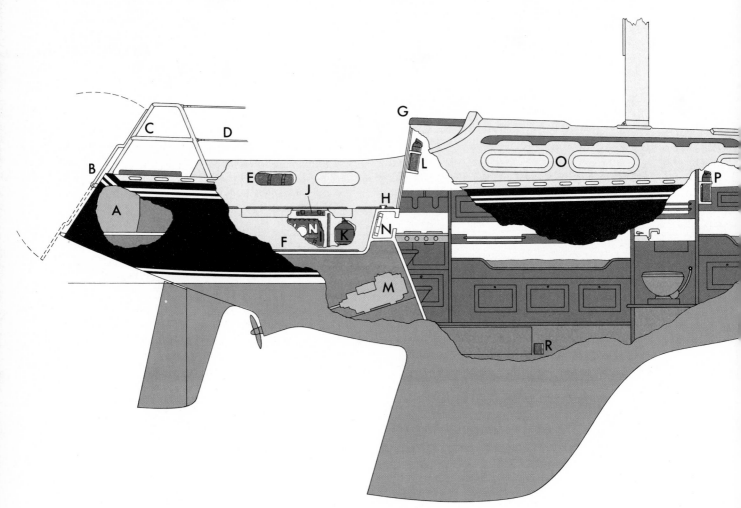

bilges due to evaporation of the spilt fuel. Once the latter has happened a small spark from an ignition switch or starter motor could cause an explosion. After refuelling it is imperative to ensure that any spillage has been thoroughly cleared up and that the bilges are free of petrol vapour before starting the engine or using any naked flame.

Cookers Normally cookers in small boats burn either calor gas or paraffin, though there is also a small proportion of methelated spirit cookers. Paraffin and spirit do not constitute the same danger onboard that petrol does but obviously sensible precautions in their use and stowage are important.

Calor gas or Camping Gaz are undoubtedly the most popular methods of cooking and if properly installed and correctly used they present no dangers. The gas bottle should be installed in a compartment that drains over the side in order that any leak from a faulty regulator or valve does not find its way into the bilges. All pipe work should be properly installed away from any possible mechanical damage and clipped up at regular intervals, and flexible connections to gimballed cookers must be inspected regularly for chafe. It is good practice to turn off the gas at the bottle when the cooker is not in use. Bilges should be checked regularly to ensure that no build up of gas occurs, and

in this connection the installation of a gas detector alarm may be considered. Remember that the modern diaphragm bilge pump is also a good air pump and if used regularly will ensure no accumulation of gas occurs in the bilges.

Fire Fighting In the event of a fire on board, no matter how small, treat it as a major incident immediately – a small fire can become a big one in an incredibly short space of time. The first step is to get to work with a fire extinguisher on the seat of the fire while someone stops the boat or alters course so that the wind does not spread the flames. All ports and hatches should be closed so that draughts near the fire are reduced to a minimum.

If there are adequate fire extinguishers on board and they are used promptly the fire should be rapidly brought under control, but if this is in doubt immediate preparations should be made to abandon ship. The presence of V.H.F. radio could be a great asset in contacting other ships or the coastguard. The life raft or inflatable dinghy should be launched complete with 'survival kit', water, food and distress rockets.

It should not be inferred from the comments in this section that fire is a common occurrence in small boats at sea. This is far from being the case, but hopefully the points made above will inspire the owner to take a long look at his boat and its safety appliances with a critical eye. Full details of recommended safety appliances will be found in Appendix 2 (see page 220).

Flares
Flares are a vital part of the equipment of any sea-going yacht. They must be properly

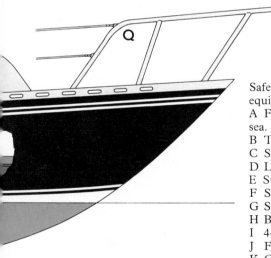

Safety points to look for on a well equipped boat.
A Fuel tank in locker with breather to sea.
B Transom ladder.
C Strong pushpit.
D Lifelines.
E Survival kit stored in cockpit locker.
F Self-draining cockpit.
G Strong hatch – not over large.
H Bridge deck.
I 4-man liferaft.
J Flares in cockpit locker.
K Gas bottle in locker draining over the side.
L Fire extinguisher accessible from cockpit.
M Engine installed with fuel supply to starboard, exhaust system to port.
N Flares.
O Strong ports.
P Fire extinguisher accessible from forehatch.
Q Pulpit.
R Gas detector.
(Lifebuoy and dan buoy not illustrated.)

stored where they cannot become damp or physically damaged, and should be replaced when they become 'time expired'. Above all the crew must know how to operate them, if necessary in the dark. The following notes refer to the general principles of use. For the various types and quantities to be carried on board reference should be made to the Department of Trade and Industries Recommendations in Appendix 2 (see page 223).

Assuming it is necessary to signal for assistance when in sight of the shore, a hand-held red distress flare should be fired, which must be followed by another one within thirty seconds to one minute. The second one ensures that anyone who only caught a glimpse of the first has his sighting confirmed and, in addition, he may be able to get a bearing on the ship's position. Assuming that no acknowledgement is made (this would be a white

star shell from a Coastguard or Life Boat Station) a second pair should be fired within ten to fifteen minutes. During daylight hours a smoke signal should be used, preferably in conjunction with a flare. In poor visibility a flare should always be used. When out of sight of land, or near land but in poor visibility, parachute flares should be used, with a twenty second gap between the first two which should be followed by another pair about ten to fifteen minutes later. When assistance is in sight, be it life-boat or helicopter, another flare should be discharged to make sure that the vessel in distress is not overlooked. This is particularly important if a heavy sea is running. When a helicopter is searching in daylight hours a smoke signal is an effective way of indicating one's whereabouts. In addition to distress flares, it is a wise precaution to carry on board some white flares for use when in close quarters among big ships.

Apart from flares for use on board, every yacht should carry sufficient 'personal' flares of the pocket-size variety for issue to each member of the crew in the

event of abandoning ship for the life-raft or inflatable dinghy.

Distress flares are available in packs of different sizes to cover a variety of requirements e.g.: dinghy pack, cruise pack and off-shore pack, thus making the correct selection of flares easy for everyone.

Search and Rescue Procedures You tend to feel rather solitary in a small boat off-shore and this feeling is certainly accentuated when you find yourself in any sort of trouble. It is comforting to understand the extensive assistance which will be made available if or when the occasion demands it.

Most maritime countries operate some form of life-saving service for vessels in distress round their coasts, which supplement the efforts of ships at sea. The arrangements differ from one country to another but coastal radio stations naturally play a large part in alerting ships in the vicinity of the incident and the other authorities involved. All these helpful organizations have one thing in common however – they must be alerted in the first place! This is so obvious it hardly seems necessary to state the fact, but, nevertheless, it is essential for the owner of any yacht to see that she is properly equipped with distress rockets and flares, even if he is also fortunate to be equipped with V.H.F. radio.

Her Majesty's Coast Guard is the authority for initiating and co-ordinating the search and rescue procedure (S.A.R.) round the coasts of the United Kingdom. The Coast Guard maintain continuous radio and visual watch from some fifty stations, half of which are designated 'Rescue Headquarters', who co-ordinate

Below: A selection of Pains Wessex distress flares and watertight container. *Opposite:* A helicopter of Royal Navy Rescue towing a small cruiser offshore into deeper water.

Below: One of the very fast semi-inflatable inshore rescue boats operated around the coast by the R.N.L.I.
Right: An R.N.L.I. lifeboat out on an engine test run.

the S.A.R. operation. There are also a further one hundred intermediate stations where watch is maintained during busy periods and bad weather, and, lastly, about one hundred and fifty stations where only visual watch is maintained during bad weather. The coastal radio stations already mentioned are operated by the G.P.O. and, in addition to their other duties, maintain continuous watch on V.H.F. channel 16 and the distress frequencies. The coverage is extensive and frequently a small craft is observed to be in trouble and the rescue operation is started before she has even fired her distress rockets . . .!

In the event of an S.A.R. operation being carried out the Coast Guard Rescue Headquarters can call on ships and aircraft, including helicopters and the Royal Air Force. The latter is primarily responsible for providing S.A.R. cover for R.A.F. and civilian aircraft round the coasts of the U.K. but it will also assist ships in distress, operational commitments permitting. When the vessel in trouble is located, or perhaps before depending on circumstances, the Rescue H.Q. contacts the local secretary of the Royal National Lifeboat Institution who arranges for the lifeboat launch and the subsequent rescue operation.

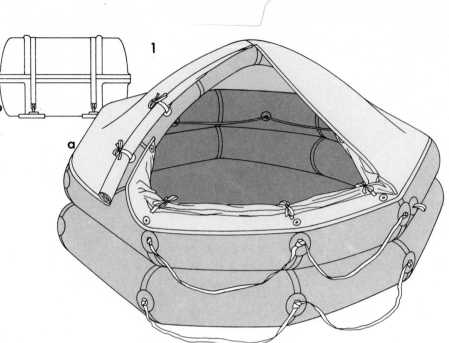

Below: A transom hung ladder, as here fitted on the *Copalu*, is extremely useful in the event of picking up a man overboard.

1 (a) 4-man liferaft with twin buoyancy chambers and self-erecting canopy. (b) Liferaft canister. In an emergency the canister is thrown into the sea and the firing lanyard pulled, the liferaft then inflates from its own CO_2 supply.

2 In an emergency when the boat, A, is in danger of sinking, the crew should abandon ship and climb into the liferaft, B. However, it is a wise precaution to remain attached to the yacht by a long line. This makes it easier for a searching helicopter to spot the yacht and thus rescue her crew.

Coastguard Service to yachtsmen H.M. Coastguard have a reporting system designed specifically for yachtsmen (and which is free of charge) which enables them to initiate S.A.R. procedures rapidly, should the need arise. At the beginning of the cruising season the owner fills in form CG66[A] which embodies full details of his boat and normal cruising grounds and he then sends it to his local Coastguard Station.

Before proceeding on any lengthy trips he completes two copies of form CG66[B], including details of his cruise, and gives one copy to the Coastguard Station and one to a friend, who will act as his agent. He tells his agent his E.T.A. at the destination and arranges to telephone him when he arrives there. If his agent does not hear from him on the appointed day he informs the Coastguard that the yacht is overdue and the Coastguard immediately start S.A.R. procedure.

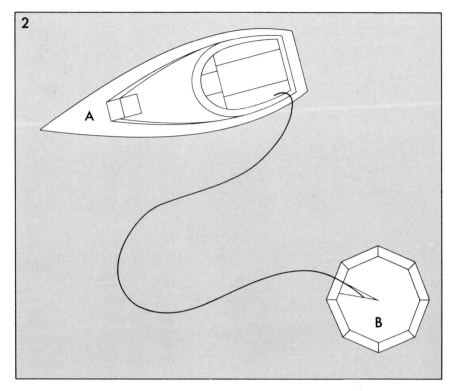

2

A

B

Apart from the life-boat there are two other methods of rescue which may be employed when a vessel is in distress: the Coastguards' Breeches Buoy equipment and the helicopter rescue. The former is normally only used on rocky coasts when the vessel in distress is close to the shore and is therefore unapproachable by a life boat while at the same time being too close to the shore for the crew to risk getting into the life-raft or an inflatable. As it is so unlikely that the small family cruiser will ever become involved in such an operation, it is not proposed to discuss it here at length, but anyone who wishes to familiarize themselves with the procedure and the signals involved should consult *Reed's Nautical Almanac* or any publication dealing with safety at sea.

The use of the helicopter is more common in rescue operations involving small craft, and so a few comments on the procedures and difficulties may be useful. When a helicopter

has begun searching, it is important to realize that a small yacht or life-raft may be very difficult to see from the air if weather conditions are bad. Therefore, as soon as the aircraft is sighted, another distress signal should be fired – not a parachute flare as this might complicate the helicopter's approach run, but rather a hand-held flare at night or an orange smoke signal during the day. The helicopter will approach from downwind and if the vessel in distress is a motor-cruiser the winchman will have no problem in landing on deck. However, if the vessel is a sailing yacht, and particularly if it is rolling heavily, then the winchman will be unable to approach closely because of the danger of his becoming entangled with the mast and rigging. The crew must, therefore, get into the life-raft or inflatable and then drift away from the vessel, at the same time remaining attached to it by means of a very long painter. If

the vessel is in danger of foundering the painter can always be cut. Otherwise remain attached to the ship as long as possible. This is particularly important if it is decided to get into the life-raft before the helicopter appears – the chances of a yacht and life-raft being spotted are much greater than a life-raft alone. If the vessel is not carrying a life-raft or inflatable, then it will be necessary for the crew, wearing life jackets, to jump into the sea to be picked up. Naturally they should not do this until it is clear, beyond all shadow of doubt, that the helicopter has spotted them. They should each attach themselves to a long rope so that they do not get separated during the rescue operation.

Once the helicopter is in position to start the rescue follow the winchman's instructions implicitly, bearing in mind that the flying time of the helicopter is limited and it may have used up a large proportion of it in the initial search.

Ch. 6
Coastal Navigation Pt. 1

Navigation is the art of getting a vessel from one place to another in safety, and the ability to pinpoint the vessel's position on the chart at any time between departure and arrival. It is not an exacting science, and in fact anyone can master it who has a knowledge of arithmetic and a little geometry coupled with a desire to understand charts and tidal systems. We shall be dealing with coastal navigation only here, that is navigation by bearings on fixed points ashore, light houses, light vessels, buoys – in fact anything which is identifiable on the chart, together with dead reckoning calculations (see page 128). Astral or celestial navigation which is navigation by 'sights', angular measurements of the sun or other celestial bodies giving position lines, is generally confined to ocean passages which are outside the scope of this book. Coastal navigation is adequate for the type of cruise normally undertaken by little ships – for example from the U.K. to France, Belgium and Holland.

Foremost amongst the equipment required for coastal navigation are the compass and the chart. On the subject of instruments it is a false economy to buy poor quality articles – they will be used for a lifetime and the best that you can afford is the cheapest in the end, quite apart from the pleasure obtained from using well made tools.

Equipment

The list of equipment below may be regarded by the little ship navigator as the minimum for safe navigation. It is followed by some additional suggestions for the navigator who takes the subject seriously and who wishes to enlarge his horizon – literally!

Charts The first essential for safe navigation and without which no vessel should proceed to sea. The chart is dealt with in some detail later on (see page 111).

Compass (ship's) The most important piece of navigational equipment on board. A great many varieties are available for small ships but probably one of the best for the family cruiser (and not the most expensive) is the grid compass. Originally developed for use in the Royal Air Force it is extremely simple in operation. On top of the compass bowl is mounted a brass ring holding a perspex plate. The ring is divided into 360° and can be rotated on the compass bowl. It is set by rotating the ring until the course to be steered is opposite the lubber line on the compass. The helmsman then keeps the North South line on the compass card parallel to two N–S lines engraved on the perspex plate. Keeping three

lines parallel is a much easier task for a tired helmsman at night than watching a rather small figure on a compass card. It is largely a matter of personal preference, however, and the dome-topped compass giving good magnification with degrees marked in groups of 5° is probably the one most commonly used.

Compass (hand bearing) In most small cruisers the ship's compass is mounted in such a position that it is not possible to take bearings with it and a small hand-bearing compass is,

therefore, a very useful piece of equipment when you want to take bearings.

Parallel Rule This rule enables a course to be laid off on the chart from the compass rose to any other position. There are specialized protractors which are much more useful in small vessels with, perhaps, rather inconvenient chart tables or even no chart table at all. The basic type consists of a perspex plate with a compass rose engraved thereon and a long movable arm pivoted in the centre of the rose. The rose is

1 Grid compass
2 Dome compass
3 Hand bearing compass
4 Echo sounder
5 Most echo sounders read off the depth of water from the transducer to the sea bed (a), and not the depth of water under the keel (b).
6 Lead line: (a) = 2 fathoms, leather; (b) = 3 fathoms, leather; (c) = 5 fathoms, white calico; (d) = 7 fathoms, red bunting; (e) = 10 fathoms, leather with hole.

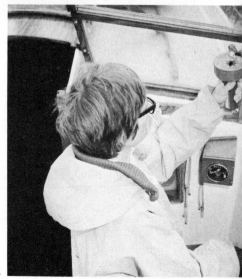

1

2

3

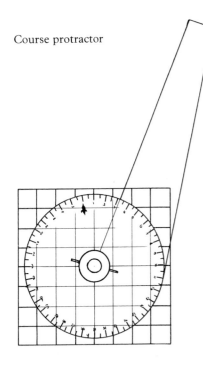

Course protractor

placed anywhere on the chart where it is desired to measure or lay off a course and the rotating arm moved to read it off directly. This obviates any possible error due to transferring back to the chart rose. Naturally the North–South line on the protractor must be parallel with any meridian on the chart.

Dividers and Pencil Compasses Simple geometrical instruments which are essential for chart work.

Barometer A necessary piece of equipment to enable the local weather situation to be fully understood. Shipping forecasts cover a wide area and a true appreciation of their implications is helped considerably by a knowledge of the local barometric trends.

Echo Sounder or Lead Line Some method of measuring depth is important in navigation. An electronic type of echo sounder is extremely good and very convenient but is not vital if a lead line is carried aboard.

Radio A simple radio set that will obtain weather forecasts is essential.

Clock Some form of timekeeper is obviously important. If you have to buy a clock it is worth considering a quartz crystal one, which need not necessarily be expensive but is useful if you have ambitions in the direction of astro navigation. If it embodies an alarm as well it will be useful to give warning of shipping forecasts.

Nautical Almanac Some form of nautical almanac is necessary for information relating to tides, lights, port entry signals, radio beacons etc. *Reed's Nautical Almanac* embodies practically all the navigational information that the little ship skipper needs to know for cruising in the U.K., on the Continental

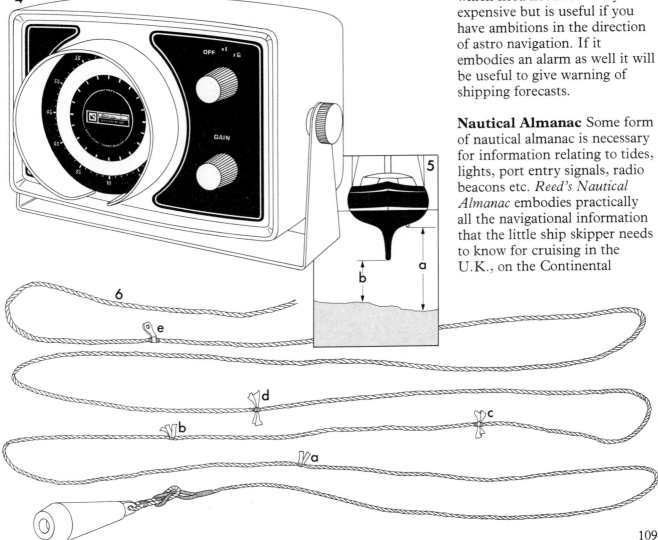

coastline and in the Mediterranean. The eastern seaboard of North America is covered, in similar manner, by the American Edition of Reed's.

Ship's Logbook It is important to keep a ship's logbook in which information relating to navigational matters is recorded. It should be written up as soon as possible after any incident and at least every hour, recording the course steered, distance run, the wind strength and any other items which may affect the passage. If calculations are made in a rough log any subsequent doubts about position can easily be rechecked and verified. A fair copy embodying all the information, which may be useful on future cruises, can then be written up at the end of the day.

Tidal Atlases Tidal stream information is provided on all Admiralty charts but for quick reference Tidal Atlases are very helpful. Issued by the Hydrographic Office in booklet form, each one covers a certain area and each page shows the whole tidal stream picture for that area, at a particular hour, related to High Water at Dover or whichever Standard port is selected. They are very useful for the small boat skipper when on or planning a passage. Most maritime countries provide this information in similar form.

Sailing Directions The British Admiralty issue 'Admiralty Pilots' covering the whole world. They contain much information which is of great use to the yachtsman but in general Admiralty pilots, whichever country produces

them, are written primarily for large vessels. However, there are commercially-published 'yachtsman's pilots' which are extremely useful to the little ship navigator as they are produced specifically for yachtsmen. K. Adlard Coles & Co. is one firm which specializes in these books.

Patent Log A Walker patent log, or some equivalent method of recording distance run (such as an inboard electronic log), is a great help in navigation and should really be regarded as essential for passages which take you out of sight of land.

Station Pointer A circular protractor with three adjustable arms, used for fixing a position from bearings taken of two or three fixed objects. They are only practical on large yachts with a full-size chart table.

Sextant Not an essential item
of equipment for the coastal
navigator but very useful for
measuring vertical angles to
obtain 'distance off' and also
horizontal angles. It need not
be expensive – some of the
plastic sextants on the market
today are capable of surprising
accuracy.

The Chart
The efforts of the little ship
navigator are centred round the
chart and a full understanding
of it is therefore important. It
contains a wealth of information
and, due to the amount
displayed, much of it is in an
abbreviated form – a sort of
nautical short-hand. To assist in
reading the chart the British
Admiralty issue booklet No.
5011 which shows full details of
the symbols and abbreviations
used. Other countries issue
similar publications for their
own charts. (In the U.S.A. the
equivalent publication is
H.O. No. 1.)

Construction There are two
types of construction or
projection used in chart making:
Mercator and Gnomonic.
A knowledge of the Mercator
projection is sufficient for the
little ship navigator, the
Gnomonic projection being of
little significance to him. If a
full understanding of the
Gnomonic projection is required
the reader is referred to the
Coastal Navigation volume, in
the Reed's Yacht Master Series.
Before the Mercator projection
can be explained, mention must
be made of Latitude and
Longitude.

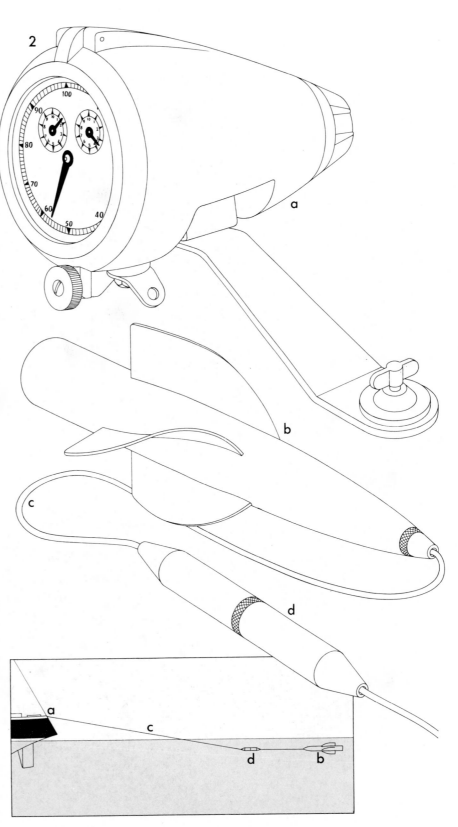

1 Sextant
2 Patent trailing log for registering
distance through the water. (a)
Register, 0–100 miles, (b) trailing
rotator, (c) braided line, (d) sinker.

Latitude and Longitude The geographical position of any place on the earth's surface may be described by reference to two imaginery lines, at right angles to each other, which cross at that point. The two primary lines are provided by the equator and the Greenwich Meridian. The equator is a line circumscribing the earth half way between the North and South poles and the Greenwich Meridian is a line passing through Greenwich Observatory in South East London and also through both the North and South poles. A circular line round the earth, parallel to the equator, is known as a 'parallel of latitude' and all points on it have the same latitude reference. Any line drawn on the earth's surface at right angles to a parallel of latitude and passing through both poles is known as a meridian. 'Meridians of longitude' are numbered from 0° to 179°W in the Western hemisphere (i.e. west of Greenwich) and 0° to 179°E in the Eastern hemisphere (i.e. east of Greenwich). They meet on the 180° meridian and so it and the Greenwich Meridian are described simply as: long. 180° and long. 0° respectively.

The latitude of a place is the angle subtended at the centre of the earth between it and the equator, measured in the plane of the meridian at that particular point. Parallels of latitude are numbered 0°–90°N in the Northern hemisphere and 0°–90°S in the Southern.

The longitude of a place is the angle subtended at the centre of the earth between the meridian of that place and the meridian of Greenwich, measured in the plane of the equator.

Mercator's Projection To transfer an area from the surface

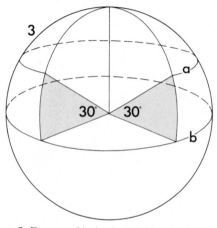
1 Plane of the equator

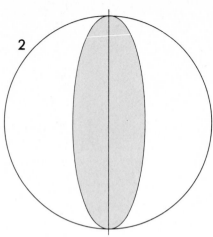
2 Plane of the Greenwich Meridian

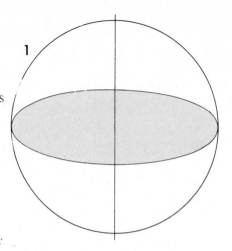
3 Degree of latitude 30° North of equator. (a) = 30° parallel, (b) = equator.

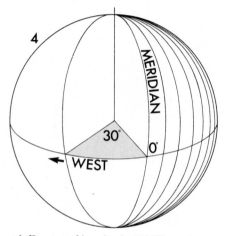
4 Degree of longitude 30° West of Greenwich Meridian at 0°.

of a sphere (the globe) to a flat surface (a chart) involves distortion of the original image, but as long as the degree of distortion is known, this presents no problem from a navigational point of view. Basically, in the Mercator projection, the sides at the top portion of the area are pulled out until the meridians are parallel and the top and bottom edges are so moved that the area is depicted as a rectangle.

Compass Rose Each compass rose on a chart consists of two concentric circles, both divided into 360°. The outer ring indicates true bearings, and the N.S. line is exactly parallel to all

meridians and at right angles to parallels of latitude. The inner ring is turned slightly so that its N point indicates the magnetic North, the difference between the true and magnetic North points being the magnetic variation at that particular point. (see page 114 for an explanation of magnetic variation.)

Length of the Nautical Mile Measurement of distance on the chart is relative to angular measurement: one minute (1/60 of a degree) measured along a meridian is equivalent to one nautical mile (1852 m or 6076.6 ft). When measuring distances on a chart, the

112

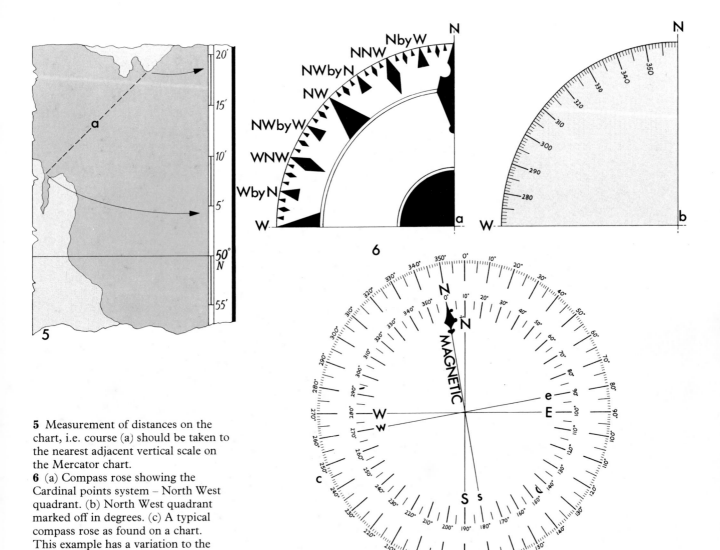

5 Measurement of distances on the chart, i.e. course (a) should be taken to the nearest adjacent vertical scale on the Mercator chart.

6 (a) Compass rose showing the Cardinal points system – North West quadrant. (b) North West quadrant marked off in degrees. (c) A typical compass rose as found on a chart. This example has a variation to the magnetic pole of 10° West.

measurement is always taken from its vertical side at the point nearest to which the measurement is required. The reason for this is that the distance between parallels of latitude expands slightly with increasing latitude due to the distortion of the Mercator projection. A cable's length is 0.1 of a nautical mile but is taken as 600 feet for practical purposes.

Depths Continental charts show depths in metres (some Dutch charts are in decimetres), whereas British charts are being gradually changed from fathoms to metres as are North American charts. It is obviously important

to note which measurement is used on any particular chart and this is clearly indicated in the title block. The depths on charts are given below chart datum (C.D.) which originally was taken as the mean level of low water springs but is now being adjusted to Lowest Astronomical Tide (L.A.T.), the lowest predicted tide in average meteorological conditions. Soundings on fathom charts are given in fathoms and in feet below 11 fathoms e.g. 6_4, and fathoms only elsewhere. On metric charts soundings are given in metres and decimetres below 20 m e.g. 15_7 and metres only elsewhere.

Drying Heights are given in feet on fathom charts and underlined $\underline{6}$ and metres and decimetres underlined on metre charts, both being above the level of C.D.

Heights of navigational features (e.g. lighthouses) are given in metres above the level of mean high water springs.

Colours On the latest Admiralty charts the land is buff coloured, and drying areas green. The 10 metre contour line is edged on the inside with blue, and all areas within the 5 m contour are blue. This convention may vary with the scale of the chart.

The Compass – variation and deviation

The compass consists basically of a bowl in which is mounted a compass card marked in degrees, from 0° to 360°, in a clockwise direction around its circumference. Attached to the bottom of this card are two or more magnets and the card is mounted on a needle-fine point bearing to minimize friction. The bowl is filled with liquid which is usually a mixture of distilled water and alcohol to damp down the movements of the card. The lubber line is marked inside the bowl, and the compass is mounted exactly on the fore and aft line of the vessel, not necessarily exactly on the centre line, but parallel to it. As mentioned earlier, the grid type compass is slightly different in construction as there is a movable ring mounted on top of the bowl graduated 0°–360° and the card has an arrow on the north-seeking pole of the card with two lines parallel to it, coincident with its magnetic axis.

Variation The Magnetic North pole does not coincide with the True or Geographic North but swings to either side of it over a period of several hundred years. Due to this displacement it follows that there will be a variation between True North and Magnetic North which varies round the surface of the earth. At the present time this is about 25°E on the western seaboard of North America and 5°W in the North Sea. This variation will apply to any magnetic bearings taken in that particular vicinity. The amount of 'swing' of the magnetic pole in any particular area is shown by the compass rose on the chart concerned, e.g. 'Variation 5°W 1977 decreasing about 5′

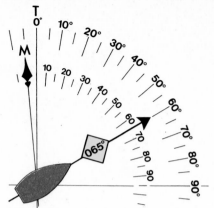

Example of variation at 5° West

annually'. In other words the magnetic meridian at that particular point is moving closer to True North by 5′ annually. The little ship navigator must fully understand how variation (and deviation, see page 115) affect his calculations.

Assume that a true course of 060° is required to be converted to a magnetic course in an area where magnetic variation is 5° West. It will be seen from the diagram that the magnetic North is 5° West of the True North. The angle between the magnetic north and the course required is therefore 060° + 5°. = 065° and this is the magnetic course required. Similarly if the variation was for example 7° East then the magnetic pole would be to the right of the true North by 7° and a 060° True course would be 060° − 7° = 053° magnetic.

Application of Variation The coastal navigator is frequently called upon to convert True courses to Magnetic and vice versa and, although a deceptively simple task, it is surprising how easily errors are made – particularly if you are tired. It will naturally help if a standard routine is adopted and the first rule is 'always to work on the chart in True and then convert to Magnetic'. Similarly a sight taken by hand-bearing compass must be converted from Magnetic to True before being

plotted on the chart.

To remember that Westerly variation is added and Easterly variation is subtracted, the following little jingle may assist:
  Error West Compass Best
  (i.e. more than True)
  Error East Compass Least
  (i.e. less than True)
(The word compass here means compass course.)

Example: a true course of 070° laid off from the chart is to be converted to a compass course where Var. is 5°W.

  070° True
Var. + 5° W.

V 075° Mag.

If the variation was say 8°E it would be:

  070° True
Var. − 8° E.

  062° Mag.

When working the opposite way, converting a magnetic bearing to plot on a chart it will be necessary to reverse the procedure. The jingle still holds good 'Variation W compass is best' and therefore the True bearing must be less than the magnetic (compass) bearing.

Example: A bearing taken with a handbearing compass is 080°C. and it is desired to plot it on the chart. Magnetic variation is 5°W.

  080° C.
Var. − 5° W.

  075° T.

– the bearing to plot on the chart.

Example: Compass bearing 110°C Variation 10°E

  110° C.
Var. + 10° E.

  120° True

114

Deviation If the compass is mounted in such a position that it is completely free from any outside magnetic interference the only correction required to be made by the navigator is the Variation. In practice though the mounting of the compass in small vessels is usually a compromise, and often introduces a local magnetic error caused by some ferrous object nearby, for example the yacht's auxiliary engine. This error is known as deviation and, unfortunately, is not a constant figure on all points of the compass. For example when the ship is heading west the error might be 3°E and when heading south might be 5°W. In some vessels the compass is mounted sufficiently far from any ferrous objects for it to be free of all local magnetic influence. However, until this is known to be a fact, you should assume that there will be an error and the necessary steps must be taken to ascertain what it is on all points of the compass. Apart from the more obvious sources of interference, such as proximity of the auxiliary engine, there will be many less obvious ones such as radio loud speakers, hand-bearing compasses, tools, cutlery and, worst of all, the variable ones – such as cans of beer stowed in a locker next to the compass or a helmsman who carries a large (and magnetic) knife in his pocket! The permanent causes of error can be overcome by a professional compass adjuster who 'swings' the ship, that is, with the ship stationary, it is rotated whilst bearings are taken of a fixed object whose position is accurately known. The adjuster then places small magnets adjacent to the compass bowl to correct the deviation error. It is seldom

possible – or indeed worth while – to completely eliminate deviation and so the adjuster draws up a deviation card which shows the error on all headings of the ship. Whilst adjusting a compass is a professional job there is no reason why the yachtsman should not try to 'swing' his ship and a simple method of doing this is described on page 117. The deviation card is as below. The central vertical line represents the compass course and the curved line is the

varying deviation error. For example, when the compass course is 160° the deviation is 6°W; if it is 120°, deviation is 7°W and obviously the deviation for courses in between those shown can be obtained by interpolation. The deviation error is applied to compass courses in exactly the same manner as variation is applied, that is, westerly deviation is added and easterly deviation is subtracted from True courses. (The same rhyme as we used for variation corrections.)

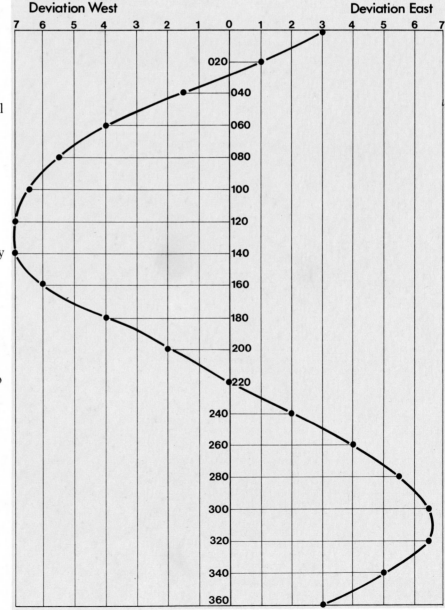

Applying Variation and Deviation to Compass Courses The inclusion of deviation, as well as variation, in the navigation calculations underlines the necessity for the standard routine of working out courses to avoid errors. Any one bearing can be written in three forms; True, Magnetic and compass and unless care is exercised confusion can arise between the two latter. The best way of remembering the steps is to memorize the letters *T V M D C*, and no doubt many yachtsmen will devise a mnemonic to impress it on their minds.

Example: The True course laid off on the chart is 090°, the variation is 5°W and deviation (taken from the ship's deviation card) is 7°E.

True	090°	
Var	+ 5°W	(error west – compass best)
Mag	095°	
Dev	– 7°E	(error east – compass least)
Compass	088′	→ Course to steer

Example: Due to a wind shift a yacht can only steer 120°C whereas the navigator wanted to make good a course of 160°T. What is the True course to lay-off on the chart to obtain the vessel's position? (Var. 6°W and Dev. 9°E).

Compass 120°
Dev. + 9°E –
(*Note reversal of sign when working from Compass to True*)

Mag. 129°
Var. – 6°W –
(*Note reversal of sign when working from Compass to True*)

True 123° → Course to lay-off on chart

In order to appreciate the magnitude of errors which can occur see the example below:

Example: The navigator has laid off a course of 120°T in an area where Variation is 7°W and the deviation error at 127°M is 8°W. What is the compass course to steer?

A Correct

True	120°
Var.	+ 7°W
Mag.	127°
Dev.	+ 8°W
Compass	135°

B Incorrect

True	120°
Var.	– 7°W
Mag.	113°
Dev.	– 8°W
Compass	105°

In 'A' the navigator has worked out correctly the compass course to be steered but in 'B' he has forgotten that 'error west compass best' and has subtracted the errors with the result that he proceeds to steer a course 30° less than he should. An error of this magnitude can, at the least, lead to serious difficulties and possibly to a dangerous situation. If he has kept a working log, however, when he becomes doubtful of his position he will be able to back track on his calculations and see where the error lies and then take the necessary action to get back on course again. Summing up, the corrections necessary to convert from True to Compass and vice versa are simple and logical, and it may seem, therefore, rather tiresome to stress the necessity of following a set pattern, but simple calculations made under difficult conditions can very easily go badly wrong unless they are made almost automatically.

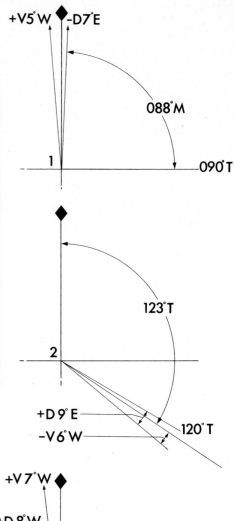

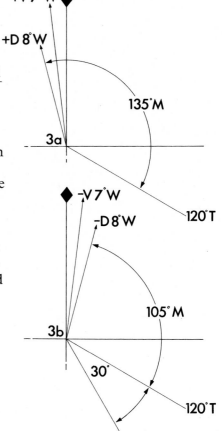

Preparing a Deviation Card

As we have seen adjusting a compass is a professional's job but the preparation of a Deviation Card is not and this should be within the capability of any little ship navigator. The accepted method of preparing a Deviation Card is to swing the ship, that is to rotate it through 360° at a fixed point whilst taking bearings of a transit whose true bearing is known. When the average yachtsman comes to carry out this operation he will usually find that it is impossible to take bearings direct from the ship's compass and he may also find difficulty in locating a suitable transit. In these circumstances an acceptable alternative is to use a Pelorus and any fixed object at least 5 miles away whose bearing need not be known.

A Pelorus consists of an adjustable compass card mounted on a base plate with a lubber line marked on it and a rotating sight centrally mounted on the card. The Pelorus is fixed in such a position that bearings can readily be taken all round the vessel and with the lubber line accurately positioned on her fore-and-aft line.

The yacht should be anchored or moored in slack water on a calm day and then rotated in a small turning circle, and sights taken of the distant object with the ship's head on intermediate headings. With the head on N (compass) the Pelorus card is adjusted to agree with the compass and then a sight is taken of the distant object (it will be appreciated that this is the same as taking a sight from the actual compass). The ship's head is then swung to 45°, the Pelorus Card adjusted to 45° and a further sight taken of the distant object. This process is continued until the ship has been swung through 360° to N again. The average of the sights will, for all practicable purposes, be the magnetic bearing of the distant object and the figures thus obtained can be used to ascertain the error, that is the deviation on each of the eight points.

The following is an example of the readings obtained and the curve produced; deviation figures in between the actual sights being obtained by interpolation.

Compass	Pelorus Bearing	Deviation	
0	123	+3	3W
45	121	+1	1W
90	117	−3	3E
135	113	−7	7E
180	115	−5	5E
225	122	+2	2W
270	126	+6	6W
315	126	+6	6W

8)963

120 = Average

The average of the Pelorus bearings is obtained (120°) from which the deviation figures (col. 3) can be produced. The curve is then drawn up and by interpolation the deviation on any compass bearing can be read off.

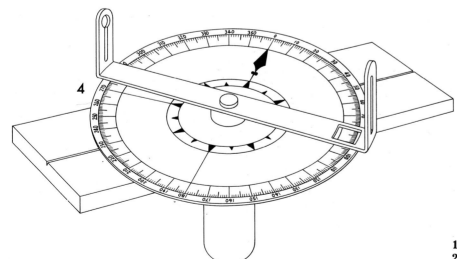

4

1 Diagram of the first example
2 Diagram of the second example
3 (a) Diagram of the correct calculation in example three. (b) Diagram of the incorrect calculation in example three.
4 Pelorus

Tides

Tides feature in the coastal navigation calculations in two ways: firstly, in problems connected with the depth of water at various places and, secondly, the effect of tidal streams on the course when on passage. Tidal theory is a complex subject but every yachtsman should have an understanding of the broad principles involved. Strictly speaking the word 'tide' should only be used in connection with the vertical movement of water whilst 'tidal stream' refers to horizontal movement.

General Theory The tidal forces acting on the mass of water on the earth's surface are a combination of centrifugal force due to the rotation of the earth, and the gravitational attractions between the sun, moon and the earth. The moon revolves in an ellipse round the earth in approximately $27\frac{1}{2}$ days, the earth revolves round the sun in three hundred and sixty-five days (approximately) and successive phases of the moon occur at approximately 30 day intervals. On the first day of the cycle the moon will be between the earth and the sun, and fifteen days later it will be on the opposite side of the earth but again in line with the earth and sun. When the moon is between the sun and the earth the dark side of the moon is towards the earth and when on the other side of the earth it is illuminated by the sun and is a 'full moon'. The combined gravitational 'pull' of the sun and moon, when in line, produce a water displacement on the surface of the globe, as in fig. 1a, when the high waters are highest and the low waters lowest, i.e. spring tides. When the moon is in quadrature (fig. 1b), the gravitational pulls of the sun and moon on the

earth are at right angles to each other and do not, therefore, directly assist each other. Due to the greater effect of the moon the resultant force is not midway between the two, as might be supposed, but as shown in Fig. 1c. In these circumstances the water displacement represents the lowest High Water and highest Low Water, i.e. Neap tides, the tides with the lowest range. Summarizing, the highest and lowest tides occur at *springs* when the earth, sun and moon are in line and the tides with the smallest ranges, *neaps*, occur when the bodies are in quadrature.

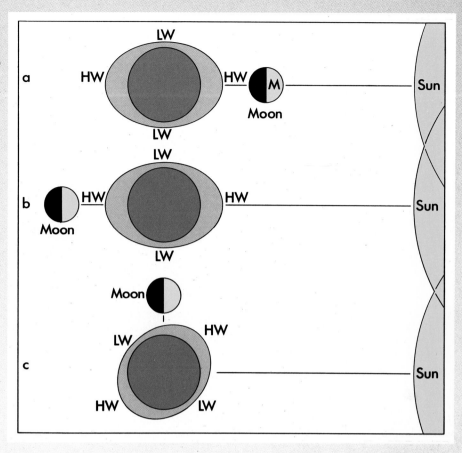

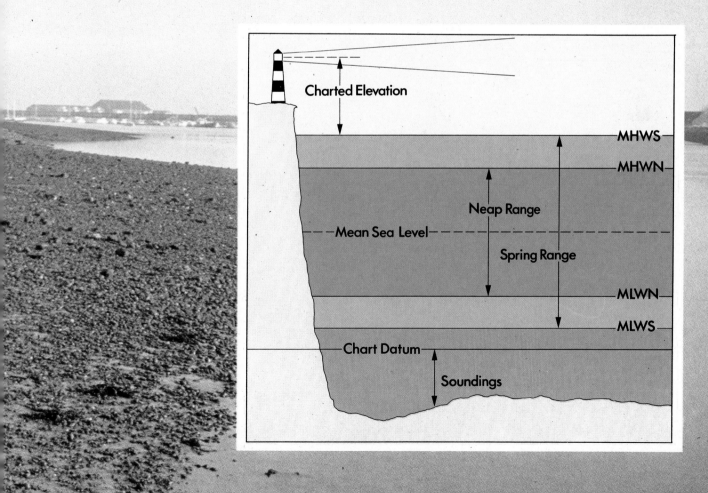

Definitions used in connection with Tides

Chart Datum (C.D.) An agreed level below which the tide very rarely falls. In the past British Admiralty Charts were normally based on mean low water springs but charts of the British Isles are now being changed to a new chart datum – lowest astronomical tides (L.A.T.). This is the lowest predictable tide calculated under average conditions – the level is rarely reached and may not even occur each year. Soundings and drying heights on charts are referred to the particular C.D. of the chart concerned. It must always be remembered, however, that, under exceptional meteorological conditions, the tidal height may exceed the predicted figure or lower levels recorded.

Height of Tide The height of water level above C.D. at any particular time.

Range of Tide The difference in height between succeeding high and low waters.

Spring Tides Tides of maximum range occurring twice a month approximately 2 days after full moon and new moon.

Neap Tides Tides of minimum range occurring twice a month when the sun and moon are in quadrature.

Perigee Tides As the path of the moon's orbit is elliptical its gravitational effect varies as it circles the earth. The moon is in 'perigee' when its path brings it nearest to the earth, and in 'apogee' when it is farthest away, thus its gravitational effect is greatest in perigee and when spring tides occur at this period they will have a greater than average range. Conversely in apogee the range will be smaller than usual.

Equinoctal Tides The gravitational effect of the sun and moon are greatest at the equinox's (21st March and 23rd September) and at these periods greater than average spring tides can be expected.

M.H.W.S. The average height of high water at spring tides throughout the year. (Mean High Water Springs.)

M.L.W.S. The average height of the corresponding low water. (Mean Low Water Springs.)

M.H.W.N. The average height of high water at neap tides throughout the year. (Mean High Water Neaps.)

M.L.W.N. The average height of corresponding low water. (Mean Low Water Neaps.)

Mean Level This is the mean of all high water, and low waters throughout the year.

Soundings Depths below Chart Datum.

Meteorological effects on tides

When studying tidal curves, for example in the Admiralty Tide Tables, the yachtsman new to navigation may understandably assume that tides can be calculated with great accuracy. It must always be borne in mind, however, that there are practical limitations to tidal predictions which are based on average barometric conditions and which in themselves vary considerably. High barometric pressures will tend to depress predicted heights and lower pressures will tend to raise them. For example, a very low pressure at the time of a spring tide may raise the level by as much as a foot, with a consequent increase in the strength of tidal streams in the vicinity of the depression. Apart from barometric pressure wind can have a considerable effect on tides. Persistently strong onshore winds will produce an increase in tidal height along the coastline with consequent variations in the times of High and Low water.

The point to remember is that all tidal calculations should be regarded as approximate and that you should always err on the side of safety.

Tidal Predictions and Calculations

As it is important to regard tidal predictions as approximate, calculations based upon them must consequently be regarded in a similar manner; this is especially important when the calculations relate to depth of water on a bar that is to be crossed. It will be appreciated that to produce annual tidal data for every port in a large maritime country would mean a very considerable amount of detail, which would be expensive to reproduce and would also occupy considerable space in tide tables and almanacs. Thus the general procedure is to select certain ports, usually the most important ones, and produce the complete tide tables for them. These ports are then referred to as 'Standard Ports'. The tidal data for other ports, known as 'Secondary Ports', and navigational points on the coastline is then calculated by applying differentials to the appropriate Standard Port tidal data. Supposing you need to know the time of H.W. at Ramsgate on a certain day. Reference to *Reed's Nautical Almanac* will show that it is a secondary port and the nearest Standard Port is Dover, to which its tidal data is referred. It will be seen that the time difference is + 0.20 min. and the height difference is − 1.6 m. Reference to Dover tide tables will show that on the 1st June 1977 H.W. is 1014 G.M.T. with a height of

6.7 m. The appropriate figures for Ramsgate on that day will be 1014 + 20 = 1034 G.M.T. and the height will be 6.7 m. − 1.6 m. = 5.1 m. Results obtained in this way are perfectly satisfactory for the cruising yachtsman. It is not proposed to go into detail of the methods employed in the Admiralty Tide Tables or *Reed's*

Nautical Almanac to calculate tidal information between times of H.W. and L.W. Reference should be made to the particular volumes concerned if this is required. There is, however, a rule of thumb method of roughly calculating tidal data which quickly gives approximate figures of tidal depths. This method is known as the

One advantage of the bilge-keel hull form is its ability to take the ground comfortably between tides as shown above.

'Twelfths Rule' and has the great advantage that a little mental arithmetic quickly produces an approximation which is adequate for most purposes. The rule is based on the fact that the depth of water does not vary at a constant rate throughout the tide cycle but follows a sine wave pattern, with the greatest movement in the middle two hours. The rate of rise or fall is:

In the:

first hour   – 1/12 of range
second hour – 2/12 of range
third hour   – 3/12 of range
fourth hour – 3/12 of range
fifth hour   – 2/12 of range
sixth hour   – 1/12 of range

Example: If H.W. height is 6m. and following L.W. height is 1m. what will the depth be at C.D. 2hr. 40min. after H.W.?

Range = 6m. − 1m. = 5m.

In the first hour tide falls by
1/12 of 5m. = 0.41

In the second hour tide falls by
2/12 of 5m. = 0.82

In 40min. of the third hour tide falls by
2/3 of 3/12 of 5m. = 0.82

Total fall   = 2.05m.

As the range is 5m. and the fall 2.05 the depth at C.D. = 5.0 − 2.05 = 2.95.

Example: H.W. = 5.4m.
L.W. 0.3m.
Range = 5.4 − 0.3 = 5.1.
How soon after L.W. will there be 2.5m. on the Bar? (C.D. + 1m.).
As the depth on the bar is C.D. + 1m., when L.W. is 0.3m. the depth at L.W. will be 1m. + 0.3m. = 1.3m.
It is required to find when there will be 2.5m. on the bar i.e. when will the tide have risen by 1.2m. (2.5 − 1.3).
In the first hour rise will be
1/12 of 5.1 = 0.43
In second hour rise will be
2/12 of 5.1 = 0.86

1.29m.

As an approximation 2 hours after L.W. there will be 2.5m. on the bar.
(1.3m. + 1.29m. = 2.59m.).

As previously mentioned this rule is based on the assumption that the tidal curve is, approximately, a sine wave pattern but this is not always the case. In some places the curve is distorted for various reasons and the results obtained from the 'Twelfths Rule' may vary considerably from the results obtained using the Admiralty Tide Tables. Caution must be exercised in using the rule where it is known that the tidal wave is unusual or distorted. In cases of considerable distortion, such as occurs in the Solent on the South Coast of England, rule of thumb methods must not be used, and the Admiralty Tide Tables must be consulted for accurate results.

Whatever method you use for calculating depths it is most important never to navigate where your calculations indicate that there is only just enough water. However carefully the depths have been worked out there is always the unpredictable error occasioned by weather and barometric conditions and the prudent navigator will always allow himself a margin of safety. For example, in the case of a yacht with a draft of 1.5m. (5ft.) it would be sensible to work to a minimum depth of 2.5m. (8ft.) on the bar in settled weather conditions and much more if there was any swell on the bar.

Reductions to Soundings It frequently happens that a useful check on your position may be made by a reduction to soundings, particularly when approaching a shore line. The depths marked on charts are the depths below Chart Datum and this information, coupled with the height of the tide at the time of your sounding, will provide the navigator with some useful

information, particularly if a line of soundings is taken. Consider first a single sounding of 30m. taken at say 0800. The calculated tide height at that time is 4m., that is 4m. above Chart Datum. The charter depth is therefore 30 − 4 = 26m. at the particular spot where the sounding was taken. This information may be helpful in confirming a position but a line of soundings is a much more useful contribution when working up an estimated position. The method is simple and consists of taking a series of soundings over a measured distance, which can be done either with the aid of the log or, if no log is available, on a time basis with an estimated speed.

The soundings can be taken at regular time intervals, say every five minutes, or on the distance run at say every 1/10 of a mile. However, if a crew member can be detailed to watch the echo sounder continuously, he can note any change of depth over a fixed distance and thus do an accurate contour of the sea bottom. These depths are then worked on the edge of a piece of paper spaced to the same scale as the chart, and the paper moved about in the vicinity of the estimated position until the depths coincide with the soundings on the chart.

Opposite an example is shown of a vessel approaching a harbour in fog, with no R.D.F. and uncertain of her position. A line of echo sounder readings is taken over one mile, the depths are reduced to soundings and marked on the edge of a piece of paper, to the same scale as the chart, calling the start 'A' and the finish 'B'. This is then moved around in the area of the estimated position until the depths coincide with the charted depths. The position at 'B' is not a fix as it does not show the ship's position in relation to the harbour entrance but it does indicate the proximity of land, and, bearing in mind that the bank which is shown in the soundings is to the east of the harbour entrance, it is very probable that the estimated position is in that area. In these particular circumstances a prudent course of action would be to move into shallow water, out of traffic lanes, anchor and wait for the fog to clear. It will be seen that a line of soundings in itself will not provide a fix but when coupled with other information it can be very useful indeed. Occasionally the configuration of the sea bed in an area is so distinctive that a line of soundings can provide a reliable fix but this is unusual.

Tidal Streams You will recall that the vertical movement of the sea is described as a tide and the horizontal movement as a tidal stream. The relationship between the two is more complex than may appear at

first sight. Take, for example, a tide wave in the Atlantic Ocean approaching the English Channel. Its initial height will be comparatively low and its associated tidal stream virtually non-existent. To digress for a moment, this does not mean that there are no streams in the oceans of the world, quite the opposite in fact, but these oceans' currents are in no way connected with tides. The forces causing them are complex but the main ones are the prevailing winds on the earth's surface. A well-known example of this type of current is the Gulf Stream, which flows in a general north-easterly direction from the Gulf of Mexico to the European coast line. The Gulf Stream is part of a large system of ocean currents which rotate in a clockwise direction in the North Atlantic. The central area of this system is the Sargasso Sea where the absence of currents leads to vast areas of sea weed and marine growths. Returning to our tidal wave in mid-Atlantic,

as it approaches the Continental Shelf and shallower waters the friction on the sea bed increases and the wave begins to build up in height. An example of this, well known to everyone, is the way in which waves become higher when they are approaching a shallow beach. As the wave starts to increase in height, gravity begins to move water away from it in two directions: ahead and behind it, thus causing the tidal streams which occur before and after the maximum height of the wave (H.W.).

At this juncture it is appropriate to consider an aspect of tidal streams which may be a little puzzling to the budding navigator and which is extremely important in coastal navigation. The way in which the tidal stream is produced is obvious but it is important to understand that streams, once started, do not stop and reverse their direction immediately the tide wave has passed. It takes time for the stream to slow down and then reverse its

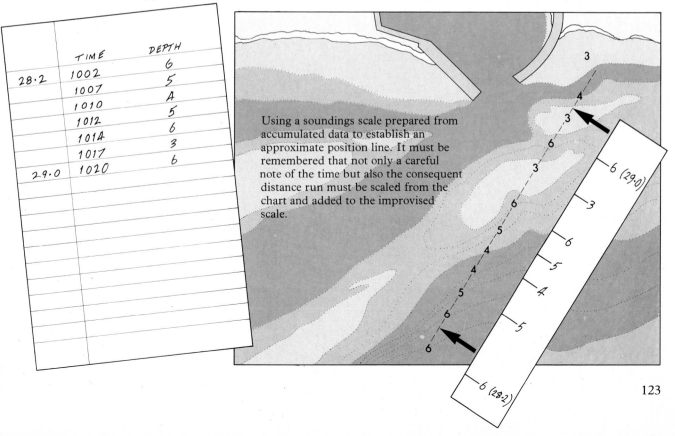

	TIME	DEPTH
28.2	1002	6
	1007	5
	1010	4
	1012	5
	1014	6
	1017	3
29.0	1020	6

Using a soundings scale prepared from accumulated data to establish an approximate position line. It must be remembered that not only a careful note of the time but also the consequent distance run must be scaled from the chart and added to the improvised scale.

direction and thus we have the situation in which the reversal may take place some little while after the time at which the tide height was at its maximum (H.W.). In other words 'slack water does not necessarily coincide with the times of H.W. and L.W., which is a rather important point to appreciate as it explains certain aspects of the Tidal Atlas which may prove puzzling to a beginner. In some cases, for example in a small harbour or creek in an estuary, the times of slack water in the entrance will correspond to the times of H.W. and L.W. locally. Other places may be quite different and, for example, off Dunkirk the tidal stream changes from 090°T to 270°T five hours after H.W. at the port.

The Tidal Atlas In coastal navigation, or pilotage as it should more properly be called, tidal streams play a large part in the navigator's calculations when on passage from one place to another. Take, for instance, the small family sailing cruiser which averages four to five knots in good conditions. It is obvious that a tidal stream of say 3 knots (depending on its direction relative to the ship's course) can very considerably affect the time taken to cover the ground. The well-planned passage will use favourable tidal streams to the greatest possible extent. Even in favourable weather there is no point in 'punching' an unfavourable tide, and perhaps remaining almost stationary for a time, if this can be avoided by good planning.

Having accepted that tidal information is so important in navigation, how does the yachtsman obtain the necessary information relating to the speed of tidal streams and, what is just as important – their direction? Around the British Isles the source of all such information is the Hydrographic Office of the Admiralty whose survey ships record the information for British waters as well as for other parts of the world. The information is then embodied in small tidal stream tables in a convenient position on the appropriate chart. Each table is lettered and the individual points referred to are marked by letters in diamonds, (see illustration below) at the point on the chart to which they refer. The tables give the rate of flow, and its direction in degrees True, for every hour before and after H.W. The H.W. referred to in the tables is usually the H.W. at the nearest Standard Port appropriate to the particular chart, which is convenient for the navigator as he will normally

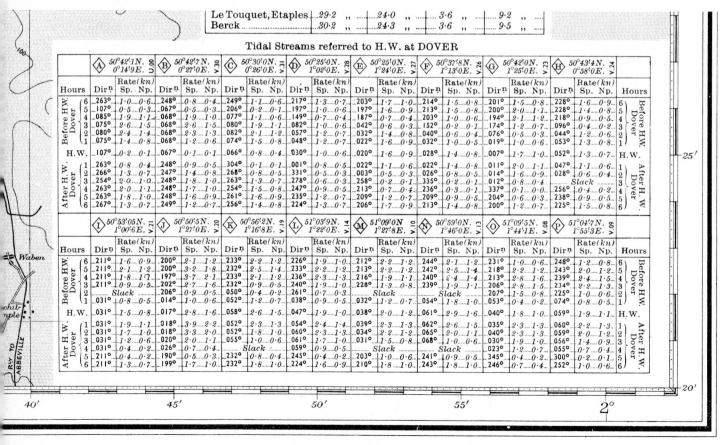

Produced from portion of BA Chart No. 5066 with the sanction of the Controller, HM Stationery Office and of the Hydrographer of the Navy.

be using that port for other calculations in connection with his passage.

In addition to the information on charts the Hydrographic Office issues detailed Tidal Atlases for all sea areas surrounding the United Kingdom. Similarly, most maritime nations issue information regarding tidal streams in various forms. The great advantage of the Tidal Atlas over the tables on the chart is that one can see the complete tidal stream picture over the whole of a particular area, at a glance. Each page shows the direction and rates (springs and neaps) of the tidal streams for a particular hour between one H.W. and the succeeding one. As a specific example of the use of the Tidal Atlas, take that for the Thames Estuary – an area familiar to all East Coast yachtsmen and many visitors from the Continent. It is a fascinating and difficult complex of sandbanks and channels, and is covered by two Admiralty charts: Thames North and Thames South, on each of which there are tables giving tidal information for many points in the area. To plan a crossing from, say, Brightlingsea in the north to Ramsgate in the south, utilizing the tides to the best advantage and taking short cuts across sandbanks, it is essential to be able to see the overall picture of the streams. It is extremely difficult to visualize this overall picture from the detailed tables on the charts but a glance at the tidal atlas shows the whole position very clearly. A further point in connection with the Atlas is its use on passage. Assuming that H.W. at Sheerness (the relevant Standard Port) is, say, 1000 hours, this time will be pencilled on top of

the page marked 'High Water'; each succeeding page is then marked with the actual time – the one giving 'One hour after H.W.' with 1100 hours and so on. The tidal stream situation is now readily available at any time during the crossing without the necessity for detailed examination of charts.

General Remarks In view of the snags associated with accurate predictions of tidal heights and times, you will now realize that it is even more difficult to accurately predict tidal streams, owing to the marked effect of wind strength on the force of the stream. Estimated positions in strong tidal waters should therefore be treated with caution until they can be confirmed with bearings. This is not to infer that tidal stream information is uncertain or doubtful – far from it in fact. The information on charts and tidal atlases is remarkably accurate under average meteorological conditions, being based on observations by survey ships. It is the unusual meteorological condition and, in some instances changing sand banks, that cause unexpected variations in the streams.

There are certain fairly standard aspects of tidal streams which are not always obvious from the Tidal Atlas, owing to its small scale, but which are nevertheless important to small ship navigation. When you are passing a bay, for example, it should be remembered that there is nearly always a tide inset into it. This is important from two points of view: firstly, when sailing along the coast in foggy weather a vessel will be pushed into the bay unless due allowance is made for the pull and, secondly, if she is working a foul tide it might pay to get

out of the strong offshore stream into the weaker currents in the bay.

Another 'standard' effect is the way in which the rate of a stream sometimes increases sharply by a headland, particularly if the headland sticks out from the general run of the main coastline. If the projection is very pronounced it can lead to strong eddies in its immediate vicinity which in bad weather could be difficult, or even dangerous, for small craft. It is also quite common for soundings to reduce when you are approaching a headland, and when this feature combines with a fast-running tidal stream, it produces a disturbance known as 'overfalls' – or in particularly violent examples, a 'race'. The disturbed water usually appears down tide of the 'hump' in the sea bed.

If the overfalls are of a potentially dangerous nature, such as those off Portland Bill in the English Channel, they are usually marked on the chart. The prudent small boat navigator should then avoid the area, for even in moderate conditions the sea may be sufficiently disturbed in an irregular manner to be dangerous to small vessels.

In a similar way to the 'acceleration' of tidal streams by some headlands, surprising local increases may occur across the entrances to man-made harbours, particularly if the entrance projects out from the coastline. These effects are mostly too local to be shown in Tidal Atlases but are usually mentioned in the appropriate Pilots. A good example is Calais where the tidal stream across the pier heads is considerably faster, particularly on the ebb, than the stream, say, half a mile out.

Ch.7
Coastal Navigation Pt.2

The fundamental knowledge required of the navigator to carry out successful coastal navigation (or pilotage) consists essentially of the ability to read a chart, to plot a course, to work the tidal streams and to take bearings. Tidal streams and compass work have already been discussed in the previous chapter and now we shall investigate the other aspects of pilotage which complete the coastal navigator's skills. A short glossary of navigational terms and symbols is given on page 128 and the reader is strongly recommended to memorise them and to use them whenever work is being carried out on the chart. The little ship navigator may think that it is rather pretentious to follow 'Big Ship Practice' but, it is equally important – if anything more important – to have a proper, standard system for chartwork when you are working in the cramped conditions of a small cruiser than it is when blessed with the facilities of the stable and uncluttered chart table of a large merchant ship.

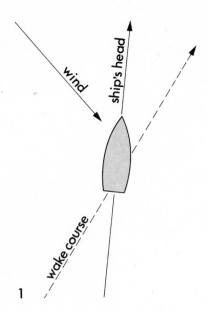

1

Glossary

Course The single word 'course' should always be thought of as a triumvirate:

True Course: as plotted on the chart in degrees True.

Magnetic Course: the application of Variation (see page 114) to the True Course converts it to Magnetic Course.

Compass Course: if you have to allow for Deviation, the Magnetic Course is converted to Compass Course by applying the correction from the Deviation Card (see page 115). This refers only to the vessel's fore-and-aft line, i.e. the direction in which she is pointing.

Leeway Due to the pressure of the wind on the hull of a vessel, it also slips sideways while it is moving forward but by how much depends on wind pressure and the shape of the hull.

Leeway Course or Wake Course The direction of the vessel's passage through the water, (fig. 1).

Track The line showing the ship's passage 'over the ground' after making due allowance for tidal currents and leeway.

Course Made Good (C.M.G.) The same as 'Track'.

Dead Reckoning Position (D.R.) A position obtained by taking the course steered and distance run from a previously known point. A D.R. position is marked on the chart with a + and the time: e.g. + 2035.

Estimated Position (E.P.) A position obtained by adjusting the D.R. for leeway and current, which is then marked thus: △ 1030, (fig. 2).

Fix A firm position obtained from bearings of two or more terrestrial objects (lighthouse beacons, buoys etc.) and marked with a circle and the time, thus: ○ 0930.

Position Line (P.L.) A line showing a bearing from a terrestrial object.

Transferred Position Line When the first Position Line is transferred to cut the second Position Line in a 'Running Fix' it is shown thus: ↞——↠

E.T.A. Estimated Time of Arrival.

Construction of a typical
E.P. Figure 2 shows the way in which to calculate an Estimated Position. You will note that the wake course is shown thus: ——→——, the tidal stream thus: ——↠——, and the estimated track is shown by ——↠——. These conventional symbols should always be used, which will help considerably in reducing the chance of errors in your chartwork.

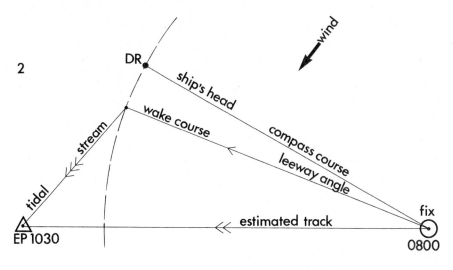

2

Planning the Passage

General A successful passage depends to a large extent on the preparatory work being carried out before the cruise begins. It is very much easier to do this work in an unhurried way without any distractions, for example, at home during the long winter evenings before the sailing season opens when all the necessary information will be available to you except the state of the weather! If it is to be your maiden cruise it is wise not to be too ambitious, and due allowance for bad weather must always be made. For example, if the plan calls for a certain distance to be covered each day and the weather becomes unfavourable during the latter part of the cruise, it could result in the return trip having to be carried out under difficult conditions.

When you have decided upon your destinations, the first step is to buy the necessary charts, which should be of the largest scale available to provide the maximum detail. If the projected cruise traverses several large-scale charts, then one small-scale chart covering the whole area should also be purchased for use as a 'track chart' – to show the overall picture. The proposed track is pencilled in on the chart, from the point of departure to the ultimate destination, including of course any ports-of-call which you hope to visit en route. The next step is to carefully examine the route to see what navigational hazards exist in its vicinity. For example, does the track pass through an area with adequate depths but which is marked with overfalls? Does the track pass close to rocks? Remember that rocks may be clearly visible in good conditions but what

happens if fog suddenly surrounds you and you are not quite certain of your position? Are you proposing to sail over a sandbank which will have adequate depth at high water, but which if you are delayed may become a hazard? These points may seem, and indeed are, obvious but they are of the sort which sometimes get overlooked with unfortunate results. Therefore, when you are examining a proposed track it pays to cultivate a pessimistic outlook and imagine it from the point of view of unfavourable weather conditions. It is surprising what a difference this attitude makes to one's feelings about the selected track . . .!

A further basic point when planning a passage is the availability of good navigational marks on, or near, the proposed track. For example, one leg of the course might consist of a twenty mile stretch out of sight of land, and if headwinds are encountered or perhaps tidal streams are under-estimated, the E.P. after four or five hours sailing might be pretty dubious? However, if there is a Light Vessel or Main Channel Buoy a mile or so off the track it would pay to adjust the course to come sufficiently close to get a fix in passing. A passage broken down into shorter navigational stretches in this way enables the navigator to be much more confident of his position and progress, and so it reduces the chance of the E.T.A. producing nothing more than a lonely horizon. Similarly, sea passages such as the crossing from Harwich to Flushing – which may appear daunting to the beginner – can also be broken down and thus make life much easier for the navigator. When you have studied the navigational hazards to stay well away from,

and also the navigational marks which you hope to sight, the proposed track will probably look rather different to the original one. Indeed it may look much more complicated but it will make navigation more simple and therefore more safe.

The next step is to look at the track with tidal streams in mind. The more use that can be made of favourable streams the better. Obviously if you are sailing at four or five knots, tidal streams which may reach three knots or more must be given careful consideration, if the passage is going to be completed in reasonable time. For example, if you were planning a short passage in a small yacht from Brightlingsea to Pin Mill, on the River Orwell, it would be best to leave Brightlingsea just after H.W. (High Water). The ebb tidal stream would then be favourable and would assist the vessel out of the River Colne to the mouth of the River Blackwater and thence in a N.E. direction along the coast to Harwich – by which time the flood should have started which will then carry the vessel up the River Orwell to Pin Mill. Conversely, if the trip was badly planned and adverse tides were met for the greater part of the trip, it would take considerably longer, especially if it was undertaken at spring tides and with an unfavourable wind.

It is important when planning passages anywhere to have due regard for tidal streams and more especially where they are fastrunning and complicated – for example in the Channel Islands and the Thames Estuary. In addition to tidal streams, due attention must be given to tide heights, which are particularly important to the little ship navigator when he is planning passages in shallow waters, again such as the Thames Estuary and also to parts of the Continental coastlines. On occasions it may be necessary to accept the existence of an adverse tidal stream in order to ensure that there is adequate water for the vessel at all times. As an example, if your E.T.A. at a harbour bar was at L.W. with a depth of 2 m. (6½ ft) and the vessel's draft was 1.5 m. (5 ft), then obviously it would be necessary to alter the time to introduce a much greater safety factor. Your aim should always be to arrive at difficult points with a rising tide and not a falling one.

These remarks may make the process of planning a simple passage sound complicated, but this is not really so in fact. All the same the first time the 'tyro' navigator sits down with the chart, the Tidal Streams Atlas, the Pilot and *Reed's Nautical Almanac* he may, excusably, feel slightly daunted . . .!

Recording the Planning Information

Finalising the route will result in most of its problems coming to light and being solved before the trip even begins. What happens at sea will seem different to the anticipatory picture on the chart. For example, buoys are not always as visible as might be imagined from the chart; they will seem much farther apart and, curiously enough, they will not always appear in the position you expected them to be! The background knowledge built up during the planning stage will make the little ship navigator familiar with what he *should* see, and if the correct information is then readily to hand during the passage he will be in a very good position to deal confidently

with any problems that may arise en route. It is quite surprising how these problems diminish in direct proportion to the amount of planning undertaken beforehand. . . .
It is a temptation to note as much of the detailed information as possible on the chart but this must be resisted. The only information that should be put on a chart is the proposed track line, preferably in a chain dotted line so that it cannot be confused with any course lines that are subsequently drawn during the trip.

One simple, handy and straightforward way of recording the information is to write it out in what might almost be regarded as a 'theoretical log'

of the trip. A suggested form is shown below which could be the left-hand page in a 'ring binder' with a blank page on the right-hand side, the latter being used as the rough log, for recording information and rough workings.

All important navigational information required on the trip is entered in chronological sequence and it is thus quickly available without having to refer to several books. Courses to steer are Magnetic Courses corrected for any deviation and variation. If it is not possible to sail that actual course because of wind direction, then the information is still a useful background and ensures that the navigator is less likely to make a mistake in

Navigational Mark	Distance	Compass Course	Remarks
Chart No. 9			
N Goodwin			Light Vessel
NE Goodwin	2.5	172°	Red can buoy
E Goodwin	2.3	172°	„ „ „
E Goodwin	2.5	172°	Light Vessel
M.P.C. Buoy	8.0	156°*	E Cardinal Light Buoy (pass about 2.5 miles on S. hand)
Outer Ruytingen SW Buoy	2.5	156°	BL. Pillar top mark ▲ Light Buoy
C.A.2	4.0	156°	N Cardinal Light Buoy QK.FL.
Chart No. 10			
C.A.2			
C.A.10	2.25	166°	Red Pillar top mark ◣, Gp. O.C.C. (2) R 6 Sec.
Calais	1.0	140°	Calais Lt. house Gp. FL (4) 15 SEC. E. Pier head LT Gp. FL (2) R 10 SEC W. Pier head LT ISO G 3 SEC.

Note This course passes midway between the M.P.C. Buoy and Sandettie L.V. so that drift in either direction will bring one of them into view. In fog without D.F. set, listen for Sandettie fog signal.

laying-off alternative courses and, if he does so, the mistake will be reasonably obvious. The distance between points is useful if only to help you to estimate when the next buoy or mark should be sighted. In the 'Remarks Column', details of buoys, light characteristics, appearances of marks etc. are all useful information to have readily to hand.

A typical extract from such a planning sheet is shown, and is part of the information required for a trip from the Thames Estuary to Calais; there are two or three points worth noting. Firstly, the charts covering the area have a folio number. As soon as more than just a few charts are carried on board it is worth giving each one a folio number and keeping a card with the descriptions of the charts and their folio numbers conveniently close by the chart stowage. Secondly, some of the information shown may seem unnecessary but it is surprising how useful it is to be able quickly to refer to the sheet and see exactly what type of buoy you are looking for without having to make a close examination of the chart (possibly under difficult conditions). The third point is that, as the end of the trip may be made in gathering darkness, the characteristics of lights are included.

In the example opposite the Calais Port entry signals might well be added, together with the V.H.F. Channel of Calais Port Control if the yacht is fitted with V.H.F., while it would also be helpful to put in information relating to any 'escape routes' which could be considered in the event of bad weather. This would be of a more simple nature – such as depth of water on the harbour bar for example

Setting out on passage in the first light of dawn.

– but still facts which would enable a decision to be made promptly in the event of a change of plan being required.

Perhaps you may be thinking that this suggested procedure is rather unnecessary, and admittedly as experience is gained the amount of work does become less as each individual evolves his own system. It is however worth thinking about what would happen should the skipper-navigator-helmsman of the small family cruiser have an accident. It is comforting to know that in the event of an emergency the crew member who will have to take over would at least start with a ready-made 'guide' to help them on their way.

Navigation on Passage
When you have settled the route and recorded all necessary information in a readily available form, it is necessary next to consider what practical navigation exercises will need to be carried out whilst on passage. There are two factors which constantly affect the course to steer: leeway and tidal current. The first step is clearly to understand the simple vector diagrams which enable the required course to be readily calculated.

131

Leeway and Current Diagrams The first consideration and the simplest is the leeway angle of the vessel's track caused by the pressure of the wind on her sails and hull. This factor is easily calculated by observing the angle between the fore-and-aft line of the vessel and the wake stretching out astern. The wake, or 'wake course', will be seen up to windward of the fore-and-aft line as the wind is pressing the vessel down to leeward (fig. 3). The angle between the wake and the fore-and-aft line, or ship's head, is the leeway angle and varies according to the wind strength and direction. In general the average smaller cruiser will have a leeway angle of approximately 5° to 8° when sailing at her optimum angle to windward, say 50° to the wind, in normal conditions. Every opportunity should be taken to check this angle in different conditions to improve the accuracy of Estimated Positions.

Fig. 4 shows the simple case of the ship's head and the wake course. If the ship's head is on 090°T, which is the desired course, the actual course made good would be 095°T. It would, therefore, be necessary to steer 085°T as in fig. 5 to counteract the leeway angle and make good a course of 090°T. Now look at the same situation with a tidal stream of 2 knots at 150°T, vessel's speed 5 knots and the ship's head at 090°T (fig. 6). AY represents the ship's head and AZ the wake course. Using a suitable scale draw AB representing the distance covered by the vessel in the first hour, i.e. 5 miles. From B draw the tidal vector of 2 miles to the same scale 150°T. This vector shows how the vessel would drift in one hour if no other influence (e.g. wind) was present. The line AC then represents the course and distance made good in the first hour. This diagram shows what would occur if no allowance was made for leeway and currents. The problem however is to calculate the course necessary to achieve the desired course of 090°T, and to do this the vector diagram is built up slightly differently as shown in fig. 10. For the sake of clarity the leeway angle has been omitted as this adjustment can be made afterwards. Line AY, (course to be made good) is first drawn at 090°T from the fix at A. The current vector is then drawn to a convenient scale representing 2 miles at 150°T – AB. This represents the distance the vessel would drift in one hour if it was unaffected by wind. From B, an arc is drawn representing the distance that the vessel will cover in one hour, that is 5 miles, to the same scale as the tidal vector. The line BC is then drawn to the point on AY cut by the arc and represents the course that the yacht would have to sail to counteract the current. If AD is drawn parallel to BC it gives the course steered and distance run, and D is the D.R. position, the E.P. being at C (it will be remembered that the D.R. is solely the distance run and course steered while the E.P. is the corrected position allowing for leeway and current). Summing up, the procedure is:

1. Draw AY – course to be made good in degrees T.
2. Draw current vector AB.
3. With centre B describe an arc representing distance covered by vessel in 1 hour cutting AY at C.
4. Draw AD parallel and equal to *BC*.
5. Correct AD for variation.
6. Apply leeway correction.
7. Correct for deviation (if any).
8. The result is Compass Course.

It will be found in practice that it is better to draw the current diagrams on squared paper to a convenient scale rather than construct them on the chart, leaving the latter for course made good, D.R.s and E.P.s etc., though this is really a matter of personal preference. In the example above no variation in ship's speed or tidal current occurs but in practice this is rarely so. Let us now see what will happen if the wind drops, and in the first hour the vessel is found to have logged only 3.5 miles instead of 5 miles.

The vessel has steered the compass course originally planned but instead of proceeding 5 miles (BC) in fig. 8 she has only made 3.5 miles along the track and at the end of the hour will have reached Z. The vector AZ is therefore the course made good and here E.P. is at Z. From this E.P. a further vector diagram will be necessary to calculate the new course required. In this instance the reduced speed of the vessel has made the effect of the current relatively stronger which has thus pushed her South of her course. On the other hand if the wind had strengthened to increase her speed to, say, 6 knots, this would have resulted in her working up North of the required course.

While it is important to be familiar with the construction of current diagrams, there is no reason why you should not use approximate methods provided you understand their limitations. In *Reed's Nautical*

Almanac tables are given which enable a quick calculation to be made of course correction factors and there are various course correction calculators on the market which are very useful in the rapid solution of current diagrams.

Fixing the Position
We have now scanned the routine process of checking tidal streams and making the necessary corrections to courses. The next problem which faces the navigator on passage is that of fixing his vessel's position. The prudent mariner should take every opportunity of getting a 'fix' – even when everything seems perfectly normal: visibility good and no navigational hazards on the route. Fog may descend unexpectedly and transform a very pleasant sail into one far less pleasing. . . . Fog at sea is probably the most difficult of circumstances with which the small boat navigator is likely to be called upon to deal. If he is shrouded in thick fog and he has only the vaguest notion of his whereabouts – then he really shouldn't be at sea at all (and no doubt is fervently wishing he wasn't)! Even on a short coastal cruise it is unwise to rely on being able to see and identify objects on the coast continually. Quite apart from the importance of always knowing your position the confidence you acquire through getting regular 'fixes' is a great asset when the time eventually comes to take a quick sight under difficult conditions. Never miss an opportunity of getting a 'fix'.

There are various ways of fixing the vessel's position and so let us now examine all the usual ones – bearing in mind that while one always *hopes* for

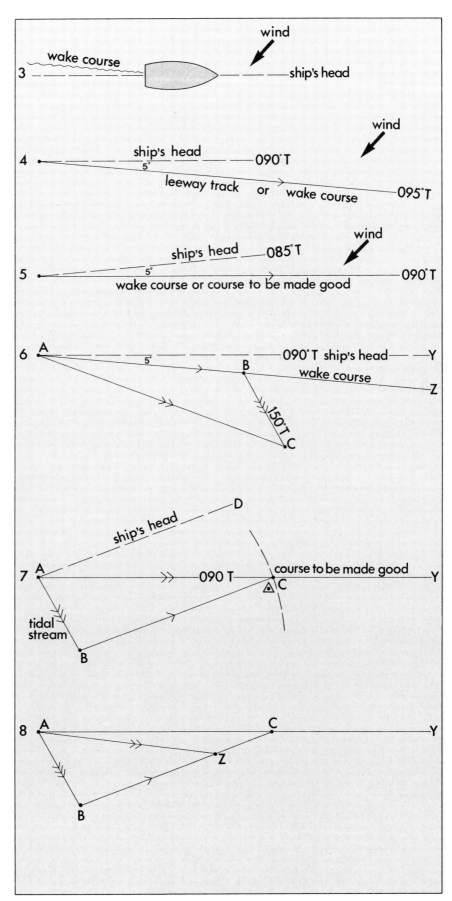

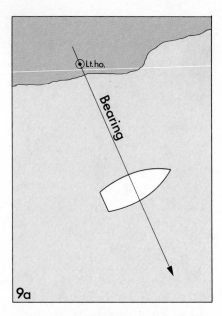

9a

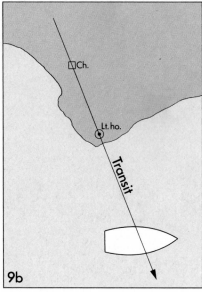

9b

*From a strictly practical point of view the Four Point Bearing and the Horizontal Sextant Angle Fix are infrequently used but they are included as they usually crop up in any Navigational Course or examination.

three nicely spaced objects to give a small 'cocked hat', in practice things usually turn out to be less convenient. For this reason a good knowledge of the various methods of fixing the vessel's position is essential.*

Single Position Line As the name implies a Position Line (P.L.) is not a 'fix' but simply a line somewhere along which the vessel is situated. There are two types of P.L.: the compass bearing of a known fixed object (i.e. one clearly marked on the chart) and the other from a transit of two known marks. The latter is much more accurate than the compass bearing due to the inherent difficulties of taking an accurate bearing from a small, moving and unstable platform. The compass bearing must be corrected for variation and deviation (if any), before being plotted on the chart in the same way that any compass course must be converted to True before it is plotted. Examples of both types of P.L. are shown in fig. 9.

Cross Bearings If the bearings of two known objects are taken simultaneously the vessel must be at the point of intersection of the two lines and, provided the objects have been carefully chosen, the fix should be accurate.

The reason for the qualification 'carefully selected' is explained in fig. 10. In 'a' the angle of cut between the two bearings is about 90° and an error in the compass bearings will not necessarily produce a large error in the fix. In 'b' however the angle of cut is about 15° and it will be obvious that a comparatively small error in the bearing of the Bn., for example, will move it up or down the church P.L. by a

significant amount. The dotted line indicates the probable area with a 3° error in one of the bearings. In 'a' the area of doubt is comparatively small whereas in 'b' it is much larger. Ideally aim for a cut of about 090°; cuts similar to that shown in 'b' (or where the angle is say 150°) should be treated as suspect! In addition, time interval between the two bearings should be as short as possible.

Three Point Fix or 'Cocked Hat' Occasionally one is fortunate enough to find three objects suitably placed from which to take bearings. The result should be a good 'cocked hat' which is a much better fix than the apparently accurate, pin-point position obtained from two P.L.s. The cocked hat is much more reliable, as it indicates the probable area in which the boat is located and does not in general lead the navigator to assume that he has an absolutely precise fix as may appear to be the case with a two P.L. fix. If the cocked hat is comparatively small and compact (fig. 11) then it is reasonable to assume that all three bearings are roughly comparable in accuracy and the position can be accepted with confidence. The converse is that the larger the cocked hat the less accurate the position.

The boat can be anywhere in the cocked hat, and if she was bound in a westerly direction the careful navigator would assume that she was at A, the nearest point to the navigational hazard off the headland, and then lay his course accordingly to give the rocks adequate clearance.

Running Fix or Transferred P.L.

If only one object is available for an observation the yacht's position may be found by taking a running fix (fig. 12).

A bearing is taken of the selected object and at the same time the log reading is noted, or if there is no log, the time is noted and the speed estimated. It is assumed in this example that there is no tidal current or leeway to complicate the exercise. The vessel runs on her course of 100°T until the bearing of the object shows a reasonable difference from the first bearing, say 60° or more. A second bearing is then taken and at the same time the log reading is noted or time taken. Both P.L.s are then plotted on the chart and it is assumed that the vessel was at position A when the first bearing was taken. The distance run and course, AB is then plotted from A and a line parallel to the first P.L. is drawn through B, cutting the second P.L. at C.

Point C is the position of the yacht at the time the second bearing was taken. It will be understood that the assumed position on the first P.L. is not important. For example, if it had been plotted at D the distance run and course would have terminated at E, and the transferred P.L. would still have cut the second P.L. at C. Should you want to know the actual position on the first P.L., this can be obtained afterwards by drawing a line through C and parallel to AB. Where it cuts the first P.L. at F. is the actual position the yacht was in when the first bearing was taken.

Now look at fig. 13 in which due allowance is made for leeway and tidal current. The two P.L.s (taken from different bearings) are drawn in as before and the initial position of the

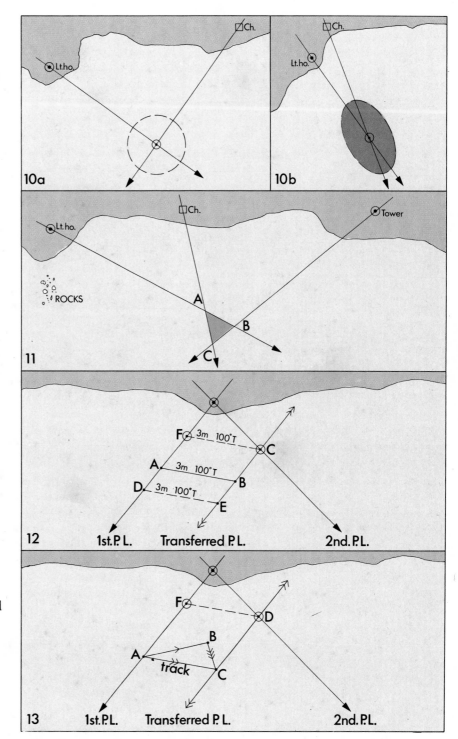

yacht is assumed to be at A. The wake course AB is laid-off representing distance run and the tidal vector BC is plotted at the end of the wake course. AC then represents the yacht's track and the transferred P.L. is drawn through C cutting the second P.L. at D, which is the yacht's position when the second bearing was taken. As in the previous example (fig. 12) if a line is drawn through C parallel to the track, the point F at which it cuts the first P.L. will represent the yacht's position when the first bearing was taken.

In connection with running fixes, note that two objects can be used if this is convenient. Perhaps the first object disappears from view before it is possible to take a reasonable second bearing on it. Then a second object comes into view. See fig. 14, in which a bearing is taken on a North Cardinal buoy and the log is read; the vessel then runs on until the West Cardinal buoy appears – a bearing is taken and the log reading noted. The two P.L.s are drawn, wake course AB and current BC are plotted from any convenient point A. The transferred P.L. is then drawn through C, parallel to the first P.L. and where this cuts the second P.L. at D is the yacht's position.

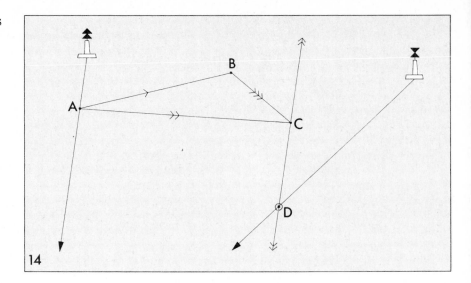

14

Doubling the Angle on the Bow If leeway and current are negligible a running fix may be obtained without the necessity for plotting it on the chart.

In fig. 15 two bearings of the L.H. at B are taken, one at A when the *relative* bearing to the ship's head is 30° and the second at C when the relative bearing is 60°. Angle BCD is 60°, angle BCA must be 120° and therefore angle ABC is 30°. The triangle ABC is therefore an isosceles triangle with AC = BC. The distance logged between A and C (where the bearings were taken) must therefore be equal to the distance BC. With this distance and the actual bearing of B, the vessel's position will be C. The 'Four Point Bearing', a particular example of doubling the angle on the bow, is shown in fig. 16. A reading of the log is noted when the Light Vessel bears 45° relative to the ship's head and a second reading is taken when it is abeam, i.e. bearing 90° relative to the ship's head. The distance run, 2 miles, will then equal the distance off the Light Vessel at the time of the second bearing. Incidentally the reason for calling them 'four

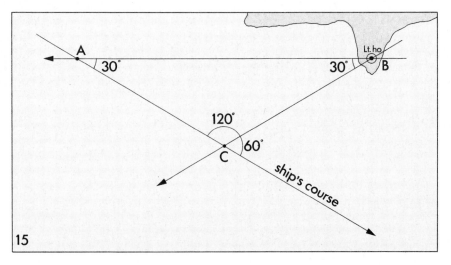

15

point bearings' is that 45° is 4 points (a point is $11\frac{1}{4}$°).

A running fix cannot be considered as accurate as a fix obtained from cross bearings because of the variables involved and no opportunity should ever be missed to check the vessel's position at the first opportunity after taking a running fix. If tidal current and leeway are present it is most important to remember that the relative bearings must be taken in relation to the ship's track and not her head. The reason for this is obvious as the distance from the Light Vessel is required *over the ground*, so then the distance run must also

be *over the ground* – in other words the ship's track.

Distance off by Vertical Sextant Angle If the navigator has a sextant very accurate fixes can be obtained from objects ashore whose exact height above M.H.W.S. is known. In fig. 17 the yachtsman has measured the vertical angle between sea level and the light of the Light House and finds it to be of 0°29′. The height of the light is 40m. and the distance-off can therefore be calculated trigonometrically. This distance can however be read off instantly by means of the 'Distance-Off' Tables in *Reed's*

Nautical Almanac at 2 miles 5 cables. A compass bearing of the Light House is taken as soon as possible after measuring the vertical sextant angle and with this P.L. and the distance off of 2 m 5 c the position is accurately plotted. A point to note is that the height of the light (not the height of the tower) is given above M.H.W.S., and therefore if the tide is lower than this, the effective height of the tower is increased by the difference between M.H.W.S. and the actual tide height. If the height of the light is considerably more than this tidal discrepancy then, from a practical point of view, it can be ignored. Any error will place the vessel apparently nearer to the headland than it really is and therefore in most cases will introduce a margin of safety. Similarly the height of eye of the observer, which will normally be of the order of 2 m (6–7 ft), can also be ignored.

Fix by Horizontal Sextant Angle This method, which produces a reliable fix, is included for those yachtsmen who are, or wish to become, proficient in the use of the sextant. In the author's opinion a horizontal sextant angle is more difficult to take than a vertical angle unless the sea is calm. Bringing down an object to the horizon when measuring a vertical angle is easier than measuring a horizontal angle, when the sextant has to be steadied in two planes. The method is free of any compass errors and the bearings can be plotted directly on to the chart, and if a 'station pointer' is available in the navigator's kit the fix can be established quite rapidly. In fig. 18, with three known objects, A, B and C, the horizontal angle between A and

B is 60° and between B and C is 45°. One arm of the station pointer is set at 60° to the centre arm and the other at 45°. The station pointer is then moved around on the chart until the three arms cut the positions A, B and C, and the fix is at the centre of the

protractor on which the three arms are mounted (fig. 19). If no station pointer is available then a Douglas protractor will do equally well. Alternatively the problem may be solved by simple geometry in the following manner (fig. 20). Join the two points A and B, and then draw

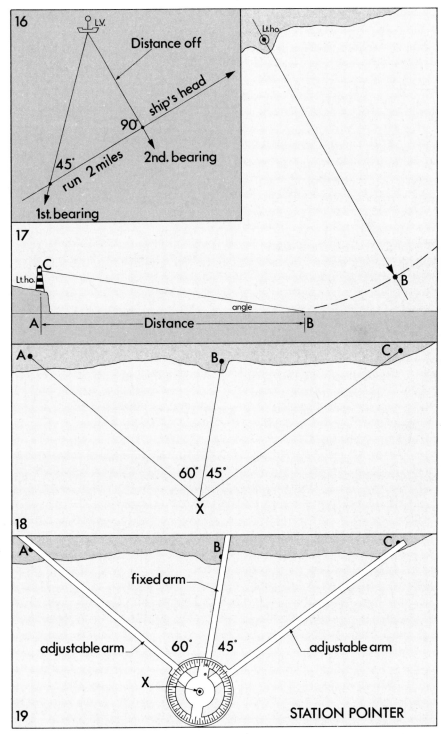

STATION POINTER

a circle of such diameter that it cuts A and B and angle ADB is 70° (the horizontal angle in this case). As all angles in a segment of a circle are equal, the segment will give a circular position line. The method of construction is:–

1. Join A and B.
2. Subtract the horizontal angle from 90° i.e. 90°–70° = 20° = Base angle
3. Lay off angle on base line AB at each end (on same side as yacht).
4. The intersection of the two lines is the centre of the circle on which A, B, and the yacht lie.

Note: if the horizontal angle is greater than 90°, then 90° is subtracted from the horizontal angle and the triangle constructed on the other side of the base line, i.e. away from the yacht.

The horizontal angle between B and C is 80° so the base angle will be 10°. The circle is then drawn in a similar manner to the first one and the position of the yacht is where the two circles cut each other.

There are certain limitations to this method but conditions under which it gives accurate results are:

1. When the three objects are more or less in line.
2. When the middle object is nearest the yacht.
3. When the yacht is inside a triangle formed by the three objects.
4. When the yacht is on or near a line joining the two outer objects.

The easiest and quickest method of fixing the position after the angles have been measured by sextant is to use the Horizontal Sextant Angle Fix Tables in *Reed's Nautical Almanac.* Using this method no measurement of angles is required on the chart, the only instrument needed being compasses to describe the circles. It is certainly an extremely simple and quick method which gives a very accurate fix.

Fixes by R.D.F. A radio-direction-finding set (R.D.F.) is a great asset as an aid to navigation but it must never be regarded as a substitute for normal navigational procedures.

The majority of sets available for use in small craft are easy to operate and, provided their use and limitations are clearly understood, they can make a significant contribution to the small craft navigator's work. Basically there are two types of R.D.F. suitable for this kind of work: the ferrite rod and the loop-type aerial. Some sets come complete with a small built-in magnetic compass, thus enabling a direction bearing of the beacon to be taken while others work with a verge ring which gives a bearing relative to the ship's heading, from which the beacon bearing is then obtained. In both types it is necessary to correct the magnetic bearing to True before plotting it on the chart. The principle of operation is simple. A directional aerial gives maximum volume when it is broadside on to the beacon and minimum volume when it is pointing directly towards it. The procedure is to tune the set to the appropriate group frequency so as to get maximum volume and then as soon as an identification signal is heard to rotate the aerial until a null reading is obtained and the latter will be the bearing along which the beacon lies. Of course the beacon can be on either the direct bearing or its reciprocal, but cross bearings will quickly establish the ship's position.

Marine Radio Beacons are listed in the *Admiralty List of Radio Signals, Vol. II* and *Reed's Nautical Almanac.* Up to six radio beacons operating on the same frequency are grouped together to cover a particular area, the beacons operating in a listed sequence which starts on the hour, with each beacon radiating for one minute. The characteristic transmission for each beacon is standardised as follows:

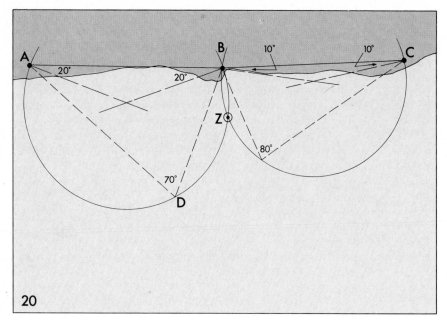

20

1. Identification signal
   3 to 6 times   22 secs.
2. Long dash lasting
   for   25   „
3. Identification signal
   once or twice   8   „
4. Silent period of   5   „
                       ——
                        60   „
                       ——

As the duration of the group transmission is 6 minutes, once the set has been tuned to the correct frequency it is a comparatively simple matter to to get bearings on several different beacons of the group thus enabling a fix to be obtained. After completion the group sequence repeats. Recently, a modification has been made to the type of transmission from certain selected non-directional Marine Radio Beacons which may cause some confusion among yachtsmen who are unaware of the situation. There are several types of transmission used by Beacons, but the yachtsmen need only be concerned with two types known as A2 and A2*, the latter being the possible source of confusion.

Basically, the A2 transmission consists of a single carrier wave which is interrupted to produce the long dash and the morse identification signal, and thus presents no problem to any type of small ship R.D.F. set.

Automatic D.F. sets of the type normally carried by Merchant Shipping require a constant uninterrupted carrier wave onto which the set automatically 'locks', thereby giving a constant bearing of the Beacon. This requirement is met in the A2* transmission which has two carrier waves, one constantly transmitted and the second one which is interrupted to give the long dash and morse identification. The continuous carrier wave requires an oscillator in the receiving set, known as a Beat Frequency Oscillator (B.F.O. for short), to convert it to an audio frequency. The more moderately priced or simple types of D.F. sets do not normally have a B.F.O. and thus have no difficulty in receiving either A2 or A2* transmissions. Sets that have a B.F.O. should use it when tuning to the required frequency and should switch it out to receive the morse identification signal. In some sets the B.F.O. switch may be marked 'NAV' or 'CONSOL', and if the B.F.O. is not switched off when receiving an A2* transmission, the constant carrier-wave signal will mask the identification signal. The yachtsman's problem arises if he has a set with a B.F.O. which cannot be switched out, and in these circumstances, identification of the Beacon will have to be effected by determining its position in the tuning sequence of the group of Beacons.

In some cases, it may be possible to retune the receiver slightly to eliminate the B.F.O. tone sufficiently to make the identification signal audible. For the technically minded, the A2* transmission is known as double side band transmission and in the U.S.A., a slightly different method is used, but the end result, as far as yachtsmen are concerned, is the same.

In addition to Marine Radio Beacons, considerable use may be made of some Aeronautical Beacons which have the advantage that their transmission is continuous. Aerobeacons situated well inland should be avoided due to errors caused by refraction.

It is important to remember the limitations of the inexpensive types of R.D.F. sets used in small vessels and to treat the results obtained from them with caution. Apart from the inherent limitations imposed by the design of the set there are three main types of error: quadrantal, night and coastal refraction. 'Quadrantal error' is a local error or distortion of the radio signal caused by a metal structure or hull and it is usually negligible in a wooden or fibreglass boat. Closed metallic circuits – such as rigging or steel-wire guard rails – will also cause the error and whereas the rigging circuits can be split up by the insertion of insulation in the rigging itself, it is hardly worthwhile in the average yacht. However, where the steel-wire guard rails are shackled to both pulpit and pushpit it *is* worth breaking the loop by substituting lashings for the shackles or senhouse slips at one end of the rails. 'Night error' is caused by the increased reflective capacity of the ionosphere at dusk and dawn producing stray signals which may make the location of a 'null' difficult on occasions. 'Coastal refraction' occurs when the bearing of a beacon makes an oblique angle with a coast-line; the radio beam is bent towards the coast and thus indicates that the vessel is nearer to the coast than it is in actual fact.

Fix by Rising and Dipping lights Another way of fixing your position – and one which is particularly useful in night navigation when making a landfall, is the use of the rising and dipping light range, but naturally the method can only be used in very clear visibility. The light must be a powerful one which becomes visible the instant it rises above the horizon, and if a bearing is taken at that moment a reliable fix can be obtained. Usually the loom of the light indicates its presence in good time so that its first appearance above the horizon can easily be noted.

The principle of the fix is shown in fig. 21 where A is the distance from a L.V. to its sea horizon and B is the distance from the observer's eye to his horizon. At the instant the observer first sees the light his distance from it is A plus B. These distances can be calculated if the respective heights are known, or alternatively the information can be extracted from *Inman's Tables* ('Distance of the Sea Horizon') or from the 'Dipping Light' tables in *Reed's Nautical Almanac*, which also gives the heights of lights in the 'Visual Aids to Navigation' section. For example, a yachtsman sights the Bishop's Rock light on a clear night and wishes to know his position. His height of eye is 3m and the height of Bishop's Rock light is 44m. By interpolation in the 'Dipping Light' tables of '*Reed's*' his distance from the light is 17.5 miles and this, coupled with the bearing of the light, gives a good fix.

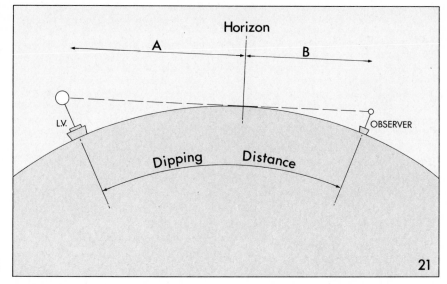

21

The Pocket Calculator as an Aid to Navigation

Coastal navigation is a continuing process of obtaining fixes from terrestrial objects, and any method which can facilitate and simplify the procedure should be used if practicable. The electronic calculator can reduce the amount of chart work and consequently speed up position fixing – particularly so in weather conditions which render the chart table a difficult place to work. It is important to remember that the calculator is a piece of electronic equipment which, although extremely reliable, can nevertheless fail. Therefore, it must not be relied upon to the extent that the navigator is unable to solve his problems without its aid. There are three main types of calculator: the simple arithmetical type with decimal base; the scientific calculator with algebraic, trigonometical and log functions with several memories: and thirdly, the more expensive calculator which can be programmed either manually or by magnetic card. The middle range of scientific calculators provide all the facilities that the cruising yachtsman really needs, and they are fairly inexpensive bearing in mind the service they provide.

Calculator facilities naturally vary in relation to the cost of the equipment, but as a general rule the better the calculator the fewer are the key sequences that need to be carried out for a specific operation. For normal navigational problems all that is required, in addition to the usual arithmetical functions, are SIN, COS, TAN and INVERSE or ARC keys, together with at least two memories. One of the disadvantages of the 'Doubling the Angle on the Bow' methods of position fixing (see page 136) is the obvious one of

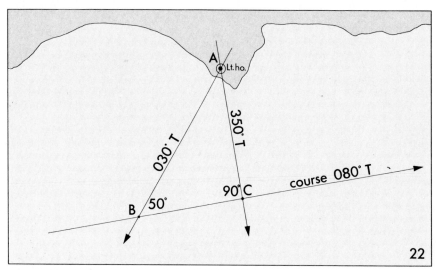

22

having to use specific angles. If you use the calculator this is not necessary and the bearings can be taken at any convenient moment. Consider the case in fig. 22 in which for simplicity, leeway and tidal set are ignored and it is required to find the distance off when abeam of A.

The first bearing of the L.H. at A is 030°T and the relative bearing to the course of 080°T will be 50°. The vessel runs on until the relative bearing is 90° when she will be abeam the L.H. which will then bear 350°T. Distance run is 4 miles.

ABC is a right-angle triangle and therefore:

$$\text{TAN } 50° = \frac{AC}{BC}$$

$$\therefore AC = \text{TAN } 50° \times BC = 1{-}19 \times 4 = 4.76 \text{ miles.}$$

$$\therefore \text{Distance-off when abeam} = 4.76 \text{ miles.}$$

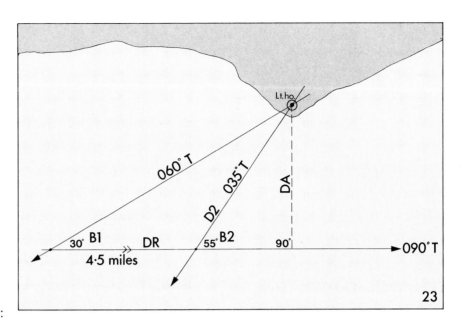

23

In fig. 23 a yacht is steering a course of 090°T and a bearing of point X is taken: 060°T – the relative bearing is therefore 30°. When the log indicates 4.5 miles the headland bears 035°T and the second relative bearing will therefore be 055°. It is required to find the distance off at the second bearing position and also the distance vessel will be off the headland when it is abeam. Again for the sake of simplicity tidal current and leeway are omitted, although it will be appreciated that the 'distance run' must be corrected to give 'distance over the ground' in actual practice. The calculation of the required distances is a simple matter, but if it is carried out step by step it involves something like twenty keying sequences on the normal calculator. However, formulae have been derived which reduce this effort considerably and these are given below (anyone interested in their derivation should consult *Reed's Nautical Almanac*):

Formula for Distance-off at 2nd Bearing:

$$D2 = \frac{DR \text{ SIN } B1}{\text{SIN } (B2 - B1)}$$

Where D2 = Distance-off at 2nd bearing
DR = Distance between 1st and 2nd bearing
B1 = 1st relative bearing
B2 = 2nd relative bearing

In fig. 23 this becomes:

$$D2 = \frac{4.5 \times \text{SIN } 30°}{\text{SIN } (55° - 30°)} = \frac{4.5 \times 0.5}{0.42}$$

$$= 5.35 \text{ miles}$$

Formula for Distance-off when Abeam:

$$DA = D2 \text{ SIN } B2$$

Where D2 = Distance off at second bearing
B2 = 2nd relative bearing
DA = Distance off when abeam

again referring to fig. 23

$$DA = 5.35 \text{ SIN } 55$$
$$= 4.38 \text{ miles}$$

Formula for Calculating the Tidal Correction Angle:

$$\text{SIN T.C.A.} = \frac{\text{T.S.} \times \text{SIN. (REL)}}{\text{Ship's speed}}$$

Where T.C.A. = Tidal correction angle
T.S. = Tidal speed
REL. = Angle between tidal current and the course to be made good (always 90° or less).

All the above calculations can be made very quickly and without any working on the chart until the fix is plotted, which is a great advantage to the short-handed crew or when conditions are difficult.

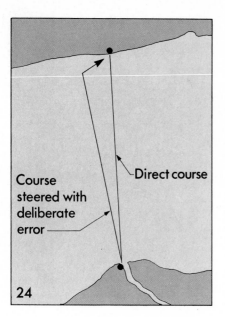

Course steered with deliberate error

Direct course

24

The Deliberate Error When you are making a day-light landfall on a coastline with few distinguishing marks, it is worth considering the introduction of a 'deliberate error' into the navigation. If the correct course is steered for the destination but, unfortunately, on making the landfall, the destination is not in sight, the navigator will be in a quandary as to which way to steer. However, if he aims at a point several miles away from his destination, then the course alteration required will be obvious when the landfall is made (fig. 24) When deciding the direction of the deliberate error some thought must be given to wind and tide, as for example it would be unfortunate to make a landfall downwind and downtide of your destination.

The Inevitable Errors. The real art in plotting D.R.s and E.P.s is to assess the probable errors which may have occurred in recording the information. The inexperienced navigator may tend to make one of two mistakes. He either has little confidence in his plot, or else he assumes that his log reading and the course steered are both accurate and his D.R. position must therefore be correct – an assumption which can be dangerous. It is much better to regard the plotted position in a doubting or questioning frame of mind. What are these errors which almost inevitably occur and which can put the E.P. well away from the actual position?

Let us first take the log where the error does depend to a certain extent on the type of instrument you use. With modern equipment it is usual for the manufacturers to state that it has accuracy of $\pm 1\%$ but, taking a charitable view, an error of $\pm 2\%$ under practical

conditions should be expected and, with an impellor-type log in very light weather, this figure may well be exceeded and might even reach 4–5%. Now consider the compass course steered and, assuming that variation and deviation (if any) have been correctly applied what of the helmsman himself? Has he or she really steered, accurately and consistently, the compass course they were given by the navigator? A good helmsman will normally work up wind of his course by virtue of the fact that he will automatically luff-up in the gusts. This is compensated for, to a certain extent, by the increased leeway which occurs as the wind strengthens. An error of one degree over a distance of sixty miles results in an error of one mile at the end of the distance run. Therefore, if an error of five degrees on the course steered occurs as a result of either compass or helmsman's error, the result will be an error of an arc of five miles at the end of a sixty mile run. Add to this a log reading error of, say, $+4\%$ – which will create a mileage error of 2.4 miles – and the net result of the two errors becomes an area of uncertainty of twelve square miles! This may seem a depressingly large area from which to start to establish an E.P. but, if the navigator assesses the errors, then the area of probability can be reduced and thus provide a better base from which to work-up the plot.

Having established a reasonable D.R. the matter of tidal current now requires consideration, and again a little thought about possible errors is necessary. As we have seen meteorological conditions affect tides to a surprising degree (page 120) and although it is not possible for the amateur

Opposite: A youngster's enthusiasm at sighting landfall after a hard day's sailing.

142

navigator to evaluate the effect of, say, a wide-spread high pressure area on tidal currents, it is worth bearing in mind the probable variations which may occur in the strength of tidal streams – and thereby improve the 'probability area' of the E.P. When you are pondering the effects of tidal streams it is also worth thinking about surface drift. When a strong-to-gale-force wind has been blowing for sometime, say two days, in sea areas like the English Channel, it will tend to produce a surface current which may reach a knot, and the effect on tidal streams, particularly if two tides are involved, can be appreciable. From the foregoing remarks the newcomer to navigation might be foregiven for concluding that the whole business of fixing one's position when out of sight of land is pretty hopeless anyway, but in practice this is far from true – always provided the presence of errors is accepted. Perhaps the term 'error' is not quite correct – one might regard them as normal factors which help to build up the overall picture.

Every small ship navigator has his own ideas about keeping his plot up to date on the chart, but however meticulous he may be, it is good practice to work up an E.P. as accurately as possible at the onset of bad weather. Inevitably the accuracy of the D.R. drops off when weather is bad and the navigator is tired, possibly worried, and probably slightly seasick; in these circumstances a good E.P. is a great help in keeping the situation under control.

While we are on the subject of errors, another is the visual error which must be guarded against – that is the assumption that a mark is the correct one because it appears at the time

and in the place you expected it to. It is a fairly common failing to convince oneself that the buoy or headland which has just become visible is the mark one has been searching for particularly when you are not feeling too well. When you are making a strange landfall in poor visibility it is frequently difficult to reconcile your view of the coastline with the picture on the chart. Low-lying objects such as harbour walls do not show up in conditions of poor visibility to the extent that one might assume from their appearance on the chart, particularly if the coastline itself is fairly high. Thus it is very important when you are making a landfall to look carefully at the features marked on the chart which should stand out *really* clearly – large vertical objects – such as church spires, tall buildings and so on – which fortunately are shown as 'conspic'. Even a familiar harbour can look surprisingly different in haze or if it is approached from an unusual angle, and the little ship navigator should assume that, when he sights a harbour for the first time, it will not look like the mental picture of it which he has built up. His sensible line of action is to consider before the approach what 'objects (conspic.)' he will use (a) to identify the harbour and (b) to establish his position in relation to the entrance. There is no great difficulty in identifying harbours under normal conditions – or even in abnormal ones – provided one has pondered on the various recognition features in advance such as approach buoys, conspicuous buildings, radio beacons *et al*.

The errors discussed above sound depressing in sum but,

provided the navigator acknowledges them and takes them into account when plotting his position and in identifying strange harbours, he will achieve results the accuracy of which may well surprise him. They may also give him enough confidence to 'go foreign' and thus achieve that memorable moment: the first foreign landfall – 'dead on the nose'!

The Beam Bearing When you are taking a beam bearing during position fixing it is worth remembering the error which can creep in if the necessary correction for leeway angle is forgotten. The correction is obviously small, and the resultant error, should it be overlooked, may not be particularly important. Nevertheless the navigator should be aware of its presence.

In fig. 26 a vessel is steering a course of 280°T but is actually making good a course of 270°T. The church is abeam when angle A is 90° and the church bears 180°T. It will be seen that, if the bearing of 90° was taken relative to the course steered, then the apparent abeam position would occur at point X instead of the true position at point Y.

Lee-bowing the Tide Planning a passage and considering the effects of tidal currents is comparatively simple when the currents are parallel to the course to be made good. However when there are cross tides on the passage lee-bowing the tide may have a significant effect. Lee-bowing the tide, as the name implies, is to keep the tidal stream pressing against the leeward side of the vessel and thus reducing the leeway. When there is a commanding wind for

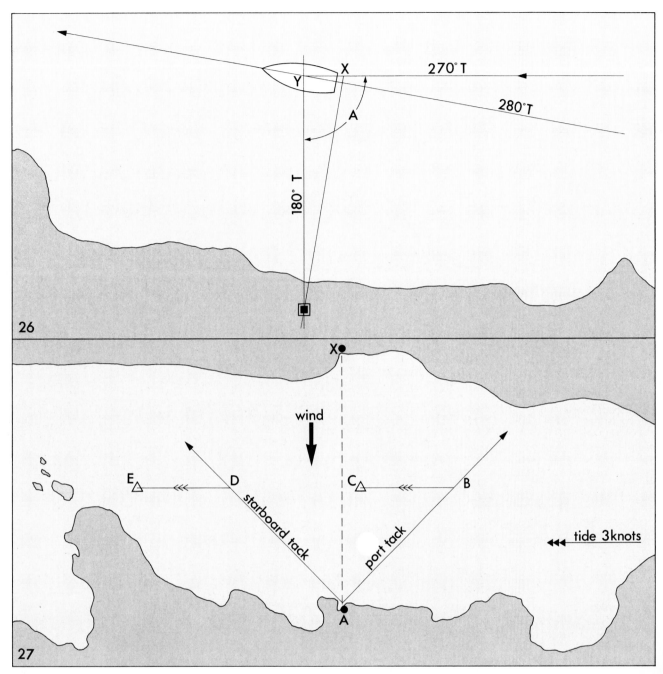

26

27

the course to be made good this is helpful, but it becomes progressively more important as the wind draws ahead.

The simplified example shown in fig. 27 will illustrate the basic principle. Two vessels leave point A for point X both of which are capable of 6 knots at 45° to the wind, with a tidal set of 3 knots westerly and a due northerly wind. One boat leaves on the port tack and,

after one hour, her E.P. would be at C. The other boat leaves on the starboard tack and her E.P. after one hour would be at E, which is much further from the desired track than C. However, when lee-bowing with a spring tide, the apparent wind direction, and therefore the close-hauled angle, will alter with the strength of the tide and the outcome will be that the yacht at C will be farther north,

while the yacht at E will be more S.W. of her apparent position at E. The drawing is a simplification of the problem but it does illustrate the care needed to utilise tidal currents – unless of course the crossing will take two tides which will cancel each other out. Even in this instance it is important to maintain a constant plot on the chart in case there is a wind shift which calls for a new course.

145

Ch.8 Meteorology

Meteorology is a complex subject but the yachtsman is only interested in two of its aspects: the wind strength and direction, and the possibility of fog. The ability to understand shipping forecasts and to relate them to local conditions does not require an expert knowledge but merely an understanding of certain fundamental phenomena.

Wind Circulation

The primary movement of air in the troposphere (a layer of air, about 10 km (6.2 miles) deep on the earth's surface) is caused by the temperature differential between the Equator and the Polar regions. The high temperature at the equatorial regions causes the air to expand and to rise to the upper troposphere, where it flows North and South, while slowly cooling, and eventually it sinks back to earth between Latitudes 30° and 40°. On reaching the earth's surface it splits – and then flows N. and S. once again.

The Polar regions generate an air-flow at ground level towards the Equatorial regions, which meets the warmer air streams coming from the 40° Latitudes and the point at which they meet is known as the 'Polar Front' – where the cold air stream undercuts the warm one thus causing it to rise (fig. 1).

High and Low Pressure Areas

In the areas with which we are mainly concerned – the latitudes

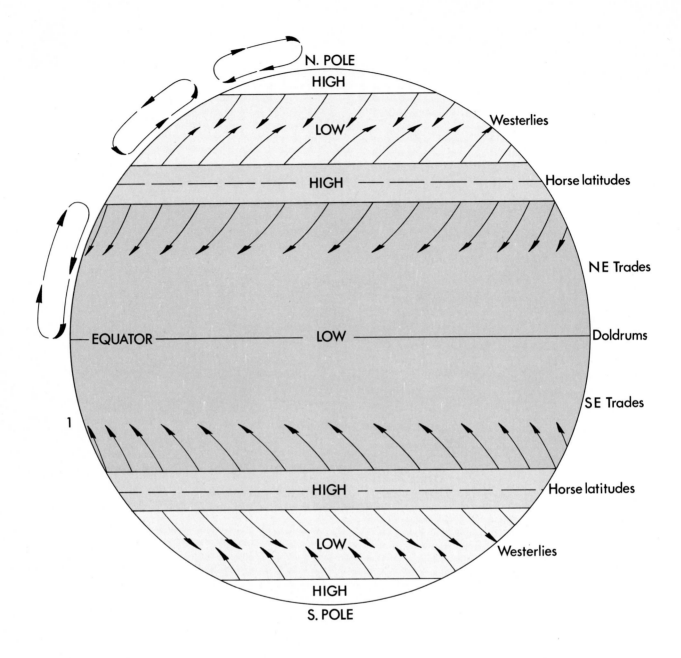

N. POLE

HIGH

LOW — Westerlies

HIGH — Horse latitudes

NE Trades

Doldrums

EQUATOR — LOW —

SE Trades

1

HIGH — Horse latitudes

LOW — Westerlies

HIGH

S. POLE

of the Westerlies – the weather is considerably influenced by the depressions which form on the Polar Front and generally move in an easterly direction. These depressions have occasional ridges of high pressure between them, producing a period of more settled weather.

Low Pressure Areas These are caused by warm air rising and cooling, bringing about the variable weather usually associated with rain and strong winds.

High Pressure Areas These are caused by air from the upper levels of the troposphere sinking to the ground – a more stable condition which is associated with dry weather and light winds.

Atmospheric pressure at any given point is the actual weight of the atmosphere at that spot; at sea level it is roughly 15 lb per sq.in. Barometric pressure is expressed as the height of a column of mercury in a tube which the air pressure will support. In average meteorological conditions this is about 30 inches (1000 millibars) at sea level.

Air Movements The secondary movement of air over the earth's surface is affected by the interaction of high and low pressure areas. Fig. 2 shows typical high pressure and low pressure areas as they appear in

148

the Northern Hemisphere, and you will see that the wind direction is reversed in the Southern Hemisphere. Note that the wind does not flow in directly towards the centre of the low pressure area, but moves in at an angle of about 20° to the isobars. Similarly with the high pressure area, the wind moves outward at an angle to the isobars. This is because wind in the Northern Hemisphere is always deflected to the right by the earth's rotation. Thus, in the case of the low pressure system, instead of the wind moving directly into the centre, it is deflected in an anti-clockwise direction. In the Southern Hemisphere the position is the opposite. From these sketches an important rule (Buys Ballot's Law) regarding wind direction in the Northern Hemisphere will be learned: *In the Northern Hemisphere an observer facing the wind will have low pressure on his right and high pressure on his left.* (The reverse applies to the Southern Hemisphere).

Cross Winds Rule In addition to 'Buys Ballot's Law' a further rule known as the 'cross winds rule' can be derived which is helpful to the observer in forecasting the weather pattern. In fig. 3, a normal depression is moving eastwards under the influence of a high level wind blowing in an easterly direction.

At X, ahead of the depression, the surface wind is blowing in the normal E to SE direction and it is obvious that the weather at this point will deteriorate, hence the first part of the rule is, with your back to the wind if the upper wind is coming from the left, the weather will deteriorate.

At position Y the weather will improve as the centre of the

depression has passed. At this point with back to the surface wind, the upper wind (as indicated by high level clouds) will be coming from the right. To sum up – with your back to the surface wind, if the upper wind comes from the left – weather will deteriorate; if from the right, it will normally improve.

It will be appreciated that the angle between the surface and upper level winds will depend on the position of the observer

relative to the centre of the depression. In the Southern Hemisphere the wind directions will of course be reversed.

Wind speed varies according to changes in barometric pressure in relation to distance (the barometric gradient) – the closer the isobars, the greater will be the gradient and thus the stronger the winds. As a rough guide a gradient of 1 millibar in thirty miles will give a surface wind speed of twenty four knots.

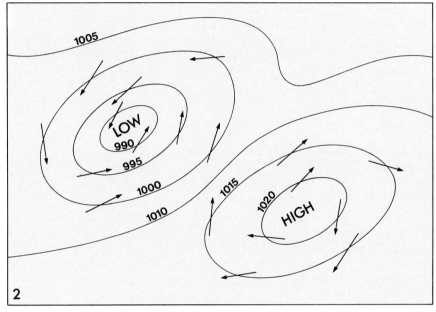

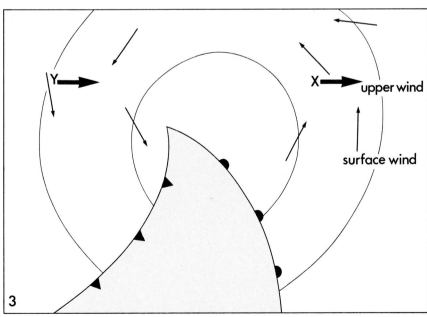

Formation of Frontal Depressions

The term 'depression' alerts the prudent yachtsman to the possibility of impending trouble, and, in the same way that knowledge of one's enemy helps in his defeat, so an understanding of depressions and the way they behave can help the yachtsman to avoid trouble – or at least to know what to be prepared for. . . .

A depression usually starts off as a small kink, or wave, of warm air protruding into the cold air of the Polar Front (fig. 4(a)). The kink grows at an accelerating rate as pressure in it falls so, it assumes the shape in (b); and it then develops into the fully-fledged depression as in (c). The term 'frontal' is derived from the two 'fronts' in the depression – the warm front which is the leading edge of the warm sector and the cold front which is the leading edge of the cold air which is following the warm sector. The warm front is shown thus ⌒⌒⌒ and the cold front ▲▲▲.

Movements and Depressions

The approximate direction of movement of the depression will be on a line roughly parallel to the line of the isobars in the warm sector, and at a speed about the same as the air speed in the warm sector. It should be noted that a small vigorous depression will move much more rapidly than a large, more stable one. Again, because of its usually steeper isobaric pattern, there are much stronger winds confined to a small area which, together with its high speed of travel, means that its progress must be carefully watched and its arrival anticipated as far as possible. These small depressions usually follow the

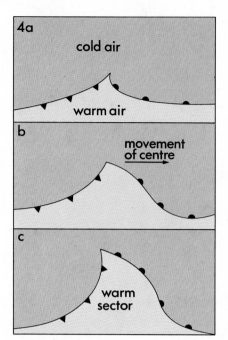

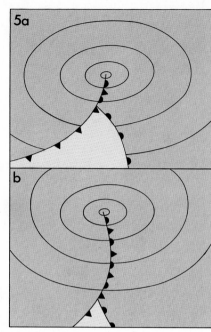

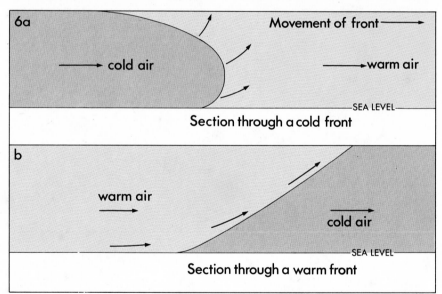

Section through a cold front

Section through a warm front

general air flow of the area, for example, round the perimeter of a large high pressure area.

Occlusion of a Depression

This is the term used to describe the condition which presages the collapse of the particular frontal depression.

The cold front travels at a higher speed than the warm front, thus gradually over-taking it, and in the process the warm air in the warm sector is eliminated. When this happens the movement of the depression can no longer follow the lines of the isobaric pattern in the warm front. The depression then slows down and follows the general air pattern and may take up to two or three days to fill and disperse. Fig. 5 shows the normal stages leading to an occlusion which starts at the centre of the depression and then moves outwards until the warm air sector is eliminated. The air pattern is shown in cross-section for both warm and cold fronts in fig. 6.

Secondary Depressions A secondary depression is one that has formed within the isobaric pattern of a larger, or primary, depression (fig. 7). It often develops within a primary one when the latter is occluding, and while it may hasten the end of the primary, it frequently develops into an even more active depression than the primary from which it originated. Due to the speed at which the secondary depression normally forms and travels, it can be a source of possible difficulty to the yachtsman if he is caught unawares. Not all secondaries are violent in their manifestation – some may pass quietly and almost unobserved, except perhaps for a slight fall in barometric pressure of the primary low. At its worst, however, it can make life distinctly unpleasant and the probability of one occurring must always be born in mind. . . .

The routine construction of daily weather charts when cruising is an invaluable guide to the possibility of trouble in store. Each chart should be kept for at least 10 days so that the pattern of movement becomes obvious and the occlusion of a large depression should be regarded as a possible warning sign of a 'secondary' occurring. In weather forecasts, any reference to a wave depression should also be looked upon as a distinct pointer to the formation of a 'secondary', while reports from Coastal Weather Stations showing an unexpected drop in pressure after the passage of a cold front, should also alert the yachtsman. Above all, of course, your own barometer readings, logged every hour, give an invaluable guide to what you may expect next . . . !

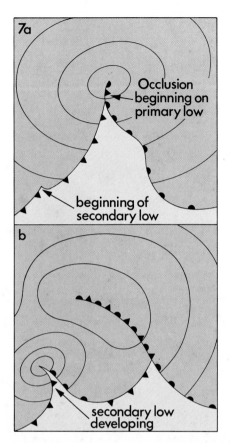

7a Occlusion beginning on primary low
beginning of secondary low

b secondary low developing

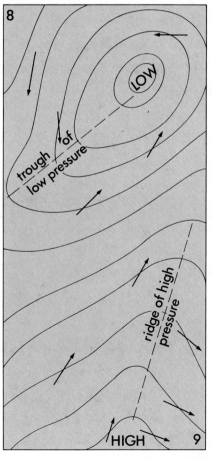

8 trough of low pressure
LOW
ridge of high pressure
HIGH 9

Troughs of Low Pressure
Fig. 8 shows a trough of low pressure extending outwards from the middle of the depression and it is indicated by the more sharply curving system of isobars along the trough line, the lines of isobars being concave. A trough may be referred to as 'deep' or 'shallow' according to the curvature of the isobars. If the latter is acute then the trough is deep but, if it curving more gently then it is a shallow one; the deep trough causes a more rapid fluctuation in the wind strength and direction than does a shallow one.

Ridge or Wedge of High Pressure A ridge of high pressure occurs when a high pressure area extends in a wedge form between two low pressure areas, the isobars assuming their greatest curvature along the line of the ridge. As with a trough of low pressure, the more sharply curved the isobars are along this ridge, the faster it moves. Ridges are usually associated with fair weather, often having very light winds along the central portion (fig. 9).

Thermal Depressions or Lows Thermal depressions are often caused by strong surface heating over islands or peninsulars, when the land temperature is much higher than the sea temperature and the barometric pressure gradient is very slight. Under these conditions there is normally very little wind and they are therefore favourable for the formation of a thermal low. The warm air over the land rises, and the colder moist air from the sea flows into the low pressure area thus created. The ascent of the cold moist air produces condensation and the formation of towering cumulus clouds which makes for an unstable condition. If it is particularly marked, thundery showers accompanied by sudden squalls and wind shifts, and frequently a complete reversal of wind direction in the vicinity of thunderstorms, will result.

Anti-cyclones Convergence of the air-streams at the upper level of the troposphere (see fig. 8) causes air to sink to the ground and thus increase the barometric pressure over a limited area. The surface air then flows outwards, anti-cyclonically, towards the areas of lower pressure. The air at the upper level being dry and becoming warmed as it descends, the central area of the anti-cyclone is nearly always associated with fine, dry weather. The British Isles is particularly affected during the summer by high pressure area or anti-cyclone which is normally positioned over the Azores. If this anti-cyclone is relatively weak in the summer, frontal depressions tend to move further south producing unsettled weather and greater than average rainfall in the area of north-western Europe.

Cold anti-cyclones are ones in which the air is colder than in the surrounding areas and these normally build up during the winter over the centre of large land masses – the Siberian one particularly effects north-western Europe. Occasionally a ridge of high pressure extends from the Siberian high to the British Isles during winter and produces exceptionally cold weather from the easterly winds associated with it.

Clouds

Apart from the barometer and thermometer the greatest source of information regarding approaching weather available to the amateur meterorologist are cloud formations and in in order to understand and interpret the situation correctly, knowledge of the different types of cloud and their relationship with fronts is very useful.

The ability of an air parcel to hold water vapour (which is invisible) is directly related to the temperature: the higher the temperature the greater the volume of water which can be absorbed; conversely, as the temperature drops it can hold less. An air parcel which contains the maximum amount of water at a certain temperature is said to be saturated and has reached its dewpoint temperature. If the temperature drops below this figure the water vapour condenses into visible droplets, either cloud or fog. The basic pattern of cloud formation is therefore simple. A parcel of air at low level rises, cools and thus lowers its capacity to hold water vapour. When its dewpoint temperature is reached the water vapour condenses and cloud formation commences. The height and type of cloud formation which occurs is determined largely by the altitude at which the dewpoint temperature is reached – for example at high altitudes the dewpoint will produce ice crystal formations (Cirrus, Cirro Stratus and Cirro Cumulus).

Cloud Classification Cloud names are derived from the Latin and are classified according to their shape and height:

Cumulus – a heap
Stratus – a layer
Cirrus – a thread
Nimbus – rain
Fracto – broken

All high clouds above 18000 ft (5500 m) are formed of ice crystals and called Cirrus or Cirro. Clouds at medium level (6500–18000 ft = 2000–5000 m) are described as 'Alto'; e.g. Alto Cumulus whereas low level clouds at 1000–6500 ft (300–2000 m) are 'Stratus', e.g. Strato Cumulus. The high, towering clouds with low base are Cumulus and, if rain is falling, Cumulo-nimbus. The term 'fracto' is applied to broken cloud e.g. fracto cumulus etc.

Group	Cloud Formation		Height Range
High Clouds	Cirrus	(Ci)	18000 to 45000 ft
	Cirro Cumulus	(Cc)	(5500 to 14000 m)
	Cirro Stratus	(Cs)	
Medium Clouds	Alto Stratus	(As)	6000 to 18000 ft
	Alto Cumulus	(Ac)	(1800 to 5500 m)
Low Clouds	Nimbo Stratus	(Ns)	1000 to 6500 ft
	Strato Cumulus	(Sc)	(300 to 2000 m)
	Stratus	(St)	
Towering Clouds with low level base	Cumulus	(Co)	1000 to 45000 ft
	Cumulo-nimbus	(Cb)	(300 to 14000 m)

Fog

Fog is defined as a condition in which visibility is less than 1000yds (900m) and haze or mist when visibility is between 1000 and 2200yds (2000m). As we have seen in the formation of clouds, water vapour becomes visible when, because of a drop in temperature, the dew point is reached. This drop in temperature is not necessarily caused by an ascending column of air but can be caused by radiation (land fog), or advection (a horizontal air movement).

Radiation Fog This occurs at night, usually during the Autumn or Winter, and is caused by the rapid radiation of heat from a land surface into the atmosphere. The temperature of the land drops sharply and cools the layer of air immediately above it so that the dew point of the air is reached. A slight ground wind of three to four miles per hour is needed to stir up this layer of air and the turbulence, coupled with the dew point being reached, causes a shallow layer of fog to form. Although it cannot form over the sea it may drift out from land for a mile or two and persist for several hours. This type of fog is more likely to occur on nights when there is no cloud cover, as the presence of cloud cover tends to act as a thermal insulating layer which reduces radiation and the likelihood of fog.

Advection Fog This can occur on land or sea at any time of the day or night and is caused by the horizontal movement of warm air on to a colder surface, the temperature drop being sufficient to bring the air mass down to its dew point. The formation of advection fog

over sea may be caused by the warm air over a land mass flowing over a cold sea surface, which can happen in the Spring when the land has already heated up but the sea is still cold. It will also form in areas where an air stream heated by warm ocean currents meets a cold ocean current – a good example of this is the southerly air stream flowing over the cold Labrador current and causing frequent fogs off the coast of Newfoundland.

From the yachtsman's viewpoint the great difference between radiation and advection fog lies in the wind speeds associated with them. With radiation fog, as already mentioned, a slight breeze of three to four miles per hour is needed to cause the necessary turbulence which assists in the fog formation, and anything much in excess of this speed will dissipate the fog. Advection or sea fog however will persist in much stronger wind forces, even up to Force Six when the conditions are really favourable for its formation.

Weather Patterns associated with Depressions and Anticyclones

The types of weather described in the following paragraphs are the classic ones associated with the particular fronts. Actual weather conditions can vary considerably because of the infinite variety of the factors involved – barometric pressure, temperature, humidity and so on. It is in the interpretation of the general situation, coupled with intelligent use of the barometer and visual signs such as cloud formations, that the small boat navigator can soon learn to predict the conditions he may expect to meet in a period of, say, twenty-four hours.

153

1

2

3

4

5

6

7

8

9

1 Cirrocumulus. High ice clouds. Outbreaks of rain likely in 24–28 hours.
2 Cirrocumulus and Altocumulus. High ice clouds. If decreasing – fair weather. If increasing – outbreaks of rain, perhaps thundery, within 48 hours.
3 Altostratus Perlucidus. Middle ice and water clouds; thickening grey sheet, with sun as behind ground glass becoming obliterated. Forming slowly – rain within 12 hours. Forming quickly – rain within 2 or 3 hours.
4 Nimbostratus. Low water clouds. Rain prolonged if winds steady SE–SW, but heavier though shorter if winds squally and variable.
5 Stratocumulus Cumulogenitus. Low water clouds. With Westerly winds backing to Southerly – scattered showers being replaced by general, and gentler, rain within 12 hours.
6 Cumulus Congenitus. Low water cloud towering. Sharp squally showers in vicinity. On NW winds, thunderstorms on Western Seaboard even in winter.
7 Cirrus Fibratus. High ice clouds indicating, if little apparent movement, fair weather.
8 Cirrostratus (with faint halo). High ice clouds. If steadily thickening – rain within 24 hours.
9 Stratocumulus. Low water clouds. With W–SW winds, dull but not bad weather; SW–SE, rain and cooler weather within 12 hours; NE–SE, fair weather in summer or in winter drizzle or light snow.

Sequence of Weather at a Warm Front
Showing characteristics as the front approaches and passes

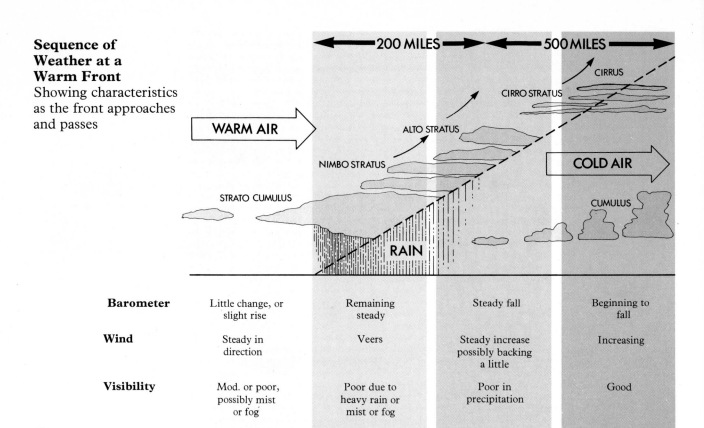

Barometer	Little change, or slight rise	Remaining steady	Steady fall	Beginning to fall
Wind	Steady in direction	Veers	Steady increase possibly backing a little	Increasing
Visibility	Mod. or poor, possibly mist or fog	Poor due to heavy rain or mist or fog	Poor in precipitation	Good

10

Sequence of Weather at a Cold Front
Showing characteristics as the front approaches and passes

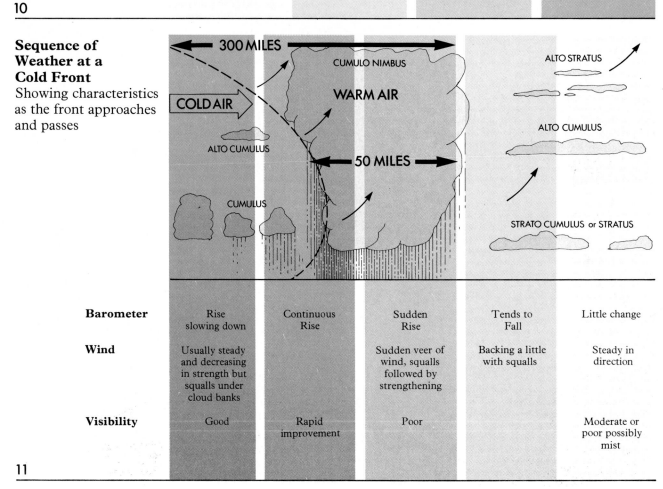

Barometer	Rise slowing down	Continuous Rise	Sudden Rise	Tends to Fall	Little change
Wind	Usually steady and decreasing in strength but squalls under cloud banks		Sudden veer of wind, squalls followed by strengthening	Backing a little with squalls	Steady in direction
Visibility	Good	Rapid improvement	Poor		Moderate or poor possibly mist

11

Warm Front The general pattern of weather on the passage of a warm front is shown in fig. 10 from which it will be seen that the high level cloud formation may start approximately 500 miles (800kms) in advance of the front. The high wispy clouds of ice crystals (cirrus) may be the forerunner of bad weather, particularly if the threads are twisted into 'Mares Tails'. This formation may be followed by Cirro Stratus which frequently causes a halo round the sun, and is further confirmation that bad weather can be expected. Alto Stratus, and Strato Cumulus following, will precede the arrival of the front. As the actual front approaches the cloud level becomes lower, precipitation starts and gradually increases until the actual front has passed. Note that the term 'precipitation' is used in weather forecasts as it covers rain, hail, sleet or snow, any of which may occur according to the ambient temperature at the front. Winds will normally increase in strength as the front approaches and possibly back a little.* The strength will then steady as the front passes and veer slightly in the warm sector. Visibility, which will be good prior to the arrival of the front, will gradually decrease as precipitation increases and may become poor because of mist or fog at the actual front and in the warm sector itself.

*A wind is said to 'back' when its direction shifts in an anti-clockwise manner. For example a westerly wind shifting southwards is said to 'back'; when the shift is in a clockwise direction, say from west to north, it is 'veering'.

Cold Front Fig. 11 shows the average weather pattern as a warm sector, followed by a cold front, passes over. The general weather conditions in the warm sector as the cold front approaches are moderate-to-poor visibility, wind probably in the SW quarter, and a steady barometer. As the front gets near, the barometer tends to fall, the wind increases and becomes squally, while visibility shortens because of the increasingly heavy rainfall. If the barometric gradient is sharp, squalls could be very strong and a careful look-out should be kept. As the front passes the barometer will rise steeply, and will be accompanied by a rapid increase in wind which will veer sharply – possibly as much as 90°.

Land and Sea Breezes Sea breezes are of some importance to the inshore sailing man, particularly if he is engaged in racing. When the land is rapidly heated up during the day in late Spring or early Summer, there is a considerable difference in temperature between the land and the still-cold sea. Thermal uplift occurs and it creates an air flow from the inshore waters to the land which will normally persist until late afternoon. The air speed is comparatively low and is easily disturbed by any prevailing strong winds. Sometimes, if the prevailing wind is on shore, it may strengthen the sea breeze, although if the former exceeds say Force 4 (see page 159) it will break up the thermal uplift which causes it.

Occasionally a reverse effect happens when, because of the more rapid cooling of the land mass at night in relation to the water, there is an outflow of air from the land. Usually this is comparatively slight but there is an exception which occurs under certain well-defined atmospheric conditions. Where high ground slopes down to the sea and, because of the more-rapid cooling of the ground at high altitude, there is a large air flow down to the sea which is known as the Katabatic wind. It is particularly marked if there are valleys sloping down to the sea which cause a funnelling effect and increase the wind speed considerably.

Weather Maps
One of the tasks that the yachtsman undertakes when cruising is the regular compilation of weather maps, or more technically, synoptic charts. Blank weather maps are readily obtainable in the form of a tear-off pad, and one should be completed every day, preferably on the basis of the first shipping forecast in the morning. Usually the first few charts you prepare are rather disappointing, but with a little practice, leavened with an increasing knowledge of meteorology, results rapidly improve. Mention has already been made of 'isobars' – points of equal barometric pressure – and to complete a good weather map it is necessary to have as many readings as possible, properly spaced over the chart. Unfortunately one always seems to need more of them than are readily available, although this varies from country to country. However, it is usually possible to interpolate isobars into the remaining gaps when only a few barometric readings are available and, provided this is done carefully, it will be quite a help in building up the weather picture. Other information given in weather forecasts – such as position and probable

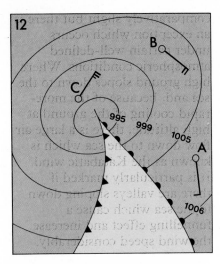

movements of 'highs' and 'lows', together with wind direction and strength – all add up to complete the picture and enable a reliable chart to be drawn up.

Few forecasts are given at dictation speed, so some form of shorthand is necessary, preferably by using the standard meteorological symbols – actually a small tape recorder is a very useful piece of equipment in this context. . . . Once the maximum amount of information has been noted the work of plotting the weather map requires a little careful thought. But the result will give one a much more clear picture than may be obtained by merely listening to a forecast. Bearing in mind that the forecast areas cover many hundreds of square miles, forecast information must inevitably be of a specific nature, and, therefore, your own weather map, specifically concocted with reference to a certain part of a shipping area, can be of great value – and particularly if it seems that the 'general forecast' is not working out as predicted.

Fig. 12 shows how wind arrows in weather maps are usually drawn. The small circle c represents the position of the Reporting Situation and is the head of the arrow, which

is pointing in the direction of the wind flow. The 'feathers' represent wind strength on the Beaufort Scale, each full member denoting 2 units on the Scale and each half member: 1 unit. Thus the arrow at A represents a Force 2 breeze, B Force 4 and C Force 5. The 'feathers' are always drawn on the same side as the low pressure area. Each chart should be kept for a period of ten days so that at any one time you have a ten day record which clearly shows the pattern of movement and helps considerably in making reliable predictions.

The importance attached to an understanding of meteorology can be judged by the fact that, in the United Kingdom, the R.Y.A. Yachtmaster's Certificate curriculum includes the ability to prepare and understand a weather map.

The Beaufort Wind Scale
The Beaufort Wind Scale was devised by Admiral Sir Francis Beaufort, R.N., in 1808, as a means of estimating wind force from the appearance of the state of the sea. Although it is now universally used there is a growing tendency to refer to wind speed in knots since instruments for measuring speeds are comparatively inexpensive and are becoming common place fittings on yachts. The relationship between the Beaufort Scale and the open sea is the important one to understand. The actual state of the sea for a given wind force may vary considerably according to the location in general – the farther from land the more regular will be the sea and thus the safer the situation. A small family cruiser which would be perfectly safe, although admittedly uncomfortable, in a

Force 6 well off-shore, could be in difficulties with the same wind force under wind-over-tide conditions in a tide-rip off a headland. . . . When you are sitting in harbour listening to a forecast, remember to relate the wind force it gives to the area you want to cover, and to the state of the tide. When in doubt, however, go out and have a look at it, unless of course it is a rapidly worsening forecast.

Until you have had some experience of bad weather at sea it is naturally difficult to estimate what your boat can stand. In truth it really comes down to what the crew, and not the boat, can stand – provided of course that the boat is well-found, and equipped with adequate gear. An attempt has been made on page 160 to relate the Beaufort Scale to the performance of three typical yachts:
One – a small family twin-keeler, with a self-draining cockpit, a small auxiliary of, say, 10 hp, 25 ft L.O.A. (7.5 m), and not really intended for serious off-shore cruising although capable if properly handled.

Two – a well-designed and built 30 ft L.O.A. (9 m) off-shore cruiser with a robust auxiliary of, say, 20 hp.

Three – a rather different type, a high-speed planing motor cruiser 30 ft L.O.A. (9 m), a popular type but one which should sensibly return to sheltered water before the advent of bad weather.

It is stressed that the probable behaviour of these vessels should not be regarded as their automatic performance. So much depends on their design and construction, plus the knowledge and preparedness of their crews.

Beaufort Wind Scale

Beaufort Number	Limits of Wind Speed in Knots	Descriptive Terms	Sea Criterion	Probable Height of Waves in Metres and Feet	Probable Maximum Wave Height in Metres and Feet
0	Less than 1	Calm	Sea like a mirror.	—	—
1	1–3	Light Air	Ripples with the appearance of scales are formed but without foam crests.	—	—
2	4–6	Light Breeze	Small wavelets, still short but more pronounced. Crests have a glassy appearance and do not break.	0.15 (6in)	0.30 (1ft)
3	7–10	Gentle Breeze	Large wavelets. Crests begin to break. Foam of glassy appearance. Perhaps scattered white horses.	0.60 (2ft)	1.0 (3ft)
4	11–16	Moderate Breeze	Small waves, becoming longer; fairly frequent white horses.	1.0 (3ft)	1.50 (5ft)
5	17–21	Fresh Breeze	Moderate waves taking a more pronounced long form; many white horses are formed. (Chance of some spray.)	1.80 (6ft)	2.50 (8½ft)
6	22–27	Strong Breeze	Large waves begin to form; the white foam crests are more extensive everywhere. (Probably some spray.)	3.0 (9½ft)	4.0 (13ft)
7	28–33	Near gale	Sea heaps up and white foam from breaking waves begins to be blown in streaks along the direction of the wind.	4.0 (13½ft)	6.0 (19ft)
8	34–40	Gale	Moderately high waves of greater length; edges of crests begin to break into spindrift. The foam is blown in well-marked streaks along the direction of the wind.	5.50 (18ft)	7.50 (25ft)
9	41–47	Strong gale	High waves. Dense streaks of foam along the direction of the wind. Crests of waves begin to topple, tumble and roll over. Spray may affect visibility.	7.0 (23ft)	9.75 (32ft)
10	48–55	Storm	Very high waves with long overhanging crests. The resulting foam in great patches is blown in dense white streaks along the direction of the wind. On the whole the surface of the sea takes a white appearance. The tumbling of the sea becomes heavy and shock-like. Visibility affected.	9.0 (29ft)	12.50 (41ft)
11	56–63	Violent Storm	Exceptionally high waves (small and medium-sized ships might be for a time lost to view behind the waves). The sea is completely covered with long white patches of foam lying along the direction of the wind. Everywhere the edges of the wave crests are blown into froth. Visibility affected.	11.30 (37ft)	16.0 (52ft)
12	64 +	Hurricane	The air is filled with foam and spray. Sea completely white with driving spray; visibility very seriously affected.	13.70 (45ft)	—

Beaufort Wind Scale:
Possible Behaviour of Typical Craft

25ft Bilge-keel family sailing cruiser

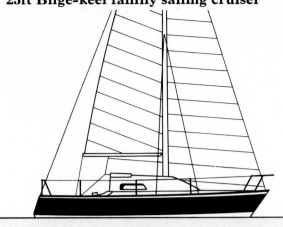

Force	Wind Speed	
0	—	—
1	1–3	Full rig – just steerage ways.
2	4–6	Full rig, making 2–3 kts at about 45°–50° off
3	7–10	true wind.
4	11–16	Full mainsail at F4 but would probably need 3 rolls in the main at F5 (with small foresail set). Makes 3–4 kts at, say, 55° to wind. Leeway increasing.
5	17–21	
6	22–27	At least 6 rolls in main and storm jib. Probably making 2 kts at 55° to wind. Considerable leeway.
7	28–33	Deepest reef in main and storm jib. Impossible to work to windward and dangerous to run. Possible square drift to shelter?
8	34–40	Survival action needed. Towing warps or lying a'hull. Latter probably dangerous if a high profile hull with large windows.
9	41–47	—
10	48–55	—
11	56–63	—
12	64+	—

Sources of Weather Information

Today's yachtsman has little excuse for being caught out by bad weather conditions in view of the number of weather forecasts available to him. Admittedly if he is on a long passage he may have an uncomfortable time occasionally, but he should never be caught unawares – except perhaps on the rare occasion when a small, very fast-moving secondary depression outstrips all the forecasts. The National Radio Services of all maritime nations broadcast weather information, some of them in English as well as their native language. In addition there are the Coastal Radio Stations broadcasting information relating to more local areas together with, in Britain further broadcasts for yachtsmen and fishermen from some commercial radio stations situated near the coast. A radio set which will receive Long wave, Medium wave and

31 ft Off-shore Fin-keel cruiser   **30 ft Planing Motor-cruiser**

—

Full rig – steerage way.
Full rig, making 4–5 kts at about 35°–40° off
true wind.

Full main but genoa changed for working
headsail. Making 5–6 kts at 45° to wind.

3–4 rolls in main (more if a large one). Small
foresail. Making probably 5 kts at about 48° to
wind. Leeway increasing.

Deeply-reefed main and storm jib. Could
probably work to windward at 3 kts 50° to wind,
considerable leeway, say 10°–12°.

Heave-to if under-water profile suitable and
searoom available. Little probability of more
than 2 kts to windward, unless engine can be
used, dependent on size.

Survival action needed. Towing warps or lying
ahull.

Planing at full speed
,,   ,,   ,,   ,,
,,   ,,   ,,   ,,

Getting very bumpy dependent on sea
conditions, will have to slow down to
displacement speed.

Slowed down still more. Danger to crew by
by being thrown about.

Situation becoming critical if not a well-
designed cruiser.

Survival action needed. Keep head to seas or
run if practicable. Avoid cross seas which
could roll her over.

If engines fail, a large sea anchor probably
only course of action possible.

Trawler band (1.5–3.5MH) is
comparatively inexpensive to
buy, and it is true to say that in
the waters of the North
Western European seaboard it
is possible to tune-in to various
shipping forecasts at least seven
or eight times a day. It is also
important to remember that the
'land forecasts' should always be
given the yachtsman's attention.
These normally give weather
information relating to the
subsequent 48 hours, whereas
shipping forecasts are only good
for 24 hours. Thus it is possible
to obtain advance information
from the land forecasts which
may be very useful. Finally, the
skipper with the V.H.F. set can
always obtain information from
the Coastguards if he has
contrived to miss all the other
broadcasts. . . .

Detailed information on all
official shipping forecasts is
published annually in *Reed's
Nautical Almanac* and the
R.Y.A. publication *Weather
Forecasts*.

Ch. 9 Signalling, Collision Regulations and Buoyage

SIGNALLING

Many learners in cruising tend to first shy off the subject of signalling as they are under the mistaken impression that it only concerns the Professional Seaman! In fact the ability to communicate with other vessels or shore stations is extremely useful. Quite apart from the obvious importance in the life-saving extremity it should be realised that some busy commercial ports exercise a strict control over the entry and exit of all vessels. Thus a small yacht which is unable to communicate with Port Control may find she has to wait longer for entry than she would if she could signal on arrival.

From a life-saving point of view the ability to communicate is vital – even if this only takes the form of distress flares – but the yachtsman who takes pride in being a seaman will at least learn the Morse Code and see to it that he has a reasonable signalling lamp on board. There is no need for him to attempt to attain the speed of a 'professional' but just to be able to send a message and receive one. It may be very useful indeed one day. . . .

Basically communication between vessels at sea and shore stations may be carried out by means of radio, International Code Flags, and Morse Code using a flashing light. Radio can of course be subdivided into Radio Telephony and Radio Telegraphy. Semaphore signalling has little practical use and is not worth bothering about so far as the yachtsman is concerned. Technically speaking the use of sound apparatus in conditions of restricted visibility is 'signalling' – but this is normally restricted to the signals of the International Collision Regulations indicating movement: whether the vessel is at anchor, aground or whatever.

Radio Receivers In addition to the Long and Medium Wave Bands the radio receiver carried on a yacht should also have the Marine Wave Band (1600–4000 KHZ) which will enable the Coastal Radio Stations to be picked up, thus providing another source of information apart from the main shipping forecasts. The average cruising yachtsman really has no need to buy a specially-designed marine receiver – there are several good, portable, and reasonably-priced transistor radios available which include a Marine Waveband. One of them should certainly be regarded as an essential item of equipment in any well-found cruising yacht.

Radio Transmitters A few years ago it was unusual to find radio transmission equipment on small yachts but the rapid development of transistorised units over the last decade or so has resulted in the production of small compact and very efficient transmitters in the V.H.F. range, which is really the only waveband of interest to yachtsman. The cost is of course well above that of a radio receiver but the V.H.F. set should not be looked upon merely as a handy means of booking a berth for the night in a marina but as an extremely effective piece of emergency equipment. In the event of trouble it is far more likely to bring help quickly than would the firing of a parachute flare and it also offers the very comforting knowledge that your distress call has been heard and acknowledged. Let us assume that you have decided to buy one of the small standard production sets which, incidentally, give the maximum power out-put permitted – 25 watts (G.P.O. Regulation for Great Britain). The first problem to be solved is – which specific channels will you require in the particular area in which the yacht will be sailed? The less-expensive sets have a restricted number of channels fitted with crystals as standard, together with some spare channels to accommodate the particular wave-lengths which the owner may require. Certain channels – Channel 16, the International calling and distress channel, together with Channel 6, the first inter-ship channel, are mandatory and these will always be included in the standard equipment.

Naturally there are strict regulations covering the installation and use of radio transmitters in every country. In the United Kingdom, for example, the sets have to be of a type approved by the Post Office and the installation must be licenced, for which an annual fee is payable, and in addition the owner or person responsible must have a Certificate of Competency to operate the equipment. In the case of a V.H.F. installation in a yacht the examination for the Certificate of Competency is carried out by a Ship Radio Inspector of the Department of Trade and is a comparatively simple matter. It does however ensure that the correct procedures are fully understood, together with the proper discipline which is so essential when you are working in crowded radio channels.

Radio Telephone Procedures – General It is not intended to discuss in detail the full V.H.F. procedures but rather to give some idea of the types of facility which will be opened up to the yachtsman who invests in a V.H.F. set. For full details of the procedures reference should be made to the *Handbook for Radio Operators*, published by H.M.S.O.; *V.H.F. Radio Telephony for Yachts*, published by the R.Y.A.; *Reed's Nautical Almanac* or other national handbooks.

Standard Phraseology

It is important that the operator of a transmitting set should be conversant with the correct procedures and standard phraseology used on the air. The average yachtsman who has just acquired a V.H.F. set may be a little daunted at the thought of using standard phrases and the phonetic alphabet – indeed he may even question the necessity for standard phrases. However, it must be appreciated that they lead to economy of words which is an important factor in an already over-crowded communications system. A further point is that standard phrases are more easily picked out against a background of 'atmospheric clutter' for example a standard phrase of five words will probably be recognised if only two of the words are heard distinctly. In this connection it is essential to be familiar with the standard phonetic alphabet as it will certainly be required when you are identifying your vessel to a Coastal Station.

Rules The transmission rules are based on common sense and courtesy. One of the most important is related to secrecy of communications; under no circumstances may any correspondence or communication overhead by a radio operator be divulged to anyone. Other rules forbid the use of obscene language and the sending of any signal without giving the call sign or name of the yacht. Calling procedures for Coastal Stations and Port

Controls vary somewhat from country to country. In the United Kingdom for example the initial call is invariably made on Channel 16 after which the Coast Station will acknowledge and instruct the caller to switch to its working frequency. Some Continental stations must be called on their working frequency as any call on Channel 16 is ignored unless it is a distress call.

The greatest advantage to a yacht of the V.H.F. set is the facility to call for assistance when in distress, and also to assist others in distress who may have no radio. Messages relating to Distress and Safety are grouped under three headings and the amateur operator must be completely clear in his mind about the precise meaning of the three priorities of message.

Distress Signal The distress signal 'MAYDAY' repeated three times precedes a message stating that a ship or aircraft is in grave danger and requires immediate assistance. This call is always made on Channel 16 and takes precedence over all other traffic which must cease immediately. If necessary the station controlling the incident will broadcast a signal embodying the words 'MAYDAY – SEELONCE' which forbids any traffic other than that relating to the matter in hand. When the silence can be relaxed the station will broadcast 'MAYDAY PRUDONCE' and when the incident is finished it will broadcast a 'Mayday – Seelonce Feenee' message to all ships. A yacht hearing a 'Mayday' message has, like any other ship, a mandatory obligation under International Agreement to accept the call and take whatever action is necessary. . . . Upon receiving the message the yacht should wait for a few minutes to see if the message is acknowledged by a Coast Radio Station or another ship. If no acknowledgement is heard then the yacht must either acknowledge the message herself if she is in a position to render assistance, or if not, then she must retransmit the message as a 'Mayday Relay'.

Urgency Signal The 'Urgency' signal consists of the words 'PAN PAN' repeated three times followed by the message, which takes priority over everything on Channel 16 except a Mayday call. The words 'Pan Pan' indicate that the station transmitting has a very important message concerning the safety of a ship, aircraft or person. In other words the ship is not in imminent danger but requires assistance urgently. For example if a yacht had a crew member overboard in conditions which made it doubtful whether or not he could be picked up, then a 'Pan Pan' message should be sent immediately – if he *is* picked up, then the message can be cancelled.

Safety Signal The Safety Signal, the third category of message, is the word 'SAYCUREETAY' repeated three times, followed by the safety message containing important Navigational or Meterological information. This is transmitted on a working frequency which has been designated in the safety call on Channel 16. In the case of a yachtsman the type of incident which would warrant his sending a safety signal would be, for example, if he observed a floating object of sufficient size to be a danger to navigation.

Quite apart from these sorts

of message the ship with V.H.F. aboard provides the pleasant everyday facility of making telephone calls to subscribers ashore and of sending telegrams, as well as being called up by Shore Stations when someone ashore wishes to communicate with her.

The International Code The latest International Code of

signals was published in 1969 and it embodies the necessary information and procedures for all forms of marine communications in one volume and enables signals to be exchanged in nine different languages. For the serious off-shore cruising man an International Code book is, therefore, a useful addition to his bookshelf.

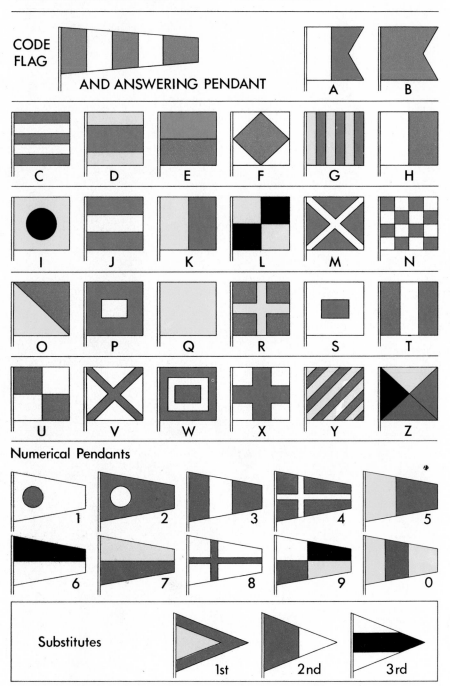

166

The Code consists essentially of three separate groups of signals:

1. Single-letter signals which are urgent, important or commonly used communications. For example, the single letter 'U' means: 'You are running into danger!'
2. Two-letter signals covering general groups of communications (e.g. the two letter signal 'RN' which mean: 'My engines are out of action').
3. Three-letter signals, all beginning with 'M', used in the Medical section.

All signals may be made by any method of communication, although there are restrictions on the use of sound in view of the requirements of the International Collision Regulations (nos. 34 & 35).

If you decide to carry a set of International Codes flags there are one or two practical aspects to be considered. Obviously the flags must be of such a size, and so displayed, that they are visible for a reasonable distance; the minimum size of flag can therefore be regarded as one of 2 ft in the hoist and it must clearly be displayed as high up as possible. The latter condition should give no trouble in the average sailing yacht but it poses an insuperable problem in all but the largest of motor-cruisers.

The complete set of Code Flags – letters, numerals and substitutes – consists of forty flags and, if they are of reasonable practical size, the space they require for stowage is considerable. From a strictly practical point of view, therefore, it is unlikely that the average family cruising yacht will find it worthwhile to carry the full set. However, it is suggested that several flags which enable the more important single letter signals to be made should be carried on board. The following ones are the most useful:

O = Man overboard.
U = You are running into danger.
V = I require assistance.
W = I require medical assistance.
CB = I require immediate assistance.

Morse Code by Flashing Light A flashing light, utilizing the Morse Code for either plain language or International Code, probably offers the best solution to signalling problems but it will be appreciated that a proper signalling lamp of the Aldis type is necessary if signals are to be made during the hours of daylight and over any worthwhile distance. A masthead lamp, fitted with a suitable morse key can be very useful at night but this is of little use during the day.

Learning the morse code by lamp should not present any great difficulties and is a useful exercise for the yachtsman to undertake. If two people can practise together, perhaps with one of the teaching aids used in conjunction with a tape recorder, there should be no difficulty in attaining a reasonable standard, certainly good enough to send messages when you bear in mind that the professional signalman, when he realises he is dealing with an amateur, will transmit much more slowly than his usual speed. Remember that it is much more important to transmit slowly with a proper rhythm than fast but in an erratic manner.

The full procedures for signalling are given in the *International Code Book* and *Reed's Nautical Almanac* but the procedure may be briefly summarised as follows:

1. Transmitting vessel calls up receiving station by signalling $\overline{AA}$ $\overline{AA}$
2. Answering signal $\overline{TTTTT}$
3. If necessary ships exchange identities. Transmitting ship sends DE followed by her name or signal letter. The receiving ship repeats this and then sends her own name or number, which is acknowledged by the other ship repeating it.
4. The message is then sent in plain language or if necessary in code, if the latter the code groups are preceded by the signal YU.
5. Each group or word is acknowledged by the receiving ship sending the letter T.
6. At the end of the message the transmitting ship sends AR which the receiving ship acknowledges with R.

Note the 'bar' over $\overline{AA}$ or $\overline{TTT}$ means that the letters are made without any gap between them.

Visual Signals *The International Code Book* also gives details of the visual signals used by Rocket Life Saving or other stations where it is not practicable for a lifeboat to operate because of rocks etc. and where the use of morse is impracticable (e.g. a yachtsman who is unable to transmit or receive). In addition to the 'control' signals mentioned above there are also the acknowledgement signals indicating that a ship's distress signals have beeen observed. These consist of an orange smoke signal or combined light and sound signal, three single signals fired at one minute intervals for daytime use, and at night three single white star rockets at one minute intervals.

INTERNATIONAL REGULATIONS for PREVENTING COLLISIONS at SEA

Anyone who goes to sea, even in a modest way, and who takes his responsibilities seriously, should have an understanding of the 'Collision Regulations' so that he may fully understand the actions and intentions of other craft and take the correct action himself in any situation which may arise. Admittedly there are few yachtsmen who are not aware of the simple sailing rules for vessels in sight of one another, but they may have little knowledge of other equally important rules governing shipping movements, especially those referring to lights and light recognition generally. The speed at which modern ships travel, and the lack of manoeuverability of very large vessels, make it quite impracticable to think of consulting a light recognition chart when confronted with a close-quarters situation. Unless one regularly sails in the vicinity of shipping lanes at night it is surprising how difficult light recognition can become in bad weather, even with a good theoretical knowledge of lights.

A copy of the Regulations should certainly be on board every sea-going yacht and it is good practice to browse through them occasionally to ensure that they remain fresh in the memory. There are several publications giving the Regulations in full, together with explanatory notes. One of the best is issued by the Royal Yachting Association and is especially annotated for yachtsmen.

Summary of International Regulations for Prevention of Collision at Sea A brief résumé of the various sections of the regulations which are of the most interest to yachtsmen is given below.

Part A – General
This preamble to the rules explains their general application and gives clear definitions of terms used in the Regs.
Part B – Steering and Sailing Rules
Sect. I Conduct of vessels in any condition of visibility. This section deals with the general requirements of the rules regarding such things as keeping a good look-out, proceeding at a safe speed etc.
Sect. II Conduct of vessels in sight of one another. The heading of this section may seem a little odd when read in conjunction with Section I, but the word 'sight' is used specifically to exclude the situation in which two vessels can only observe each other on their radar screens.

The section contains the all-important rules governing the conduct of sail and power vessels when approaching, crossing, overtaking and so on, which will no doubt be familiar to most yachtsmen.

Sect. III Conduct of vessels in restricted visibility This section contains only one rule which lays down the code of conduct for vessels not in sight of one another operating in restricted visibility. It does not give details of the necessary signals to be made by vessels in fog.

Part C – Lights and Shapes

This section deals with lights and shapes to be exhibited and refers to all conditions of visibility, as all lights shall be exhibited at any time between sunrise and sunset when there is restricted visibility. From the yachtsmen's point of view this is probably the most difficult section of rules to memorise and apply *quickly* without hesitation.

Part D – Sound and light signals

This section gives details of the necessary signals for manoeuvring and warning when vessels are in sight of one another and also in conditions of restricted visibility.

Part E – Exemptions

This section refers to certain relaxations regarding the time when lights and sound appliances on existing vessels have to comply with the Regulations.

Annex I This section explains the positioning and technical details of lights and shapes (useful information for the amateur building his own boat).

Annex II This section gives additional signals for fishing vessels fishing in close proximity.

Annex III This section outlines the technical details of Sound Appliances.

In addition to covering the conduct of vessels both in sight of one another and in conditions of restricted visibility, the regulations give much detailed information concerning matters such as the positioning of lights, arcs of visibility and powers of illumination.

Extracts from the Regulations

It is difficult to make extracts from the Regulations covering the majority of the situations in which the average yachtsman may find himself. Indeed, in many ways it is rather risky to try to do so as so many of them will have to be left out. . . . Nevertheless the following extracts have been made in the hope that they will be read and their spirit fully digested, thus encouraging the newcomer to get a complete copy and study it for himself. It must be emphasised that the extracts do *not* necessarily cover all the information needed by a seagoing yachtsman and that they should only be regarded as a first step to reading up the subject thoroughly.

Part B – Steering and Sailing Rules

Rule 5: Look-out Every vessel shall at all times maintain a proper look-out by sight and hearing as well as by all available means appropriate in the prevailing circumstances and conditions so as to make a full appraisal of the situation and the risk of collision.

Rule 7: Risk of Collision
(a) Every vessel shall use all available means appropriate to the prevailing circumstances and conditions to determine if risk of collision exists; if there is any doubt such risk shall be deemed to exist. (b) In determining if risk of collision exists the following considerations shall be among those taken into account:
(i) Such risk shall be deemed to exist if the compass bearing of an approaching vessel does not appreciably change.
(ii) Such risk may sometimes exist even when an

appreciable bearing change is evident, particularly when approaching a very large vessel, or a tow, or when approaching a vessel at close range.

Rule 8: Action to Avoid Collision Any action taken to avoid collision shall, if the circumstances of the case admit, be positive, made in ample time and with due regard to the observance of good seamanship.

Rule 9: Narrow Channels
(a) A vessel proceeding along the course of a narrow channel or fairway shall keep as near to the outer limit of the channel or fairway which lies on her starboard side as is safe and practicable.

(b) A vessel of [less than] 20 metres [65 feet] in length, or [a] sailing vessel, shall not impede the passage of a vessel which can safely navigate only within a narrow channel or fairway.

Rule 10: Traffic Separation Schemes (c) A vessel shall as far as practicable avoid crossing traffic lanes, but if obliged to do so shall cross as nearly as practicable at right angles to the general direction of traffic flow.

(j) A vessel of less than 20 metres [65 feet] in length or, a sailing vessel, shall not impede the safe passage of a power-driven vessel following a traffic lane.

Rule 12: Sailing Vessels
(a) When two sailing vessels are approaching one another so as to involve risk of collision, one of them shall keep out of the way of the other as follows:
  (i) When each has the wind on a different side, the vessel which has the wind on the port side shall keep out of the way of the other.
  (ii) When both have the wind on the same side the vessel which is to windward shall keep out of the way of the vessel which is to leeward.
  (iii) If a vessel with wind on the port side sees a vessel to windward and cannot determine with certainty whether the other vessel has

the wind on the port or on the starboard side she shall keep out of the way of the other.

Rule 13: Overtaking
(a) Notwithstanding anything contained in the Rules of this section, any vessel overtaking shall keep out of the way of the vessel being overtaken.

(b) A vessel shall be deemed to be overtaking when coming up with another vessel from a direction more than $22\frac{1}{2}°$ abaft her beam; that is, in such a position with reference to the vessel she is overtaking that at night she would be able to see only the stern-light of the vessel but neither of her side-lights.

Rule 14: Head-on Situation
(a) When two power-driven vessels are meeting on reciprocal, or nearly reciprocal, courses so as to involve risk of collision, each shall alter her course to starboard so that each shall pass on the port side of the other.

(b) Such a situation shall be deemed to exist when a vessel sees the other ahead, or nearly ahead, and by night she could see the masthead lights of the other in a line, or nearly in a line, and/or both sidelights and by day, she observes the corresponding aspect of the other vessel.

Rule 15: Crossing Situation
When two power-driven vessels are crossing so as to involve risk of collision, the vessel which has the other on her own starboard side shall keep out of the way and shall, if the circumstances of the case permit, avoid crossing ahead of the other vessel.

Rule 18: Responsibilities between Vessels Except where Rules 9, 10 and 13 otherwise require:
(a) A power driven vessel shall keep out of the way of:
  (i) A vessel not under command.
  (ii) A vessel restricted in her ability to manoeuvre.
  (iii) A vessel engaged in fishing.
  (iv) A sailing vessel.
(b) A sailing vessel underway shall keep out of the way of:

  (i) A vessel not under command.
  (ii) A vessel restricted in her ability to manoeuvre.
  (iii) A vessel engaged in fishing.

Rule 23: Power Driven Vessels Under Way (a) A power driven vessel under way shall exhibit:
  (i) A masthead light forward.
  (ii) A second masthead light abaft of, and higher than the forward one: except that a vessel of less than 50 metres [165 feet] in length shall not be obliged to exhibit such light but may do so.
  (iii) Side lights.
  (iv) Stern lights.
(b) An air cushion vessel when operating in the non-displacement mode shall in addition to the lights prescribed in paragraph (a) of this rule exhibit an all round flashing yellow light.
(c) A power driven vessel of less than 7 metres [25 feet] in length and whose maximum speed does not exceed 7 knots may, in lieu of the lights described in paragraph (a) of this rule exhibit an all-round white light. Such a vessel shall if practicable also exhibit side lights.

Rule 24: Towing and Pushing
(a) A power driven vessel when towing shall exhibit:
  (i) Instead of the light prescribed in Rule 23 (a) (i) two masthead lights forward in a vertical line when the length of the tow, measuring from the stern of the towing vessel to the after end of the tow exceeds 200 metres [650 feet] three such lights in a vertical line.
  (ii) Sidelights.
  (iii) A sternlight.
  (iv) A towing line in a vertical line above the stern lights.
  (v) Where the length of the tow exceeds 200 metres [650 feet] a diamond shape where it can best be seen.
(e) A vessel or object being towed shall exhibit:
  (i) Side lights.
  (ii) A stern light.

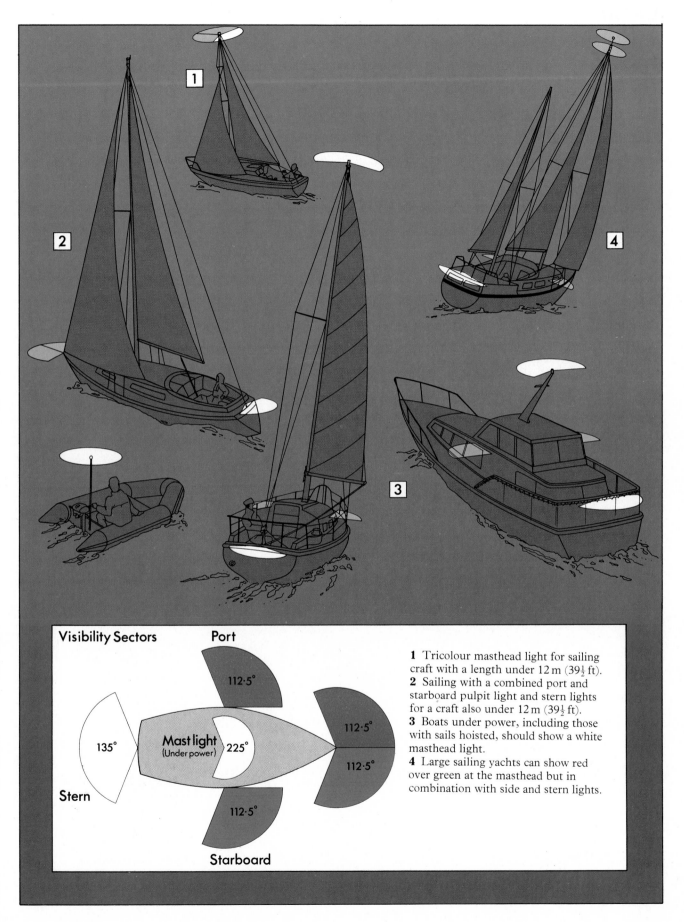

Visibility Sectors

Port

112·5°

135°

Mast light
(Under power)

225°

Stern

112·5°

112·5°

112·5°

Starboard

1 Tricolour masthead light for sailing craft with a length under 12 m (39½ ft).
2 Sailing with a combined port and starboard pulpit light and stern lights for a craft also under 12 m (39½ ft).
3 Boats under power, including those with sails hoisted, should show a white masthead light.
4 Large sailing yachts can show red over green at the masthead but in combination with side and stern lights.

(iii) Where the length of the tow exceeds 200 metres [660 feet] a diamond shape where it can best be seen.

Rule 25: Sailing Vessels Under Way and Vessels Under Oars (a) A sailing vessel underway shall exhibit:
(i) Side lights.
(ii) Stern lights.
(b) In a sailing vessel of less than 12 metres [40 feet] in length the lights prescribed in paragraph (a) of this rule may be combined in [one] lantern carried at or near the top of the mast where it can best be seen.
(c) A sailing vessel underway, may in addition to the lights prescribed in paragraph (a) of this rule exhibit at or near the top of the mast where they can best be seen, two all-round lights in a vertical line, the upper being red and the lower green; but these lights shall not be exhibited in conjunction with the combined lantern permitted by paragraph (b) of this rule.
(d) (i) A sailing vessel of less than 7 metres [about 23 feet] in length shall if practicable exhibit the lights prescribed in paragraph (a) or (b) of this rule but, if she does not, she shall have ready at hand an electric torch or lighted lantern showing a white light which shall be exhibited in sufficient time to prevent a collision.
(ii) A vessel under oars may exhibit the lights prescribed in this rule for sailing vessels, but if she does not, she shall have ready at hand an electric torch or lighted lantern which shall be exhibited in sufficient time to prevent a collision.
(e) A vessel proceeding under sail when also being propelled by machinery shall exhibit forward, where it can be seen, a conical shape, apex downwards.

Rule 26: Fishing Vessels (b) A vessel when engaged in trawling shall exhibit:
(i) Two all-round lights in a vertical line, the upper being green and the lower white, or a shape consisting of two cones with their apexes together in a vertical line one above the other, a vessel of less than 20 metres [65 feet] in length may instead of this shape exhibit a basket.
(ii) A masthead light abaft of and higher than the all-round green light, a vessel of less than 50 metres [160 feet] in length shall not be obliged to exhibit such a light but may do so.
(iii) When making way through the water in addition to the lights prescribed in this paragraph, side lights and stern lights.
(c) A vessel engaged in fishing other than trawling shall exhibit:
(i) Two all-round lights in a vertical line the upper being red and the lower white, or a shape consisting of two cones with apexes together in a line one above the other: a vessel of less than 20 metres [65 feet] in length may instead of this shape exhibit a basket.
(ii) When there is outlying gear extending more than 150 metres [about 150 yards] horizontally from the vessel, an all-round white light or cone apex upwards in the direction of the gear.
(iii) When making way through the water in addition to lights prescribed in this paragraph, sidelights and stern light.

Rule 27: Vessels Not Under Command or Restricted in Their Ability to Manoeuvre
(a) A vessel not under command shall exhibit:
(i) Two all-round red lights in a vertical line where they can best be seen.
(ii) Two balls or similar shapes in a vertical line where they can best be seen.
(iii) When making way etc. in addition side-lights and stern-light.

Note: The term 'vessel not under command' means a vessel which through some exceptional circumstances is unable to manoeuvre as required by the Rules and is therefore unable to keep out of the way of another vessel.

(b) A vessel restricted in her ability to manoeuvre (except a vessel engaged in minesweeping) shall exhibit:

  (i) Three all-round lights in a vertical line where they can best be seen, the highest and lowest shall be red and the middle light white.

 (ii) Three shapes in a vertical line where they can best be seen. The highest and lowest of these shapes shall be balls and the middle one a diamond.

(iii) When making way through the water masthead lights, side-lights and stern-lights in addition.

(iv) When at anchor in addition to lights in sub-paragraphs (i) and (ii), the lights and shape prescribed in Rule 30.

(c) A vessel engaged in a towing operation such as renders her unable to deviate from her course shall, in addition to the lights in sub-paragraphs (b) (i) and (ii), exhibit the lights or shapes prescribed in Rule 24 (a).

(d) A vessel engaged in dredging or underwater operations shall exhibit the lights and shapes prescribed in paragraph (b) and where an obstruction exists exhibit:

  (i) Two all-round red lights or two balls in a vertical line to indicate the side on which the obstruction exists.

 (ii) Two all-round green lights or two diamonds to indicate the side on which another vessel may pass.

(iii) When making way through the water, in addition masthead lights, side-lights and stern-light.

(e) When the size of a vessel engaged in diving operations makes it impracticable to exhibit the shapes prescribed in paragraph (d) a rigid replica of the International Code Flag 'A' not less than 1 metre [3 ft] in height shall be exhibited.

(f) A vessel engaged in mine sweeping shall, in addition to lights prescribed in Rule 23, exhibit three all-round green lights or balls, one at the foremast head and one at the end of each foreyard, indicating that it is dangerous to approach closer than 1,000 metres [1,100 yards] astern or 500 metres [550 yards] on each side of the mine sweeper.

Rule 28: Vessels constrained by their draught A vessel constrained by her draught may, in addition to the lights prescribed for power-driven vessels in Rule 23, exhibit where they can best be seen three all-round red lights in a vertical line, or a cylinder.

Rule 29: Pilot vessels (a) A vessel engaged on pilotage duty shall exhibit:

  (i) At or near the masthead, two all-round lights in a vertical line, the upper being white and the lower red.

 (ii) When underway, in addition, side-lights and a stern-light.

(iii) When at anchor, in addition to the lights prescribed in sub-paragraph (i) the anchor-light, lights or shape.

(b) A pilot vessel when not engaged on pilotage duty shall exhibit the lights or shapes prescribed for a similar vessel of her length.

Rule 30: Anchored vessels and vessels aground (a) A vessel at anchor shall exhibit where it can best be seen:

  (i) in the fore part, an all-round white light or one ball.

 (ii) At or near the stern and at a lower level than the light prescribed in sub-paragraph (i), an all-round white light.

(b) A vessel of less than 50 metres [160 feet] in length may exhibit an all-round white light where it can best be seen instead of the lights prescribed in paragraph (a) of this Rule.

(c) A vessel at anchor may, and a vessel of 100 metres [330 feet] and more in length shall, also use the avilable working or equivalent lights to illuminate her decks.

(d) A vessel aground shall exhibit the lights prescribed in paragraph (a) or (b) of this Rule and in addition, where they can best be seen:

(i) two all-round red lights in a vertical line.

(ii) Three balls in a vertical line.

(e) A vessel of less than 7 metres [about 23 feet] in length, when at anchor or aground, not in or near a narrow channel, fairway or anchorage, or where other vessels normally navigate, shall not be required to exhibit the lights or shapes prescribed in paragraphs (a), (b) or (d) of this Rule.

Part D – Sound and Light Signals

Rule 32: Definitions (a) The word 'whistle' means any sound signalling appliance capable of producing the prescribed blasts and which complies with the specifications in Annex III to these Regulations.

(b) The term 'Short Blast' means a blast of about one second's duration.

(c) The term 'Prolonged Blast' means a blast of from four to six seconds duration.

Rule 33: Equipment for Sound signals (a) A vessel of 12 metres [40 feet] or more in length shall be provided with a whistle and a bell, and a vessel of 100 metres [330 feet] or more in length shall, in addition, be provided with a gong, the tone and sound of which cannot be confused with that of the bell. The whistle, bell and gong shall comply with the specifications in Annex III to these Regulations. The bell or gong (or both) may be replaced by other equipment having the same respective sound characteristics, provided that manual sounding of the required signals shall always be possible.

(b) A vessel of less than 12 metres [40 feet] in length shall not be obliged to carry the sound signalling appliances prescribed in paragraph (a) of this Rule but if she does not, she shall be provided with some means of making an efficient sound signal.

Rule 34 Manoeuvring and Warning Signals (a) When vessels are in sight of one another, a power-driven vessel underway, when manoeuvring as authorised or required by these rules shall indicate that manoeuvring by the following signals on her whistle:

– One short blast to mean 'I am altering my course to starboard'.

– Two short blasts to mean 'I am altering my course to port'.

– Three short blasts to mean 'I am operating astern propulsion'.

(c) When in sight of one another in a narrow channel or fairway:

(i) A vessel intending to overtake another shall in compliance with Rule 9 (e) (i) indicate her intention by the following signals on her her whistle:

– Two prolonged blasts followed by one short blast to mean 'I intend to overtake you on your starboard side'.

– Two prolonged blasts followed by two short blasts to mean 'I intend to overtake you on your port side''.

(ii) The vessel about to be overtaken when acting in accordance with Rule 9(e) (i) shall indicate her agreement by the following signal on her whistle:

– One prolonged, one short, one prolonged and one short blast, in that order.

(d) When vessels in sight are approaching each other and either vessel fails to understand the intentions or actions of the other, or is in doubt whether sufficient action is being taken by the other to avoid collision, the vessel in doubt shall immediately indicate such doubt by giving at least five short, rapid blasts on the whistle. Such signal may be supplemented by a light signal of at least five short, rapid flashes.

(e) A vessel nearing a bend or an area of a channel or fairway where other vessels may be obscured by an intervening obstruction shall sound one prolonged blast. Such a signal shall be answered with a prolonged blast by any approaching vessel that may be within hearing around the bend or behind the intervening obstruction.

(f) If whistles are fitted on a vessel at a distance apart of more than 100 metres [330 feet], one whistle only shall be used for giving manoeuvring and warning signals.

Note to Rule 35: Yachtsmen should particularly note that the sound signals for a sailing vessel in restricted visibility now take no account of which tack s she happens to be on. Whatever her point of sailing there is only one signal.

Rule 35: **Sound Signals in Restricted Visibility** In or near an area of restricted visibility, whether by day or night, the signals prescribed in this Rule shall be used as follows:

(a) A power-driven vessel making way through the water shall sound at intervals of not more than 2 minutes one prolonged blast.

(b) A power-driven vessel underway but stopped and making no way through the water shall sound at intervals of not more than 2 minutes two prolonged blasts in succession with an interval of about 2 seconds between them.

(c) A vessel not under command, a vessel restricted in her ability to manoeuvre, a vessel constrained by her draught, a sailing vessel, a vessel engaged in fishing and a vessel engaged in towing or pushing another vessel shall, instead of the signals prescribed in paragraphs (a) or (b) of this Rule, sound at intervals of not more than 2 minutes three blasts in succession, namely one prolonged followed by two short blasts.

(d) A vessel towed, or if more than one vessel is towed the last vessel of the tow, if manned, shall at intervals of not more than 2 minutes sound four blasts in succession, namely one prolonged followed by three short blasts. When practicable, this signal shall be made immediately after the signal made by the towing vessel.

(e) When a pushing vessel and a vessel being pushed ahead are rigidly connected in a composite unit they shall be regarded as a power-driven vessel and shall give the signals prescribed in paragraphs (a) or (b) of this Rule.

(f) A vessel at anchor shall at intervals of not more than one minute ring the bell rapidly for about 5 seconds. In a vessel of 100 metres [330 feet] or more in length the bell shall be sounded in the forepart of the vessel and immediately after the ringing of the bell the gong shall be sounded rapidly for about 5 seconds in the after part of the vessel. A vessel at anchor may in addition sound three blasts in succession, namely one short, one prolonged and one short, to give warning of her position and of the possibility of collision to an approaching vessel.

(g) A vessel aground shall give the bell signal and, if required, the gong signal prescribed in paragraph (f) of this Rule and shall, in addition, give three separate and distinct strokes on the bell immediately before and after the rapid ringing of the bell. A vessel aground may in addition sound an appropriate whistle signal.

(h) A vessel of less than 12 metres [40 feet] in length shall not be obliged to give the above-mentioned signals but, if she does not, shall make some other efficient sound signal at intervals of not more than 2 minutes.

(i) A pilot vessel when engaged on pilotage duty may, in addition to the signals prescribed in paragraphs (a), (b) or (f) of this Rule, sound an identity signal consisting of four short blasts.

Annex II Additional signals for fishing vessels fishing in close proximity

1. General The lights mentioned herein shall, if exhibited in pursuance of Rule 24 (d), be placed where they can best be seen. They shall be at least 0.9 metre [3 feet] apart but at a lower level than lights prescribed in Rule 26 (b) (i) and (c) (i). The lights shall be visible all round the horizon at a distance of at least 1 mile but at a lesser distance than the lights prescribed by these Rules for fishing vessels.

2. Signals for Trawlers (a) Vessels when engaged in trawling, whether using demersal or pelagic gear, may exhibit:

(i) When shooting their nets: two white lights in a vertical line.

(ii) When hauling their nets: one white light over one red light in a vertical line.

(iii) When the net has come fast upon an obstruction: two red lights in a vertical line.

(b) Each vessel engaged in 'pair trawling' may exhibit:

(i) By night, a searchlight directed forward and in the direction of the other vessel of the pair.

(ii) When shooting or hauling their nets or when their nets have come fast upon an obstruction, the lights prescribed in 2 (a) above.

General Points Arising from the Regulations The Rules appear to be quite explicit and to deal with most foreseeable situations in the three wide categories: narrow channels, traffic separation lanes, and the open sea – until the yachtsman comes to apply them practically. For example take the familiar case which can arise when a sailing yacht meets a large power-vessel in a narrow channel (Rule 9). The Rule does not, and cannot, define a narrow channel and on this point the skipper of a small sailing yacht and the skipper of a large fast-moving container ship may have different opinions. . . . What may appear to be the open sea to the former may constitute a narrow channel to the latter. In some areas, such as the Thames

Estuary or the approaches to 'Europort', a large vessel must navigate with precision and cannot deviate from her course in areas where the small boat skipper might consider it reasonable for her to do so.

In Traffic Separation Lanes the position of sailing vessels and power vessels of less than 20 m (65 ft) is quite clear – they really have no rights at all! They 'shall not impede the passage of a power-driven vessel following a traffic lane'. It is important therefore to be aware when you are in a 'traffic lane'. . . . Crossing a busy traffic lane obviously calls for considerable care. The Rule requires the crossing vessel to do so as 'nearly as practicable at right angles to the general direction of traffic flow'. Under certain conditions – for example with a strong tide parallel to the lane and an adverse wind – the course made good in a small sailing cruiser may be much less than 90° and, when viewed on a radar screen five miles away, it may appear that the vessel is crossing with little regard to the Regulations.

The situation in the open sea, away from narrow channels and traffic lanes, is quite clear. Rule 18 states that 'a power-driven vessel underway shall keep out of the way of a sailing vessel'. Thus the sailing vessel has the right (and indeed an obligation) to maintain her course and speed (Rule 17). However, if the power-driven vessel is either 'not under command', 'restricted in her ability to manoeuvre', or a vessel 'engaged in fishing', then the sailing vessel shall keep out of her way. In addition, if the power-driven vessel is exhibiting the signals for a vessel 'constrained by her draught' then the sailing vessel shall 'avoid impeding her passage'. Thus, even in the open sea, the yachtsman must be alive to the Regulations and of necessity be able to identify the category of a vessel by her signals.

Fundamentally, the object of the Regulations is 'Preventing Collision at Sea'; and the first reaction of any good seaman on sighting another vessel is – take a bearing! This should be followed a few minutes later with another one and if the bearing has not altered and the distance is decreasing then risk of collision is present. It will be appreciated that, if the encounter is in the open sea and the power-driven vessel is not 'constrained by draft', 'restricted in ability to manoeuvre' or 'not under command' (rather improbable), then the sailing boat has right of way and should stand on, leaving the power-driven vessel to alter course. If after weighing-up the position the skipper of the yacht decides to alter course, any such alteration must be made in good time – if it is left too long the power vessel may alter course at the same moment with possibly disastrous results.

What, it may be asked, is 'good time'? If one considers the case of a large, fully-laden container ship, any objects dead ahead at sea level will probably disappear from sight under the bows at least a half mile away so far as the viewpoint of the bridge is concerned. . . . Hence the necessity for course alterations to be made well in advance of any imminent 'close quarters' emergency. Judging the speed of another vessel which is some distance away is difficult at sea where there are no reference marks. For example, a V.L.C.C. (Very Large Crude Carrier) eight miles away, travelling at, say, 26 knots may appear to be hardly moving, probably due to the fact that it has the appearance of a smaller ship at half the distance and travelling at about half the speed. One tends to judge speeds by the size of the bow wave and the way the vessel increases in size and, except at fairly close quarters, this can be misleading. Whilst we are on the subject of speed it is worthwhile remembering that modern large bulk carriers have to maintain speeds in order to maintain manoeuvreability, even in confined waters, which may seem excessive to the yachtsman.

It will be appreciated that the remarks about estimating the other vessel's speed are particularly pertinent during the hours of darkness, and it is then that a good lookout is doubly important. The presence on a yacht of an adequate radar reflector, properly mounted, is probably even more important than navigational lights at night. The average small family cruiser has navigational lights which may not be visible at more than a mile and a half away unless she carries a good tricolour lamp at the masthead, which will certainly increase the range but probably not to the extent that is really desirable. However, a good radar reflector will probably produce an echo at 8 or 9.5 kilometres (5 or 6 miles) – which is a reassuring thought when you appreciate that the fast-moving commercial vessels are probably plotting echos at least up to 9.6 kilometres (6 miles) away and probably farther. . . !

BUOYAGE SYSTEMS

It is not proposed to discuss the older types of buoyage systems which are gradually being replaced by the I.A.L.A. (International Association of Lighthouse Authorities) system, which has been introduced as a result of the work of the I.A.L.A. in order to reduce the number of buoyage systems throughout the world. There were approximately thirty, nine of which were in NW Europe, all dissimilar and obviously confusing. The installation of the new system in NW European waters began in 1977 and is scheduled for completion in December 1981. It is known as the I.A.L.A. system A, the combined cardinal and lateral system, which it is anticipated will also be installed in the rest of Europe, India, Africa, Australia and most of Asia. The U.S.A. will be utilising the I.A.L.A. system (Red to Starboard) the details of which have yet to be finalised.

Although the system is new, it should not be difficult for the yachtsman to memorise, as it is basically simple and logical. It consists of five groups, the Cardinal and Lateral buoys forming the main groups, with the Isolated Danger Marks, Safe Water Marks and Special Marks completing the system.

Cardinal System is used to mark points of navigational interest and the buoy indicates on which side it is to be passed, e.g. a North Cardinal Buoy must be passed on its N side.
Lateral System Buoys are used to mark well-defined channels with a conventional direction of buoyage. In rivers and estuaries this direction is with the flood tide but not necessarily so in coastal

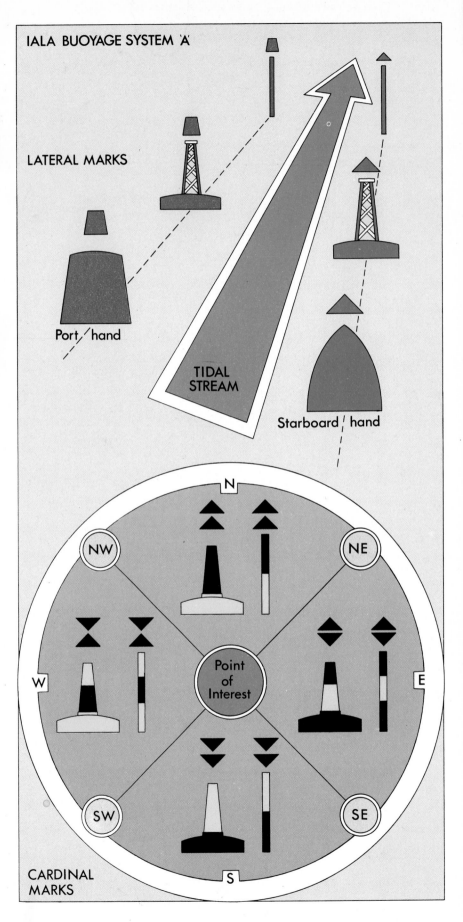

IALA BUOYAGE SYSTEM 'A'

LATERAL MARKS

Port hand

TIDAL STREAM

Starboard hand

CARDINAL MARKS

Point of Interest

N NE E SE S SW W NW

178

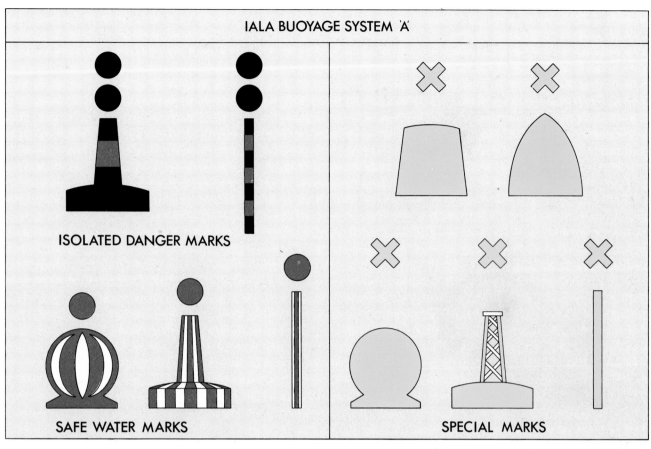

IALA BUOYAGE SYSTEM 'A'

ISOLATED DANGER MARKS

SAFE WATER MARKS

SPECIAL MARKS

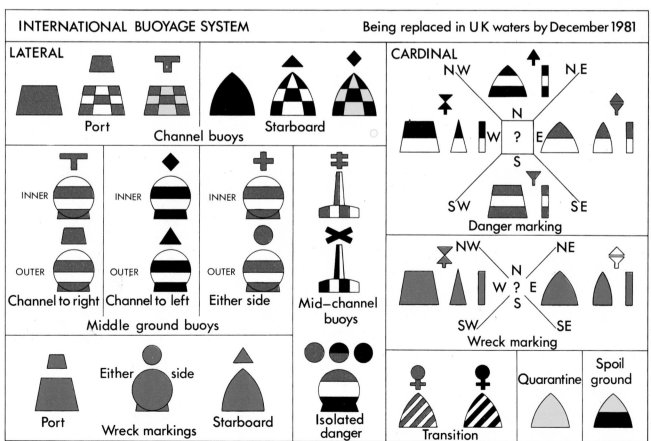

INTERNATIONAL BUOYAGE SYSTEM

Being replaced in UK waters by December 1981

LATERAL

Port

Channel buoys

Starboard

INNER

OUTER

Channel to right

INNER

OUTER

Channel to left

INNER

OUTER

Either side

Middle ground buoys

Mid-channel buoys

Port

Either side

Wreck markings

Starboard

Isolated danger

CARDINAL

NW

NE

N

W ? E

S

SW

SE

Danger marking

NW

NE

N

W ? E

S

SW

SE

Wreck marking

Transition

Quarantine

Spoil ground

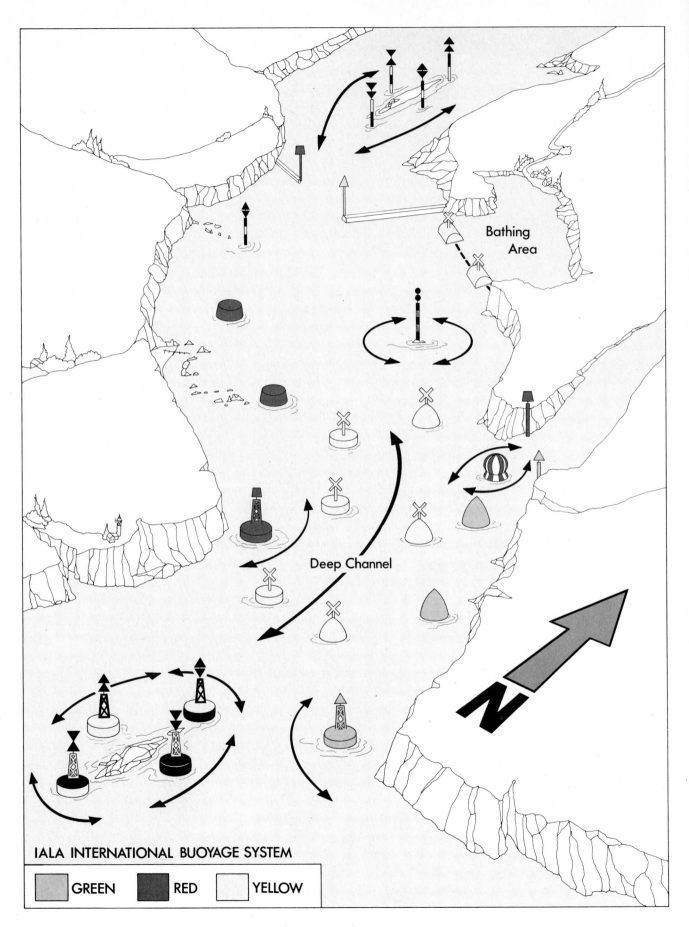

Bathing Area

Deep Channel

IALA INTERNATIONAL BUOYAGE SYSTEM

| GREEN | RED | YELLOW |

channels. Details of conventional directions are given in Hydrographic Office Publications and Nautical Almanacs.

Isolated Danger Marks indicate a small but dangerous point such as a wreck, but with clear water all round it.

Safe Water Marks indicate that there is navigable water all round the mark, e.g. can be used for mid-channel marks.

Special Marks not normally intended as navigational marks but for purposes such as 'spoil ground', cables or pipe lines etc. and may also be used as traffic separation marks where the use of other types of buoy might prove confusing.

The I.A.L.A. system has made several significant changes in relation to the older systems. A new danger, such as a wreck which has not yet been notified to all concerned, is indicated by a duplication of one of the marking buoys. Wrecks are no longer marked by green buoys but are treated as any other hazard and marked similarly. The Middle Ground Buoy is also obsolete, and Safe Water Marks are used for the centre line or mid-channel buoys and landfall buoys. The following schedule will, it is hoped, assist you in remembering the main characteristics of the buoys. The colours of the Cardinal Buoys are omitted for the sake of simplicity, as it is considered that the visual outline of the buoy is most important.

System	Buoy	Topmark	Light*	Aide Memoire**
Cardinal Marks	—	All Buoys have a double cone topmark	All have White FL. lights	
	N	Two cones point up	Continuous FL. *or* V.QK. FL.	Cones point up the North
	E	Two cones, bases together	V.QK. FL. (3) every 5 secs. *or* QK. FL. (3) every 10 secs.	Flash 3 for 3 o'clock
	S	Two cones, points down	V.QK. FL. (6) every 10 secs. *or* QK. FL (6) every 15 secs. Both followed by 1 long flash.	Cones point down to the South Flash 6 for 6 o'clock
	W	Two cones, points together	V.QK. FL. (9) every 10 secs. *or* QK. FL. (9) every 15 secs.	Cones form 'a wasp-waisted woman' Flash 9 for 9 o'clock
Lateral Marks	—	Red cans to port, with or without a red can topmark	Red flashes (any rhythm)	—
Isolated Danger Marks	—	Two black balls	Two white flashes	—
Safe Water Marks	—	One red ball	One white flash	
Special Marks	—	Yellow buoys with cross topmarks	Yellow flashes (any rhythm)	—

Note* : V.QK. FL. = flashing at the rate of 100 to 120 per min.

      QK. FL.   =   „   „   „   „   „ 50 to 60   „   „

**: the 'Aide Memoire' does not give full details of the buoys but picks out some points which assist in memorising their characteristics.

Ch. 10 Maintenance

Quite apart from being a source of pride to its owner, a well-maintained boat is a safe boat — safe in the sense that gear failures are far less likely to happen than in a boat where the owner's idea of 'maintenance' is a cursory glance round (usually after something has already broken) and a quick clean-up in the Spring! The sea is an environment which is constantly attacking a boat and its equipment, and all the materials used in its construction inevitably deteriorate to varying degrees with time. A small knowledge of the different forms of construction used in boat-building will materially assist the owner in the maintenance of his boat, and especially in anticipating potential trouble-spots. While it is true to say that maintenance is a constant fight against the elements, it should not be inferred that an owner who maintains his boat conscientiously will have less time for sailing – quite the contrary in fact. Well-planned maintenance, carried out at the proper time, means that an owner can look forward to a full, trouble-free season in a smart boat and one moreover that is maintaining its value.

Forms of Construction

Wood Obviously one of the oldest forms of construction material known to man is wood, but it is now superseded by G.R.P. (glass reinforced plastic) for the mass-produced family cruising yacht. Building a conventional wooden hull, that is one planked-up on wooden frames, calls for a high degree of craftsmanship – which nowadays regrettably is not readily available – and also for carefully selected, well-seasoned timber. The average individual buying a wooden boat now will almost inevitably be buying second-hand and therefore it is desirable to have a fair idea where deterioration can and does occur. No sensible person buys a second-hand boat without a professional survey, but a knowledgeable look over a boat which is offered for sale can show whether it is worth paying for a survey. As well as the conventional planked hull, wood in recent decades has been used in other methods of building: the cold or hot moulded hull, plywood construction and strip planking, the two latter forms having come about to suit the requirements of the home builder.

Cold moulded hulls are formed by bonding veneer strips together over a mould: the strips are laid diagonally from the deck edge down to the keel, each successive layer being laid up crossing the one below it. A cold setting resin glue is used and the finished hull is light and possesses great strength. A similar method of moulding but with a hot setting glue is also used. In this method the hull is placed in a container and pressure applied, the heat setting the glue and the pressure ensuring that no voids occur in between the veneers. Due to the high cost of production it is not a method which features in the production of family cruising yachts.

Marine plywood construction has been used extensively for the fabrication of hulls but the method naturally limits the hull form to a series of comparatively flat surfaces, as the degree of curvature which can be applied without deformation is limited, quite apart from the difficulties of bending the plywood in two planes. Planing hulls, such as speed boats, and also hard chine sailing boat hulls, lend themselves to this form of construction and the hulls are light and strong with good impact resistance. One of the more important aspects of maintenance on this type of hull is the protection of end grain to prevent delamination of the layers. At present marine plywood, as far as cruising yachts are concerned, is largely confined to interior partitions, bulkheads and decks.

Strip planking appears to be similar to conventional planking but the underlying principles differ. As the name implies the planks are actually strips of wood about 3.75 cm (1½ in) wide instead of the normal 7.5 cm to 10 cm (3 in to 4 in) of conventional planks and the tops and bottoms of the strips are usually concave and convex. After the frames have been assembled and positioned the planking is started. Each strip is glued and pinned to the one below it and to the frames. The advantages from the home-builder's point of view are that it is easier to obtain timber 3.75 cm (1½ in) wide in long lengths than planking 7.5 cm to 10 cm (3 in to 4 in) wide and the narrower timber is very much

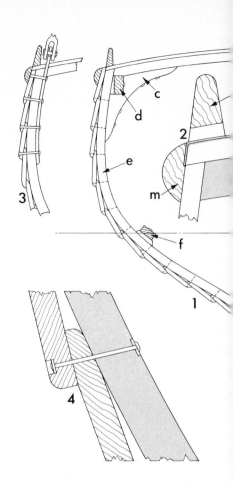

easier to lay-up to shape. It is of course important to have carefully selected and seasoned timber for this method of construction for, whereas the glued joints will not open up, should longitudinal splits occur in the strips the problem may prove difficult to deal with. This is an important point to look for when you are buying second-hand: splits allow water to penetrate to the pins (which are usually ferrous) causing rust stains to appear.

A very modern method used in wooden construction is the Wood Epoxy Saturation Technique (W.E.S.T. for short) developed by Gougeon Bros., Bay City, Michigan, which uses no metallic fastenings except those required to hold timbers in position while they are being glued. It offers considerable advantages to the home builder and would appear

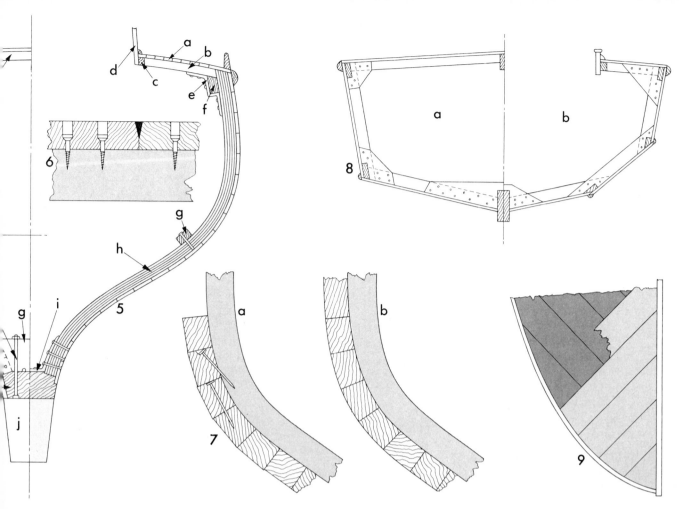

to have great potential for the future.

Steel As a method of construction steel is not really practicable under, say, 10 m (30 ft) L.O.A. Hulls are welded, and this is one of the limiting factors in construction, as welding cannot be carried out satisfactorily on very thin plates. The steel yacht is probably most common in Holland, where specialist builders have made them for many years with considerable success. The big maintenance problem is corrosion of the hull but modern shot-blasting techniques and advanced paint technology have succeeded considerably in reducing the problem. However, it is interesting to reflect that the waters of the Dutch canals and inland seas may not have quite the same effect on steel hulls as do the waters of the east coast of England with their high salinity. A welded-steel hull has greater internal space than a comparable size of wooden vessel due to the absence of the comparatively large frames of the latter. Basically, a steel hull constructed by a specialist firm of builders has much to offer but maintenance is just as important as with any other form of construction, if not more so. There is a growing interest in steel as a method for home construction and provided the builder can cut and weld, or he can call upon the services of a welder, it is a practical proposition. In general the home builder would be restricted to hard chine construction, either single or multi-chine, but the possibilities are well worth investigation if the necessary facilities are available.

Aluminium This has always

1 (*Left hand*) Section through a clinker built wooden boat. (a) Plywood deck, (b) deck beam, (c) grown knee, (d) shelf, (e) bent timber, (f) stringer, (g) oak floor, (h) floor bolt, (i) keel, (j) ballast keel.
2 Edge detail of canvas covered deck. The canvas (k), is laid under the toe rail (l), and turned down under the rubbing-strake (m).
3 Detail of shroud plate bolted through both hull planking and timber frame.
4 Detail of fastening using a copper nail and rove to clamp the strake and frame together.
5 (*Right hand*) Section through a carvel built hull. (a) Laid deck, (b) half beam, (c) carline, (d) coaming, (e) iron knee, (f) shelf, (g) stringer, (h) laminated frame, (i) iron floor.
6 Detail of laid deck using screws and wooden plugs.
7 Strip planking construction: (a) prior to fairing-up the hull, (b) with the hull faired true.
8 (a) Hard chine construction, (b) double chine.
9 Cold moulded construction.

seemed to be an attractive material for boat building but it is only in comparatively recent years that the development of new alloys, particularly in the welding field, have made it really practicable. Here again, as with steel, the limiting factor in construction is the minimum thickness of plate that can be satisfactorily be welded, but as the weight of aluminium is very much less than that of steel, it is comparatively unimportant. The cost of building a welded aluminium hull is much higher than for a steel one but the light weight coupled with strength has resulted in this type of construction making an impact on the off-shore racing scene.

Ferro Cement This is a comparatively recent innovation

for yachts, although large heavy vessels have been constructed by this method for many years.

The problem has been to reduce the weight of the material for a given area to a figure comparable with other methods of construction, without sacrificing strength. Modern techniques plus increased knowledge of the method have now resulted in the production of boats down to approximately 10.5 m (35 ft) L.O.A. becoming a practical proposition, and there is a possibility of even smaller ones.

Normally used for 'one-off' jobs, the system has great attractions for the home-builder who can carry out practically the whole of the work himself except for the final stage of plastering. When the hull is properly constructed

it should have a finish comparable to G.R.P., allied to great strength and very few maintenance problems, while the cost to the home builder should be considerably less than for most other forms of construction.

Basically, the method of construction is simple. It consists of the erection of the frame-work of rods or tubes and then tying on the mesh with soft iron wire ties. During the initial erection of the rod frame-work, welding assistance will be needed. Once the frame has been completed tying in the mesh will begin and although lengthy and laborious, this needs no special skill, patience being the great necessity and virtue. When the final stage of plastering arrives it is essential to see that the frame-work is

Opposite: A GRP *Jaguar 27* sits on its purpose-made cradle ready for launching. The boat is then lifted by the tractor-drawn cantilever crane; notice the careful positioning of the padded slings to keep the hull as evenly balanced as possible. The tractor reverses down the launching slip and the cantilever arms swing over. Finally, the *Jaguar* is lowered into the water ready for another season's sailing.
Left: The versatility of Ferro Cement in boat construction is well shown in the classic lines of the *Dulas Dragon*.

properly supported so that no sagging occurs anywhere as the weight of the mortar builds up. Many willing hands are needed for the operation, to force the mortar into and through the mesh for the plasterers to finish off outside. The work must be completed in one operation without any stoppage and then allowed to cure for two to three weeks in a humid atmosphere to retard drying out.

Glass Reinforced Plastic (G.R.P.) Undoubtedly this is the method of construction that will be most familiar to the average cruising man and therefore it is the one about which he should be the most knowledgeable.

It is probably true to say that the introduction of synthetic materials such as G.R.P. was really responsible for the 'explosion' in boating activity by introducing the economics of large-scale production runs into what before was strictly a craftsman's preserve. G.R.P. has many advantages, chief of which is the strength and comparative lightness of the hull and, above all, the minimal maintenance that is required. The first step in the production of the hull is to make the wooden plug which is the exact shape of the designed hull. A mould is laid up round the plug and the hull is then laid up in this mould, starting with the gelcoat, followed by successive layers of resin and glass mat until the necessary thickness is built up. Areas such as the keel, the stem and so on can very readily be reinforced by increasing the amount of resin

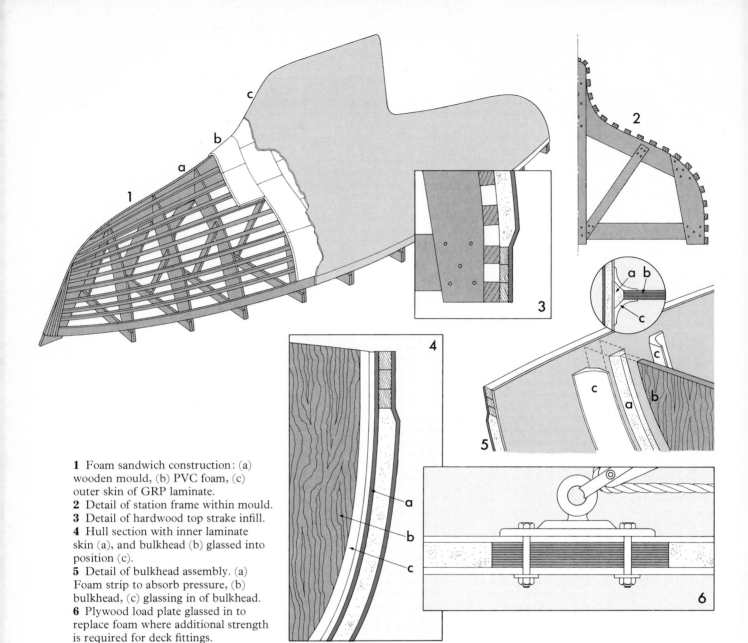

1 Foam sandwich construction: (a) wooden mould, (b) PVC foam, (c) outer skin of GRP laminate.
2 Detail of station frame within mould.
3 Detail of hardwood top strake infill.
4 Hull section with inner laminate skin (a), and bulkhead (b) glassed into position (c).
5 Detail of bulkhead assembly. (a) Foam strip to absorb pressure, (b) bulkhead, (c) glassing in of bulkhead.
6 Plywood load plate glassed in to replace foam where additional strength is required for deck fittings.

and glass during this process. Thus when the result is removed after curing it is virtually complete as far as the basic hull is concerned. The bulkheads are then glassed in and the deck moulding is fitted to complete the basic boat. The latest development in the G.R.P. concept is sandwich construction, in which there is a layer of either polyurethane foam or balsa wood between an inner and outer G.R.P. skin. In the latter form the balsa wood is known as 'end grain', i.e. the grain spanning the gap between the

inner and outer skins and not running lengthwise between the skins. A similar form of construction is used to give decks great rigidity by using marine ply as the centre core.

Laying-up
Having had a good season's sailing there is a great temptation to lay-up as quickly as possible and become involved in your winter pursuits, especially if the weather is not conducive to working outside. Laying-up is often left entirely to the yard with the thought that a really good fit-out in the

Spring will be sufficient. The man who has pride of ownership however will look at it slightly differently and will first of all make sure that the laying-up ashore is carried out properly. This means – even with the best of yards – giving them specific instructions.

Assuming that the boat is being laid-up ashore and not afloat the bottom should be scrubbed, the whole hull and deck hosed down with fresh water and then properly chocked up in the appointed place. Before the winter cover is put on, the owner should settle down with a notebook for an hour or so and list all jobs to be done, in three categories: jobs on board, work that can be carried out at home and, hopefully, a very small list of jobs for the yard to do. Naturally all those modifications which seemed such good ideas during the Summer sailing should be included under the appropriate heading. When you are looking the boat over, a critical viewpoint is needed – it is worth mentally adopting the attitude that one is about to buy the boat. What should be done?

Any work that needs to be done by the yard or outside agents, such as servicing the life raft, any major repairs etc., should be put in hand immediately to avoid delays in the Spring. For the benefit of the newcomer to boat ownership, a short list of purely routine jobs is given below which may help to ensure that the boat is properly laid up for the Winter. This is followed by a complementary section entitled 'Looking for Trouble', which may assist the novice (particularly if his boat is a second-hand purchase) in assessing the general condition of the boat.

Lay-up Procedure List

1. On wooden hulls remove any flaking paint and when dry touch up with primer to protect during the Winter.
2. G.R.P. hulls – clean down and coat with a good wax polish (*not* a silicone-based one) and do not polish off.
3. Any flaking varnish or bare brightwork should be scraped and a coat of 50% varnish and 50% white spirit brushed on. If the weather is warm, a couple of coats of varnish applied now will cut down the work in the Spring (when weather conditions may be worse).
4. Clean out and dry bilges.
5. Clean out all lockers and discard any junk.
6. Remove all portable electronic equipment such as radios, echo sounders etc.
7. Water tank: either leave it full with purification tablets in it or better still, drain off and clean out.
8. Fuel tank: either leave it full (to obviate condensation) or drain and clean.
9. Toilet: flush throughout with fresh water and disinfectant.
10. Engine: carry out 'winterising' programme as recommended by makers and then spray with a moisture repellent. If it is decided not to proceed with the full maker's treatment an absolute minimum would be: Change all filters (lubricating oil and fuel). Change engine oil and gearbox oil.
    Fit new plugs if petrol. Diesel – if engine is several years old, remove injectors for checking and replace impeller if neoprene type. Repack any greased bearings.
    If dynamo/starter/ alternator is not removed ensure thoroughly sprayed with moisture repellent.
11. Batteries: take ashore, clean and trickle charge. At least once during the winter discharge the battery completely in about 5 hours and immediately recharge e.g. a 60 AH battery should be discharged at 12 amps. This will assist in removing any sulphation from the plates.
12. Examine all electrical circuits, junction boxes etc. tighten connections and then spray with moisture repellent.
13. Clean and oil all halyard and sheet winches.
14. Wash all running rigging in fresh water before storing.
15. Sails – soak in warm soapy (not detergent) water, scrub stains with hard brush, rinse, drain and then take to the sailmaker. This treatment may seem an unnecessary chore but it preserves the appearance and lengthens the life of the sail considerably, and it certainly pays to take any sail that has had a season's use to the sailmaker, who can spot trouble before it develops.
16. Rigging: stainless steel – wash and store. Galvanised – wash in fresh water, dry and then soak in a mixture of petrol and raw linseed oil. Done annually this prolongs the life of the rigging to a surprising extent.
17. When all gear has been removed, the winter cover should be fitted (assuming the boat is laid-up in the open). The strongback (frame) should be well fitted, high enough to permit ventilation but not so high that rain can drive in at the ends and leave pools of water subsequently to freeze. The cover should be wide enough to cover the topsides and be properly secured with girth ropes to prevent any possibility of flapping.
18. The most unpleasant job of all is the bottom – a job usually left to the Spring but it should really be done during the Winter. In all probability there will be a build-up of anti-fouling resulting in a somewhat rough bottom. This can either be rubbed down with a coarse sanding block

(keeping it thoroughly wet as the dust is poisonous) or a suitable paint stripper used. Anti-fouling should never be burnt off even on a wooden hull because of the toxic fumes that would be produced.

Looking for Trouble

The great majority of yachtsmen, at least in the family cruising world, are involved with either wood or G.R.P. hulls and thus the comments on maintenance which follow will be confined to those types of construction. Dealing first with wooden hulls, the two great enemies are water and boring organisms such as the Teredo worm. It may seem a daunting prospect that water, the essential element in sailing, is also the great adversary but in fact the water which is dangerous to the vessel's well-being is not salt water but fresh water. Careful observation of a wooden jetty in salt water will show that little rot occurs below L.W.S., in fact the timber is really pickled. The maximum deterioration takes place at about mean tide level where the wood is alternately wet and dry, the deterioration is not, however, as marked as it would be if the piles were in fresh water. Fresh water, and in this context that means rain water, is the main enemy. Rain water, being very 'soft', is the biggest cause of wet rot in timber and it is therefore essential to prevent it collecting anywhere in a wooden boat and remaining unobserved. It is probably true to say that, apart from repairing impact damage and cosmetic treatment of topsides etc., 90% of the maintenance work on a wooden boat is aimed at preventing fresh water damage. Rain water alone is not the sole culprit,

condensation in the Spring and Autumn can also cause accumulations of fresh water, which if not dealt with, will eventually lead to rot.

Wooden Hulls

The following notes may assist the owner of a wooden boat, or perhaps a prospective purchaser, in looking for potential trouble points which may need preventive maintenance. Considering first the plywood hull, the main defect to watch for apart from wet rot is delamination of the ply, which could cause considerable damage before any rot occurs. Delamination is caused by water, either fresh or salt, penetrating between the layers in the ply, freezing and expanding and so splitting open the layers. Once this has occurred rapid deterioration of the plywood follows.

Important items to look for in plywood hulls are:

1. Check all butt joints for water penetration. Cracks in the paint are a useful sign that either the joint is 'working' or that water is already in the joint.
2. Examine the chines to see if the fixings and glue have come adrift – again cracks in the paint are a good indicator but an examination should also be made on the inside of the hull as any movement of the plywood sheet will show up here as well.
3. Check the 'garboard' area, that is the joint between the bottom section of ply and the keel. A careful examination both inside and out should be made here.
4. Carefully examine the transom edges and any butt joints for signs of opening up.
5. Examine the stem for any

signs of working and water penetration.
6. Look at the tops of all horizontal internal timbers attached to the outer hull to check whether fresh water, either condensation or rain water, has collected, and rot is occurring.
7. The deck edge where it joins the topside is particularly liable to water penetration and if this has happened it is important to examine the ends of any deck beams under the shelf for signs of dampness.
8. Examine load-bearing bulkheads under the mast where there are very heavy compression loads which may lead to deformation of the bulkheads.

Before going into the preventive measures which are common to *all* wooden boats, there are some points in connection with conventional planked hulls which should be regularly examined when fitting-out, or better still when laying-up, as this allows more time to deal with troubles:

1. Examine the hull for any signs of paint cracking along the line of the seams, this indicates the need for hardening down the caulking and re-stopping.
2. Examine planking ends at the transom and also the stem for any signs of water penetration. (In a very old boat there may be a need for recaulking at the stem).
3. In an old boat the garboards, (the bottom plank of the hull adjacent to the keelson) should be checked occasionally. Any softness in the hull planking usually starts at this point and may be caused by loose caulking, which should be hardened down or replaced.

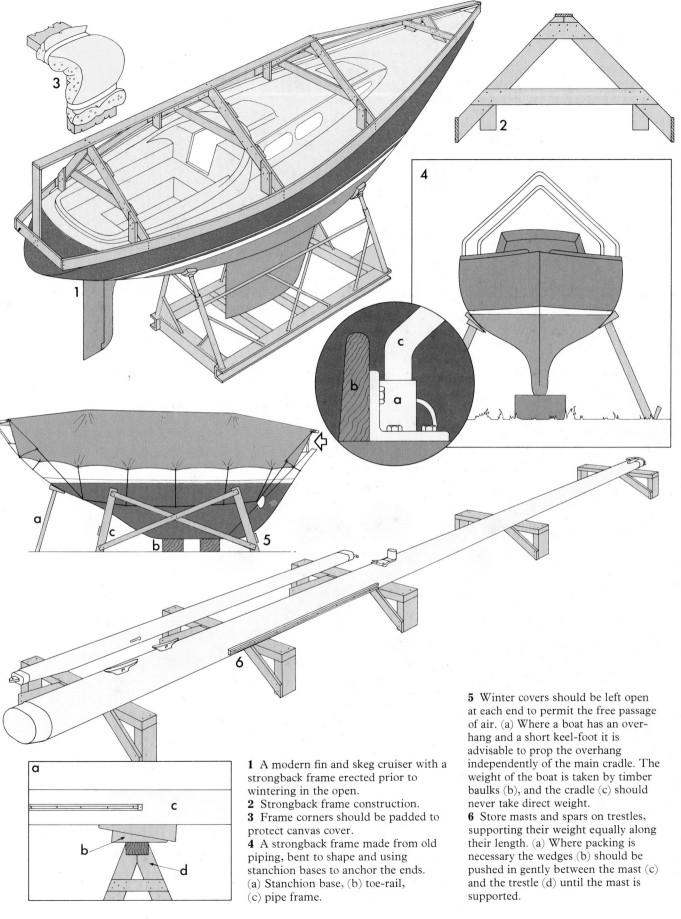

1 A modern fin and skeg cruiser with a strongback frame erected prior to wintering in the open.
2 Strongback frame construction.
3 Frame corners should be padded to protect canvas cover.
4 A strongback frame made from old piping, bent to shape and using stanchion bases to anchor the ends.
(a) Stanchion base, (b) toe-rail,
(c) pipe frame.

5 Winter covers should be left open at each end to permit the free passage of air. (a) Where a boat has an overhang and a short keel-foot it is advisable to prop the overhang independently of the main cradle. The weight of the boat is taken by timber baulks (b), and the cradle (c) should never take direct weight.
6 Store masts and spars on trestles, supporting their weight equally along their length. (a) Where packing is necessary the wedges (b) should be pushed in gently between the mast (c) and the trestle (d) until the mast is supported.

191

4. Toe rails and coamings are subject to damage and should be examined to check whether they are properly bedded down, and not loose thus permitting the ingress of water and possible damage to the shelf and deck beams, which usually occurs in a very inaccessible position.

5. Cabin topsides should be carefully examined to see if there is any evidence of the structure 'working'. Paint lifting, or discolouration under varnish, clearly indicates that this is taking place.

6. Try to think of any place on deck where water can lie, paying particular attention to the cockpit sole and the stringers and beams beneath.

7. The timber around all deck fittings should be checked occasionally to ensure that no water penetration is taking place. Cleats which are subject to strain should be closely examined for any signs of movement which will eventually lead to trouble.

8. 'Nail Sickness' shows up as soft wood around fastenings and is caused by galvanic action making the wood acid or alkaline in the immediate vicinity of the fittings and thus possibly leading to the fastenings becoming loose (see page 193 for 'galvanic action').

Reference has been made to checking for rot. This may be done in one of two ways: either by means of a spike – effective but brutal – or with a small hammer. If a hammer is used to strike suspect timber it will give out a crisp note if the timber is sound, but a dull, soggy one if there is rot present. The hammer is the best tool for checking over a hull, while using the spike in the inaccessible places. The above points are really self-evident and the man who carries out his own maintenance will soon learn where to look for potential trouble and how to deal with it before it becomes a major job.

Remedial Action – Wood

Basically, repair work on a wooden hull consists of replacing all unsound timber – a very obvious statement but one implying a line of action from which some owners tend to fight shy. It refers particularly to timbers affected by rot. If perchance, any is discovered, it is necessary, unfortunately, to cut back in all directions until sound timber is reached. This is vital because if any rot is left it may spread, so one has again to be quite ruthless in cutting it out still further. The action to be taken with broken or damaged timber is usually obvious and is quite often within the scope of an owner who is handy with tools. Methods of carrying out specific repairs are too numerous to cover in a book such as this, and no doubt some owners will prefer to have the work done by a professional shipwright. However, any owner who takes a pride in his boat and has the time to spare and/or cannot afford professional assistance, will find that he can effect many repairs provided he acquires a little knowledge of wood-working, uses good timber of the correct type and the right fixings and adhesive et al. In cases where timber is dry, and free from any contamination in the form of paint etc., the modern epoxy resin type of adhesive can materially assist in fabrication. Take, for example, a cracked rib in a wood hull that

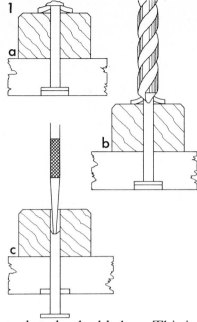

needs to be doubled up. This is not necessarily work for a shipwright. It is a simple job to laminate a curved timber to a given pattern, using thin strips of wood and a good adhesive, and the resultant piece will be as strong, or stronger, than the original timber. Once the rib is fabricated it is not a difficult job to fasten it close to the the defective one to make the necessary reinforcement. Certain major jobs, such as, for example, replacing a plank in the hull of a boat, undoubtably require the services of a ship-wright – or at least rather more skill and knowledge than the average handyman possesses. . . .

New timber should be treated with a good rot-proofing liquid such as Cuprinol (clear), followed by an aluminium sealer, after which the normal undercoating, topcoat etc. can be applied when weather conditions permit.

Keel Bolts A fixed-keel cruising yacht will carry a considerable weight of metal bolted to the wood stub keel, the bolts passing right through the latter. These bolts can corrode and waste away over a period of

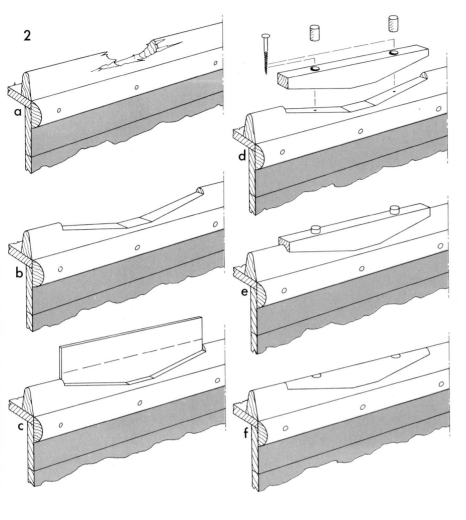

1 Removal of a copper fastening from a frame. (a) Section through frame and topside plank with the copper nail peened well over the rove. (b) Drill into the head until the bit bites into the rove. (c) Tap out the nail with a drift.

2 (a) Repair to a damaged toe-rail. (b) Cut away the damaged area. (c) Make an accurate template to transfer to the replacement timber. (d) Pilot drill the new timber for screws and counter-bore for wooden plugs which should be cut with the grain running in the same direction as the toe-rail. Also pilot drill the toe-rail for the screws to avoid splitting the wood. (e) Glue and screw the new timber in place and glue in the plugs. (f) When the adhesive has set hard, fair off the excess timber to shape and sand down ready for finishing.

years and, if they are not checked, it is possible ultimately for a keel to drop off – with disastrous results of course. . . . When a wooden boat is beginning to age, a check should be made occasionally to see whether corrosion is taking place – it can be made at the time of the annual overhaul, either by dropping a sample bolt, or alternatively (but possibly more expensively) by having the bolts X-rayed by a specialist firm. If the sample bolt shows no sign of corrosion one year, then a different bolt should be dropped at the next annual inspection as the bolts do not necessaily waste uniformally. When replacing keel bolts make

sure that they are thoroughly embedded in waterproof mastic.

Skin Fittings and Electrolytic Action Mechanical wear and tear on such fittings as propeller shafts, rudder pintles and stern bearings is easy to see and the remedial action that is required is obvious. However, galvanic or electrolytic action is not always so simply observed and thus it must be sought out with care.

Corrosion of the metallic fittings on a boat's hull is caused by the passage of a small electric current between dissimilar metals. This current may be caused in two different ways but from the boat owner's point of view the result (if

unchecked) is the same – trouble!

If two dissimilar metals are placed in an electrolyte (salt water) and connected either by touching or through some connecting link such as a copper-based antifouling, a primary cell is formed and current will endeavour to 'plate' one metal into the other. All metals may be listed in a galvanic order; a metal high on the list (the 'noble' one) attacks one lower down (the 'base' one) when both are in each other's presence and connected in an electrolyte. Thus copper for example, being higher on the scale than steel and therefore a 'nobler' metal, will attack the steel which will corrode

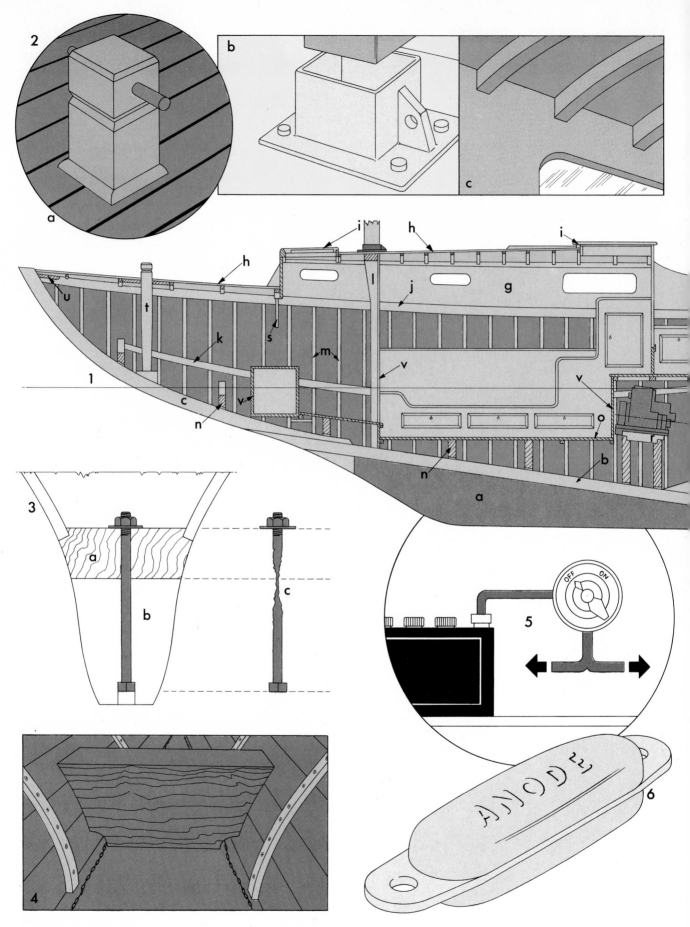

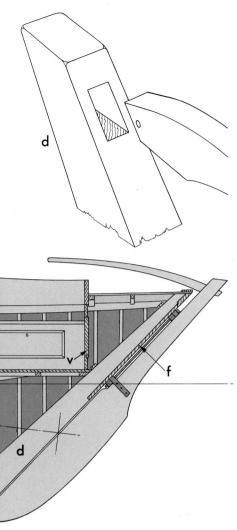

accordingly. Similarly with, say, bronze and aluminium, the aluminium being the baser metal will corrode when in the presence of bronze. The way to avoid trouble would be to use the same metal for all fittings and their fixings but this is hardly practicable; hence the need to provide some kind of protection. As mentioned above there are two ways trouble can be caused: the galvanic cell just described, and electrolysis caused by stray electrical currents. The latter can happen when a fault occurs on the boat's electrical system – for example if the boat's battery negative is earthed to the engine bedplate and a positive circuit develops a leak to a skin-fitting thus causing an electric current to flow between two points. For this reason it is always wise to fit a master switch to isolate the battery when it is not in use.

Protection against galvanic action may be achieved by using cathodic protection in which a zinc sacrificial anode is fixed to the out-side of the hull and then connected internally to all metal skin fittings, the engine and the propellor shaft. The zinc anode (being low on the galvanic scale) is 'attacked' by the other metals and consequently ensures that no wasting occurs on the skin fittings. The zinc anode should be inspected annually but it usually has a life of two or three years before it is eaten away.

The subject of electrolytic action appears at first to be a simple and straightforward one but in reality it becomes quite complex and thus makes much better sense to fit the protection rather than wait for obvious signs of corrosion.

1 This section view of the *Stella Class* cruiser/racer shows the complexity of wooden boat construction and the many areas requiring regular inspection to maintain peak condition and performance. (a) Ballast keel, (b) keel, (c) stem, (d) sternpost, (e) deadwood, (f) transom, (g) coaming, (h) deck, (i) hatches, (j) shelf, (k) stringer, (l) mast support beams, (m) frames, (n) floors, (o) cabin sole, (p) cockpit sole, (q) mainsheet post, (r) engine bearers, (s) grown knee, (t) samson post, (u) breasthook, (v) bulkheads.
2 Inspection for water penetration. (a) Deck fittings, (b) mast socket and mast foot, (c) deck beam ends, (d) rudder stock head.
3 Keelbolt securing ballast keel (a) to keel (b) and the possible result of galvanic action (c).
4 Floor limber holes can be kept clear of debris by rigging a chain to run fore and aft through them.
5 A cut-out switch built into the electrical system can isolate the battery when not in use.
6 A zinc anode or 'sacrificial plate'.

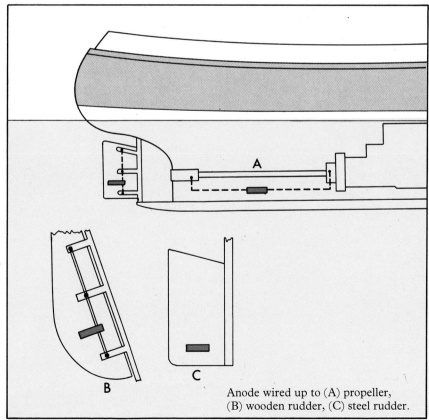

Anode wired up to (A) propeller, (B) wooden rudder, (C) steel rudder.

G.R.P. Hulls

A basic feature of G.R.P. hulls, which an owner should understand, is that the material is *not* 100% waterproof; it can and does absorb water. The glass mat is completely non-hygroscopic, but the resin used in the laying-up is not, and the gel coat (the water-proof seal as it were) can also absorb water to a minor extent due largely to the presence of colouring fillers in the resin. Hence the necessity to maintain the gel coat in first-class condition is one of the pre-requisites of good maintenance and, incidentally, this should be born in mind when you are considering the best method of laying-up for the Winter. When looking for trouble the key to success is to locate any damage t to the gel coat or cracks in it which will permit the ingress of water into the laminate.

To the new owner of a second-hand G.R.P. yacht it may sound as if maintenance is going to be as onerous as it would be with a wooden hull, but this is not so. If an owner, even an inexperienced one, examines his boat carefully, at annual intervals in a critical way – taking nothing for granted – he will very quickly learn to see potential trouble spots and take the necessary remedial action. It is assumed that a check-over will be made of all wooden fittings such as grab rails, cockpit trim *et al.* along the lines suggested for wooden boats (see page 190), paying particular attention to any plywood bulkheads.

The exterior of the boat should be carefully examined beginning with the deck fittings, to check that no fastenings have become loose. All deck fittings, and particularly those carrying strain, should be well bedded-

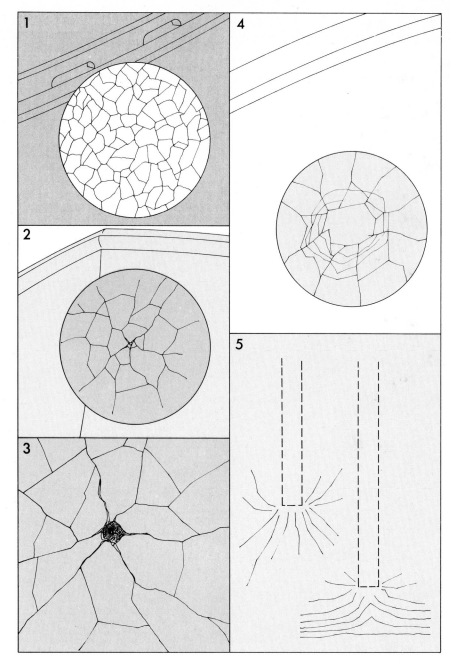

down and through-bolted to a backing plate. The G.R.P. in the vicinity of fittings should be checked for any signs of cracking which could indicate undue stress at that point. This also applies to the area round the foot of the mast, where signs of crazing or cracking could indicate stress because of the partial collapse of a load-bearing bulkhead, or stiffening under the deck, or perhaps to over-tensioning of the rigging at

sometime. Another area of possible trouble is along the edge of mouldings, such as the turn of the cabin top and the toe rail; voids can occur in the lay-up at these points and then suddenly appear as small holes due to impact or stressing of the gel coat – these edges are obviously more susceptible to impact damage and abrasion than are flat surfaces. When examining fibre glass surfaces for damage it is sometimes difficult to

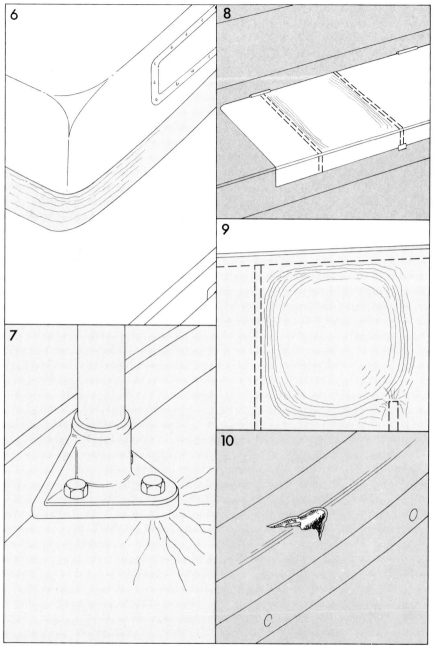

Faults and flaws in a GRP hull.
1 Crazing. Note random nature.
2 Star crack caused by impact or local stress, radial cracks emanate from a definite centre.
3 An area of shattering and damage may occur at the centre of a star crack.
4 Impact from reverse side. Note absence of definite centre.
5 Cracks due to hard spot on the reverse side.
6 Stress relief cracks at the corner of a cabin top, probably due to the deck being forced to fit the hull.
7 Radial cracks from a fastening due to overtightening or excessive strain.
8 A blunt impact leaves no mark but the moulding cracks at the bulkheads owing to sharp bending there.
9 Cracks due to flexible topsides overstrained by hard sailing. The parallel cracks roughly enclose the area of bending. Note how the bending is sharper where restrained by the bulkhead and naturally stiff hull/deck join.
10 Moulding flaw caused by poor lay-up technique.

differentiate between scratches and cracks. The former blemishes are a normal accompaniment to the life of a G.R.P. hull, and, provided they receive prompt treatment, are no cause for worry.

However, cracks are a different proposition and the reason for their appearance must be discovered before repair work is carried out. Naturally if they are the result of mechanical damage then they can be treated as an ordinary repair job. Should there be no apparent reason for them, however, the owner should be well advised to call in expert advice as they might be a prelude to more serious damage. Unfortunately cracks start as hair-line cracks which are not as obvious as surface scratches. The result is that they may be present for some time, and allow water to penetrate the laminate if the hull is only given a cursory glance once a year. A surveyor testing for cracks uses a fluorescent dye, which is wiped over the surface and absorbed by the cracks, which then subsequently shows up clearly against the rest of the hull. The last check item is the bonded joint between deck and hull – if this is possible – paying particular attention to the ends, fore and aft. The hull should then be looked over for damage, again searching carefully for any

hair-line cracks in the topsides which may have been caused by physical damage or some form of internal stressing. Apart from cracks, the presence of osmotic blisters should be sought. Fortunately this is a fairly rare disease in well-constructed hulls, it looks rather alarming and dealing with it can be expensive. If blisters appear on the hull, expert advice should be sought immediately. Keels on G.R.P. hulls are of either the external iron variety bolted-on or encapsulated, and the latter should be carefully examined on the underside if no 'shoe' is fitted, to make sure that the G.R.P. has not been damaged, thus admitting water. Bolted keels should be examined at the point of attachment to see whether there is any sign of rust, which indicates slackness and water penetration. Similarly bilge keels should be examined in the same way; if they are moulded they will probably have suffered damage at some time or another.

Remedial Action – G.R.P. To deal first with the inevitable minor scratches which occur,

Opposite: When a boat is out of the water for anti-fouling application, scrubbing down, etc. the hull should be examined for any signs of osmosis and structural defects. This ensures that the boat will be kept in good condition. *Above:* Two examples of GRP hulls in bad condition. The hull on the left has bad scoring probably caused by rubbing against a jetty whilst the hull on the right has the first signs of osmosis.

199

the cosmetic treatment for these varies according to their depth. Very slight scratches (which nevertheless show up as they gather dirt) may usually be polished out by using a rubbing-down compound followed by burnishing with a G.R.P. polishing paste or Brasso (metal polish). Scratches which obviously need more careful attention should be cleaned out, degreased with acetone (which should be used very sparingly as it softens gel coat) and carefully filled with the appropriate gel coat. As the latter does not cure properly if it is exposed to the atmosphere, it should be covered with cellophane held in position with sellotape, to exclude air. The filling should be left slightly proud and, when cured, it may be rubbed down with a 'wet-and-dry' medium-grade paper using water with a little detergent added, finishing with the finest grade obtainable. The area should then be burnished with G.R.P. polishing paste. Occasionally 'star crazing' occurs, which is a fine network of cracks rather like a spider's web, and which usually is the result of impact damage. First check to ensure that no serious damage such as delamination is involved by inspection inside, and by tapping the area with a ball-pein hammer. If there is any internal damage to the laminate it will give a dull sound in the damaged area. Should the area be found to be quite sound it should be thoroughly cleaned with acetone and gel coat rubbed into the cracks with a clean rag. Wipe off all surplus immediately, leave to cure and follow by burnishing and the usual wax polishing.

More extensive damage naturally requires more drastic

treatment to effect good permanent repairs – for example an area that has suffered a bad abrasion caused perhaps by rubbing against a quayside without proper fendering. It would be quite hopeless to consider filling the cuts and cracks individually. The only treatment is to cut back to the laminate with a rough file, build up with gel coat – making perhaps two or three applications – and then rubbing down in the usual way. However, if it has been necessary to cut right back to the first layer of glass mat, then it will be

preferable to first build-up with an epoxy putty, such as 'plastic padding', finishing up with a layer of gel coat, followed by rubbing and burnishing. Alternatively resin can be applied, but epoxy putty will be easier to use on a vertical surface. The actual techniques for handling these materials and obtaining the best results are usually adequately covered in the manufacturers' leaflets which are supplied with the product.

When major damage occurs and the laminate as well as the gel coat is badly harmed it will be necessary to cut out the

With the winch arrangement shown here the GRP deck will have been considerably reinforced to increase its strength and take the added strain put on it.

whole section after you have carefully checked to ensure that full extent of the damaged area is clearly defined. It is essential to make certain that the cut, when it is made, goes right back to sound materials. It is useless (and time wasting) to try to 'cobble up' what requires a sound repair job. Having marked out the area needing repair, the next step is to decide on the method to be employed. If the area is large and the owner is not very experienced, then it would probably be best to have the work carried out professionally. If, however, it is reasonably small – not exceeding say one square foot, and is obviously a straight-forward job, there is no reason why the average handyman should not attempt it. The intial step is to cut through the laminate making sure that all defective material is removed. Next, chamfer the cut edge so that the replacement mat is held in by the outer edge of the hull and the overlapping layer of glass-fibre mat that will be applied on the back.

The next step is to fix on the outside of the hull a former of some reasonably flexible material such as 'Formica', which will take up the curvature of hull and can be attached by self-tapping screws – or by any other method which will hold it firmly in position against the opening. A coat of wax or releasing agent should be applied to it before it is fixed to the hull, and you must be very careful not to get any of the agent on the edges of the cut. The cut should be thoroughly clean, and any paint on the inside surrounding the aperture should be carefully scraped off to ensure a good bond. With the former in position and all surfaces prepared, a layer or two of gel coat should be applied to the former from the inside. When this has partially cured, say after two or three hours, the first layer of chopped strand mat should be applied and a coat of resin stippled in. This process should be continued until the mat is built up to the thickness of the hull, resin should then be applied to the area surrounding the repair, sufficient to give a good overlap of about 3 to 4 inches. Chopped strand mat and resin should then be built up to a thickness of at least half the hull thickness (see diag.). When the repair is cured the outside former may be removed and the fixing holes are then filled with gel coat. When it is thoroughly cured,

201

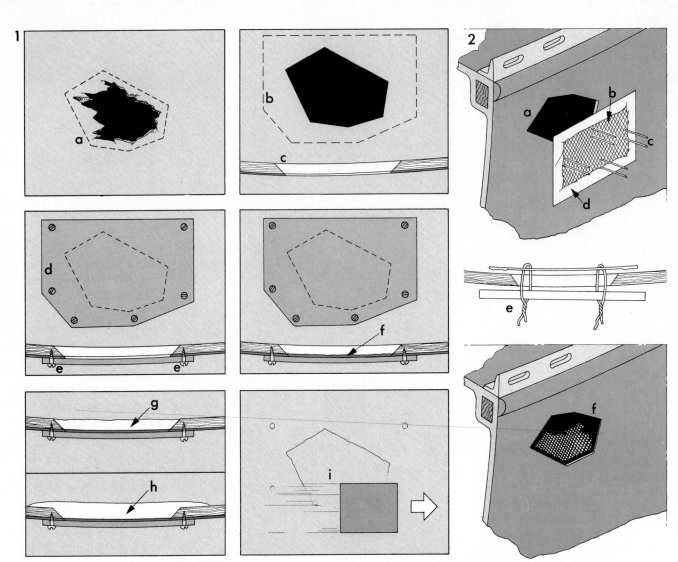

the whole area can be rubbed down with wet-and-dry paper, using a sanding block, starting with a coarse grade, (say 200), and finishing with a fine grade (number 600), after which the usual burnishing and wax polishing should be carried out.

There is no reason why anyone who has carried out minor repairs in G.R.P. should not undertake a repair of this kind. Cleanliness and temperature are the critical points to watch; temperatures below about 65° F (18° C) lengthen the curing time and should be avoided. Again manufacturers' leaflets are a useful source of information or you can consult one of the many books which are

1 Repair to a GRP hull. (a) Pencil in the area to be cut away. (b) The former required to cover the damage. (c) The skin thickness cut back at an angle. (d) Screw the former into place with self-tapping screws (e). The Gel coat (f) is applied to the inside of the former and left to harden for two or three hours. (g) Primary layers of chopped strand mat are applied and resin stippled in between each coat. (h) Apply resin around the damaged area and build up the chopped strand mat to give a good overlap. (i) Finally rub down the outer surface.

available on the subject. The materials required for the work are a thixotropic polyester resin, preferably pre-accelerated, together with catalyst, glass fibre mat about 1½ oz per sq.ft (450 gr per sq.m), the

2 Where damage cannot be reached from inside the hull: (a) cut back the damaged GRP as before, (b) cut a fine grade metal mesh sheet to overlap the damaged area, (c) thread wire tiers through the mesh (d) apply resin soaked mat around the edge of the patch, (e) push the patch through the hole and secure the tiers with scrap timber to hold it firmly against the hull until the resin has cured. (f) After hardening the tiers can be removed and layers of mat built up against the mesh former.

appropriate coloured gel coat and acetone for cleaning. Lastly, wet-and-dry paper, a stiff brush for stippling the resin into the mat and the tools which will be found in any handyman's kit.

Above: A massive extruded alloy mast from the ocean racer *Lionheart* lies on trestles waiting to be stepped. Nearby is a more humble wooden mast with deck gasket in place.

Masts and Spars Wooden masts and spars are somewhat outdated at present but they are still around and are subject to their own particular brand of trouble: wood rot caused by rainwater, the arch enemy! A well-maintained wooden mast has a very long lifespan but if maintenance is neglected its life may be considerably shortened. Trouble is usually caused by rainwater being trapped and then penetrating the wood, a particularly susceptible point being at the hounds, i.e. the place where the cross-trees, or spreaders, are attached to the mast. Some types of fitting are quite blameless but others are less so, and if they have fixings which penetrate the mast they should be watched over carefully. If the mast is stepped in a tabernacle, little trouble should

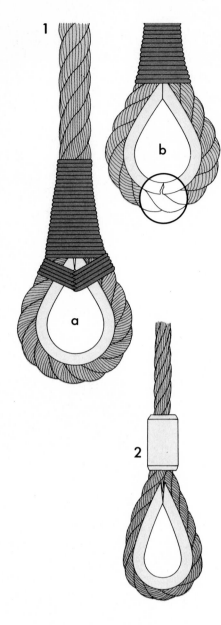

1 (a) Spliced and whipped end with thimble. (b) Thimble fracture.
2 Talurit end.

Opposite : The application of a mid-season coat of anti-fouling between tides.

be experienced at its foot. If it is stepped in the keel though, that part where it passes through the deck needs inspection when laying-up, as also do the deck timbers in the immediate vicinity.

Metal masts of course require little attention but it is worth inspecting the surface round any fittings such as halyard winches for signs of galvanic action (see page 193). If any cracks are showing seek professional advice on the cause and also the best method of repair.

Rigging The majority of yachts today have stainless steel wire (or rod) rigging which, while it has a great many advantages, does have one disadvantage in that it does not give such long advance warning of impending failure as does galvanised wire. Obviously there will be few signs of rusting on the compression joints at termination but any stray broken strands sticking out of the lay of the wire indicate the possibility of future trouble. There is little maintenance that you can carry out except giving it a thorough washing in fresh water before storing for the winter.

Galvanised wire rigging normally shows its age by starting to rust at terminations or splices, and this indicates the need for eventual replacement, the urgency being indicated by the amount of rust which is present. When it is stripped down for the winter the rigging should be washed in fresh water, dried and then soaked in a mixture of raw linseed oil and petrol before being stored away. This annual treatment will prolong the life of galvanised wire to a surprising degree.

All rigging fittings should be

carefully examined for condition. Terminations, whether spliced, swaged or Talurit ends, should be checked to see if there is any sign of cracking – if so then the end must be remade. Bottle-screws should be examined (after thorough cleaning) to check if the threads are worn or barrels cracked. If the thread is sloppy – replace!

Fitting-out
If a good 'lay-up' and Winter programme of work has been completed fitting-out should be a comparatively easy and painless job starting with a good wash down to remove the Winter's accumulation of dirt.

The Hull A G.R.P. hull should be carefully checked over to see that no minor cuts or abrasions were missed when the Autumn repairs were made. Next the hull should be thoroughly cleaned and any stains removed with a proprietory cleaner, after which it should be well waxed and polished. During the Winter the bottom should have been prepared to receive the antifouling coat and a final check should now be made to see whether any touching-up with primer is required (wood or G.R.P.). All sea-cocks and skin fittings should be checked over: sea-cocks dismantled, cleaned and greased with water pump grease, any cone-type sea-cocks being lapped-in with grinding paste before being greased and reassembled.

In the case of a wooden hull the bilges will have thoroughly dried through during the Winter and they should now be cleaned out, paying particular attention to limber holes, after which a coat of bilge paint should be applied if necessary. The topsides of a wooden hull will probably need a top coat and should be prepared in the usual way. Minor dents and abrasions should be filled with a good hard stopping, and the topsides then rubbed down with a medium grade wet-and-dry paper to give a good 'key' for the new paint. Stopping and any bare wood should be primed and under-coated ready for the application of the top coat.

If the work cannot be done under cover a day should be awaited when there is no chance of rain or strong winds to blow dust about. Manufacturers' instructions should be followed as closely as possible, particularly in respect to the use of thinners. A newcomer to painting a hull almost invariably uses horizontal strokes of the brush but in fact if the work is carried out with vertical strokes, working from one end of the boat to the other, then the number of leading or wet edges is reduced with a consequent improvement to the finished surface. The use of a paint roller will considerably increase the speed of working, but these tend to give an 'orange peel' effect. However, if the surface is gently wiped over immediately with a wide paint-brush the effect will be eradicated.

Anti-fouling the bottom should normally be the last job before launching and it should present no problems if all the preparatory work has been properly done. The only query may be the selection of the correct brand and type. Other local users will be confident that they know which gives the most satisfactory results in a particular area but the newcomer will probably be a little surprised at the diversity of the options

expressed. . . . This may be due to the fact that conditions in most countries (and certainly in Britain) vary from season to season. Thus an anti-fouling which produces excellent results one year may seem poor by comparison the following season – not because the manufacturer is trying to economise with the expensive poisons but more likely because the sea temperature happens to have risen several degrees above average resulting in a

considerable increase in marine growth. There are two main types of anti-fouling: 'hard' and 'soft'. The former is usually the more expensive, can be applied well before the launching date if necessary, and may be scrubbed without re-coating during the season. Soft anti-fouling must be applied within twenty-four hours of launching and is much easier to scrub as it tends to come away with the marine growth. It is continuously dissolving into the water and therefore re-coating may be needed before the end of the season. Whichever type you choose it is important to remember that anti-fouling is not a water-proof paint and, in the case of wooden hulls particularly, the bottom must be properly primed and under-coated to preserve the timbers. When dealing with varnished surfaces (the 'bright-work') all varnish which has started to flake, or where the wood has a grey appearance, should be scraped down to bare wood. Then, starting with a 50:50 coat of varnish and white spirit, at least two to three coats of varnish should be applied with a very gentle rub down between each, to give a key for the next coat. This is a job which, like painting, requires a warm dry atmosphere. When 'touching up', or putting another coat of varnish onto existing varnish, it will normally be found that the ordinary synthetic varnish is more satisfactory than the polyurethane variety.

The rest of the work on board – such as removal of inhibiting oil from the engine etc. – is straightforward and consists of little more than replacing equipment, the exception being the last major job: setting up the rigging, which is not a very lengthy job but certainly a most important one.

Setting up Rigging If the mast of a sailing yacht is not too heavy and if it is stepped on deck, it is well within the capability of the average owner to step it for himself. If you are in doubt, however, then have it stepped by the yard. In either case there is no reason why the average owner should not dress the mast himself – that is fit all

1 Distortion of mast athwartships caused by: (a) overtightening of the starboard cap shroud and (b) over-tightening of the starboard lower shroud and the port cap shroud.
2 On a mast rigged with jumper stays it is difficult to adjust the tension once the mast has been stepped. For this reason it is as well to tighten them up fairly stiffly otherwise when tension is applied to the backstay it will pull the top of the mast sternwards.
3 Distortion of the mast fore and aft caused by (a) overtightening of the forestay and (b) overtightening of both the lower back shrouds and the forestay.
4 As a general rule the standing rigging should be tensioned in this order: (A) forestay, (B) backstay, (C) cap shrouds, and finally (D) the lower shrouds. If executed with care the rig should only require minor tuning adjustments.
5 To establish the required mast rake a plumb line suspended from the mast head to the deck will enable the correct angle to be measured.

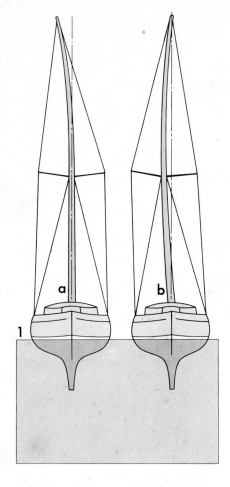

the running and standing-rigging to the mast before it is stepped. In this way he will be fully aware of the condition of all his rigging and know what is likely to need replacing in the future. All shackles should be properly moused (i.e. wired-up with monel wire), clevis pins should be fitted with new split pins, and bottle-screws thoroughly greased and fitted fully extended to make the work of connecting them up more easy. It is worth remembering that bottle-screws should be fitted with the righthand thread at the bottom, so that the bottle screw is tightened up in a clockwise direction when viewed from above. Having stepped the mast and roughly tightened up the bottle-screws, now comes the rather worrying business (at

least to the conscientious owner) of tensioning up the rigging. If it is set up too slack the boat's performance suffers and if it is too tight then the boat suffers! It is very difficult to advise on this matter, apart from setting out the general principles. The rigging should be taut but it is important to remember that, if it is over-tensioned, the compression load on the deck at the foot of the mast will become much higher than the boat's hull has been designed to take.

Starting with the boat afloat, the first operation is to ensure that the mast is vertical when viewed in the fore-and-aft plane and raked back to the correct angle, which may be read off the sail plan or alternatively ascertained from the builders. The job calls for a

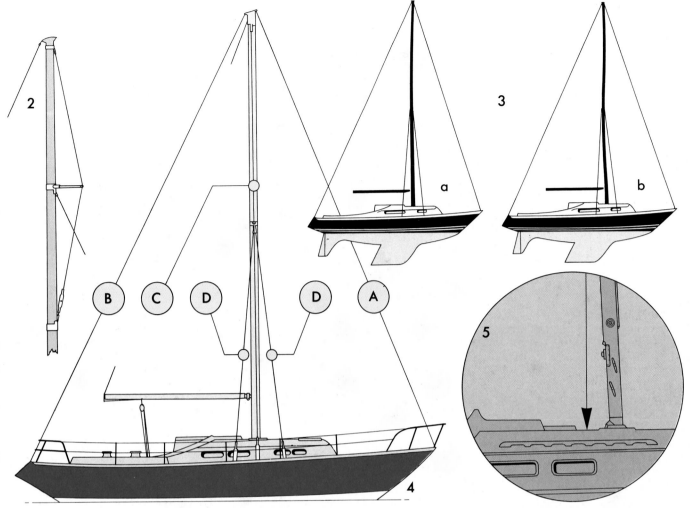

very calm day as a plumb bob will be needed from the mast head to the deck to check the rake angle. Having got the mast set in the right plane, both fore-and-aft and sideways, the next step is to check that it is absolutely straight. A dead straight mast can withstand very high compression strains but, if it has a bend in it, then it can fail prematurely under load. The best way to check is to lie on deck and sight up the mainsail luff track and then up the side of the mast. If the rig is a standard mast-head sloop rig it will normally have a forestay, back stay, cap shrouds and lower shrouds. First, set up the forestay taut followed by the backstay, remembering that with equal tensions in them the backstay will appear to be the slacker, because of its additional length. Check for any bends in

the mast and then start on the shrouds. The cap shrouds should be tighter than the lower shrouds as, because of their greater length, they will tend to stretch more. Check again for bends before doing the final tightening up. Incidentally, one way of comparing tensions is to strike the stays with a small metal rod and check that the note is the same. The forestay should now be set up tightly (one well-known builder says it should 'sing' when struck) check the tension in the back stay which will appear slightly slacker. Now set up the cap shrouds, slightly slacker than the forestay, and then the lower shrouds a little slacker still. Check the mast for bends between each operation as tightening up one bottle-screw will affect the adjustment on others.

When the setting-up is complete the boat should be taken for a short sail in reasonably calm conditions, checking the mast for curvature on each tack, both fore-and-aft and sideways. The lee shrouds will appear slightly slack but should not be 'floppy'. The forestay should remain taught on all points of sailing and should not sag unduly to leeward when beating to windward. When you are satisfied that the rigging is properly set up, the last operation when you are back on the mooring is to check all locking-nuts on the bottle-screws and then wire them with monel wire to ensure that vibration does not permit one to slacken off.

Finally, do remember to give the rigging a check-over once or twice during the season.

207

Appendix 1 - Equipment

A Guide to Additional Equipment One of the difficulties the average yachtsman has to face when he is contemplating the purchase of additional equipment for his yacht is the wide range of products available – particularly in the electronics field.

The selection of deck equipment is normally fairly straightforward. After an owner has built up experience over one or two seasons and has possibly sailed in other yachts, he will usually have a fairly clear idea of what is required to improve the performance, or the ease of handling, of his boat. Electronically, however, the position is not quite so simple, mainly due to the variety of equipment which is available and which may appear to the inexperienced owner to do the same job. It is important to weigh-up very carefully exactly what is required of the gear, for otherwise the owner may buy equipment that is unsuitable, either because it is inferior or too sophisticated for his requirements. The equipment discussed in this section will be confined to apparatus where the principle of operation, or perhaps the need for it at all, may not readily be understood by the newcomer to sailing.

Electronic Equipment

There has been a gratifying trend in recent decades for manufacturers to produce much more sophisticated equipment of a size suitable for installation in small yachts, and also at a price which is within reach of most people. Apart from the obvious transistorised radio receiver, the equipment of interest to the average yachtsman consists of:

R.D.F. equipment.
V.H.F. radio telephone.
Radar.
Echo sounders.
Electric logs.
Wind speed and direction indicators.
Automatic pilots.

Installation of Equipment

Before you start comparing the merits of equipment it is worth remembering that proper installation is essential to achieve the designed performance – a fact which is occasionally overlooked when equipment is enthusiastically installed by the new owner. The following points in connection with the installation of electrical equipment are not by any means intended to be a 'complete guide' but it is hoped that they may assist in overcoming some of the more common problems.

Apart from actual failure of equipment, electrical problems fall into two main categories: excessive voltage drop and radio interference because of lack of suppression or earthing. Taking voltage drop first, it is important to remember that the criteria for the size of an electric cable are firstly its adequacy for the load and, secondly, that it will not cause excessive voltage drop for the length of cable in question. Reputable manufacturers usually supply all the necessary information to enable their equipment to be installed and will certainly advise on cable sizes if there are any installation problems. When installing equipment which may be sensitive to voltage drop and interference, V.H.F. radio telephones for example, it is important to wire a separate circuit back to the main battery and not to tap into existing circuits even if they are ideally located. Apart from reducing voltage drop problems this avoids the possibility of an important piece of equipment being put out of action because of a fault on another circuit. An auto-pilot also should be wired back to the main battery (with adequate fusing of course) to reduce voltage fluctuations to other equipment caused by the intermittent operations of the pilot motor.

All circuits should have properly made cable terminations – wire ends twisted round a terminal are a

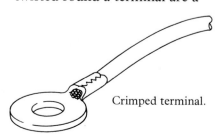
Crimped terminal.

fruitful source of mysterious happenings on electrical circuits. . . . Proper terminations, preferably crimped, which are readily available from any good auto spares dealer, should be used. Soldered connections should be avoided if possible as they may have a tendency to corrode in a salt atmosphere. The method of running the circuits is also important; single core cables should never be used, particularly in the vicinity of magnetic compasses, as the separation of wires carrying positive and negative currents may lead to the creation of electrical fields. From a radio angle it is desirable to avoid large, closed loops such as might occur if wiring was run both sides of a boat terminating in a junction box at either end. Such installation may have occurred in the construction of the boat and therefore little can be done about it, but it is at least worth knowing about the problem that it can cause.

Apart from the voltage drop problem the other trouble affecting radio equipment is the pick-up of electrical interference from equipment on board. Starting with the engine it will be obvious that the ignition circuits on a petrol engine should be adequately suppressed in a similar manner to those of an automobile engine. Similarly dynamos and alternators should be properly suppressed by the manufacturers, and if this has not been done or it appears that the suppression is ineffective, reference should be made to the manufacturers or to a really good automobile electrician. Electrical interference, generally, is considerably reduced when all equipment is properly earthed. In Chapter 10 (see page 193)

reference is made to cathodic protection, and the anode of the system can be effectively utilized as a main earth. Assuming that cathodic protection has been installed, all skin fittings, engine, gear box etc. will have been bonded to the anode and to complete the installation all other metallic equipment should also be bonded in – in fact any metallic equipment which can be tied in, should be – it can do no harm and may do good.

The closed loops mentioned above apply not only to electrical circuits but any other sizable metallic circuit – the guard rails for example (see page 139). If they form a continuous loop round the vessel they may have an adverse effect on the accuracy of R.D.F. equipment. This particular problem is easily dealt with by substituting a terylene lashing of adequate strength for the shackle or senhouse slip at the pulpit and pushpit, thus breaking the electrical circuit.

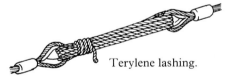
Terylene lashing.

Similarly with rigging – it may be necessary to insert insulators in the standing rigging if certain types of R.D.F. equipment are used. However, this is expensive and the results may not justify the outlay, thus it is best to seek expert advice before starting.

A further source of interference which may occur in auxiliary sailing yachts is caused by the rotation of the propeller when the auxiliary is not in use. If a prop. shaft brake is not fitted, then the rotation of the shaft when sailing may cause radio interference. This can normally

be reduced by fitting a metallic brush maintaining constant contact with the shaft, which should be located as close as possible to the stern bearing (inboard) and connected to the ship's earth or anode.

R.D.F. The prices of R.D.F. sets cover a wide range with a corresponding variation in their capabilities. It is important, therefore, for the purchaser to decide what he requires of the equipment before he looks at costs, although the average family cruising man must inevitably be largely influenced by the latter consideration. As a general rule it is fair to say that the more expensive the equipment the easier it will be to get accurate results, nevertheless comparatively inexpensive sets from a reputable manufacturer will also produce a good reliable performance, if the owner is prepared to practice with them regularly and get to know their limitations and capabilities. If you wait until life is getting difficult – fog for example – you are asking too much of the set if you expect to get a precise location if you haven't already tried it out in various conditions in which its results are easily checked.

R.D.F. sets suitable for yachts can be split roughly into three types: the completely self-contained unit with built-in compass which can be used on deck; a fixed receiver with portable sensing aerial and compass; and the fixed installation with a deckhead rotating aerial. The choice of the family cruising man will probably lie in the first or second groups, and despite the drawbacks of some models there is no doubt that the most popular instruments for the

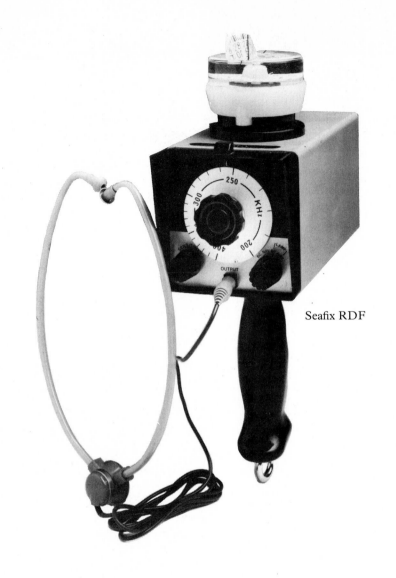

Seafix RDF

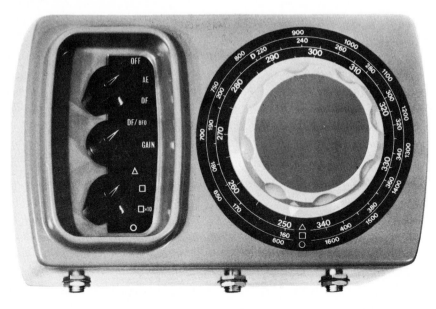

average cruising yacht lie within the first group. One of the most popular sets in this range is the 'Seafix DF', which embodies the complete set with built-in compass in one unit which can be used anywhere on deck (thereby enabling the more obvious closed loops to be avoided) and bearings may be taken directly from the unit's compass. The set also embodies a Long Wave Band receiver to enable British shipping forecasts to be obtained and it also has a small 'pea' lamp for illuminating the compass, which means that it may be used at night. The compass is admirably positioned for it to be used as a normal hand-bearing compass for visual fixes. In use, the set is tuned to the frequency of the beacon or group of beacons (see page 138), finely tuned when the signal is picked up, and then, when the beacon has been identified, the set is rotated until a null is obtained; the compass bearing is then read and noted for plotting on the chart, together with any other bearings which can be taken at the same time.

At the top end of the price range the latest D.F. set in the handheld class is the 'Aptel Digital Direction Finder' which marks a major forward step in this type of equipment. In this set the radio frequency of the beacon is selected by pressing the appropriate keys on the keyboard and the selected frequency then appears on a small display unit, confirming the frequency chosen. The set incorporates a small non-liquid compass which is locked on the bearing by the operation of the trigger when the null has been obtained. Also built-in is a quartz clock assembly which displays the appropriate time period in a six minute cycle, thus enabling ready identification of the beacons in a standard 6 group. The method of using the 'Aptel' is simplicity itself, the selected frequency is keyed on the switchboard, appropriate beacon selected, the null obtained visually on the meter, the trigger released which locks the compass in position, thus enabling it to be read at leisure on the chart table. In addition to the visual meter, stethoscope-type headphones can be used for audio tuning. Again in the more expensive price range Messrs. Brooks and Gatehouse manufacture the 'Homer Herm' D.F. set. This set has a fixed receiver and loud speaker with a portable aerial and compass, together with headphones. As it is built to a very high standard this is naturally reflected in the price. An extremely useful accessory, the 'Digitune' gives a visual display of the frequency to which the set is tuned thus avoiding the necessity for 'searching'. The sets mentioned above are self-contained in so far as the reading obtained is the direct magnetic bearing of the beacon, and it is not necessary therefore to note the ship's heading at the instant the bearing is taken.

The 'Big Ship' D.F. systems, such as Decca Omega and 'Consol', are of little interest to cruising yachtsmen, but 'Loran C', although of academic interest only to U.K. yachtsmen at present, is widely used in the U.S.A. Sets designed for yachtsmen utilizing 'Loran C' are now available (Texas Instruments). An extremely high standard of accuracy is obtainable with some of these sets, of the order of fifty yards with a 'repeatable' error of

fifty feet being possible in areas of high signal strength. Looking into the future the next generation of D.F. sets for use in small craft will undoubtedly offer a high degree of sophistication, probably utilizing the proposed chain of navigation satellites, in a price range that will bring them within the reach of many yachtsmen.

V.H.F. Sets V.H.F. radio telephone sets have gained enormously in popularity in the last few years because of the reduction in physical size and electrical loading, allied to prices which are reasonable in relation to the facilities provided. Basically the V.H.F. set provides communication between ships and ship to shore stations over distances of forty to sixty miles under normal conditions, and in addition 'link calls' can be put through a shore station to any telephone subscriber. Above all it enables immediate distress calls to be made on the International Distress Frequency, and this safety aspect is the main justification for the expenditure on the equipment in small yachts. It is also comforting to be able to talk to Coast Guard Stations when you are in trouble but not actually in need of immediate assistance. As with other equipment the facilities in general are in direct ratio to the cost, with an important exception. Any equipment used for radio transmission in British ships has to conform to Post Office specifications and the purchaser knows therefore that any equipment sold for use in yachts is built to a good standard. The choice of equipment for the average yacht lies between the small transmitting set with, say,

twelve different channels, and the large multi-channel sets with sixty or more. In addition to the number of channels, the sets also have differing power outputs and 'simplex' or 'duplex' operation, the power output varying from 10 watts to 25 watts, the latter figure being the maximum power permitted for the type of set we are talking about. 'Simplex' operation refers to an installation which cannot send and receive simultaneously and uses a single aerial with a change-over switch incorporated in the hand microphone. 'Duplex' operation permits a two-way conversation to be carried on as on a normal telephone and requires two aerials, one for sending and one for receiving, so it is naturally more expensive than a 'simplex' set.

Bearing in mind the requirements of the average family cruiser operating in a fairly limited area the probable choice would be for a twelve channel 'simplex' set, preferably with 25 watts output, although if the cruising range always lies within easy reach of port a 10 watt set could be usefully considered. One of the most popular sets in the United Kingdom is the 'Seavoice' V.H.F. radio made by Electronic Laboratories of Poole, Dorset. This is a twelve channel 'simplex' set with 25 watts output and 1 watt for close-quarters work. Eight channels are fitted as standard with four channels spare, but any of the crystals can be changed to enable other channels to be selected (except Channel 16 and 6 which are mandatory). In addition the firm also manufacture a 'simplex' twelve channel 10 watt 'Mini-Seavoice', the channels are synthesised (as opposed to crystal control) and there are no optional channels available. This set can be quickly removed from the parent craft and, with an 'emergency pack', used as an emergency transmitter in a life raft or dinghy. The 'Multi-Seavoice', a sixty-one channel V.H.F. radio has also been designed to give a comprehensive communications system for operation anywhere in the world. There are many other manufacturers producing sets too numerous to mention, and the American small boat market in particular has a very wide range of equipment to choose from, both in sophistication and price.

For the yachtsman who does not wish to pay for the full V.H.F. service but takes a responsible view of safety precautions, there are emergency packs available which are completely self-contained and designed to be used from a life raft or dinghy; two examples are the 'Safety Link' and 'Callboy', operating on 2182 KHZ. Operation is simplicity itself: the aerial is extended, the earth wire dropped into the sea, and the alarm button is depressed, which transmits the two-tone alarm signal, after which speech contact can be made with rescuing ships or land stations.

Radar Radar in general is of somewhat academic interest to the owner of a small craft of, say, 30 feet or less, and even in motor cruisers it is still a little unusual to see radar sets installed in boats of this size although, with the increasing miniaturisation of electronic circuitry, future generations of radar sets will be smaller, lighter and have even lower

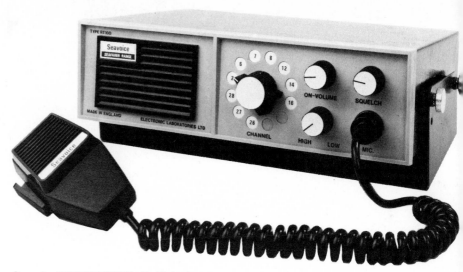

Seavoice RT 100 VHF Radio Telephone

power consumption. Radar is often regarded by yachtsmen primarily as a means of avoiding collision but it is in fact an extremely useful piece of navigation equipment, especially in fog. The limiting factors are normally the weight and size of the scanner and perhaps the electrical loading of the set, which at the present time is round about 40–50 watts for the small radar designed especially for yachts. The scanner, as it operates on line of sight, needs to be as high up as possible and in a motor cruiser a reasonable height can be achieved by using a small tripod-type mast. The average sailing yacht however presents more of a problem unless it is ketch rigged when it can be mounted on the foreside of the mizzen mast. In a sloop, however, the problem of mounting becomes acute; the scanner cannot be mounted near deck level as it will inevitably foul either the sails or rigging, whereas it would not be desirable to mount it at the masthead due to its weight (25–30 kg = 55–65 lbs) and the difficulty in maintenance. It is standard practice to enclose the

scanner in a lightweight non-metallic dome, thus reducing the motor power required to drive it in a strong wind and also making possible a much lighter scanner. At present (1979), however, its weight is still such that it constitutes a problem for the smaller sailing yacht.

As with other equipment there is a good choice to meet most requirements – particularly in the United States. In Britain probably the most popular set for medium-size yachts is the 'Sea Scan III' produced by Electronic Laboratories which has a range of sixteen miles with a power consumption of 48 watts – a figure markedly lower than many other sets of comparable range and performance. The display unit consists of a 6 inch cathode ray tube, which with a standard magnifier gives an effective picture of approximately 8 inches in diameter.

Echo Sounders One of the most useful, and certainly the most commonly-fitted, pieces of navigational equipment in yachts is the echo sounder. There are two main types of equipment: the instantaneous reading type and the recorder, in which the contour of the bottom is traced on a moving paper roll. The latter, which may also have an instantaneous readout as well, is of less interest to the average cruising yachtsman than the instantaneous type.

The recorder is widely used by fishermen as it gives a clear indication of fish shoals and the depths at which they are feeding, but its cost is considerably more than that of the instantaneous type. However, the family navigator is usually only interested in avoiding running aground and the instantaneous type is perfectly adequate for that purpose. The dual range availability is usually of the order of 0–60 feet and 0–60 fathoms with metric equivalents marked (0–18m and 0–108m). Power supply is from the main battery or internal dry batteries, the latter normally having sufficient capacity for the usual intermittent use throughout one season. Indication is by means of a rotating neon tube or light-emitting diode which shows a bright spot alongside the appropriate depth, or there is an alternative type with a normal metre display dial. Installation generally is simple, the most difficult part being the transducer which is either through-mounted in the hull, with direct water contact, or in G.R.P. hulls it can be fitted internally with a special fitting. The idea of internal fitting is attractive as it avoids the necessity for drilling another hole in the hull but, like other superficially attractive ideas, it has possible drawbacks. In a G.R.P. hull with a thickness of $\frac{3}{8}''$ for example, the depth potential of the echo sounder may be reduced by a fifth and this reduction may be as

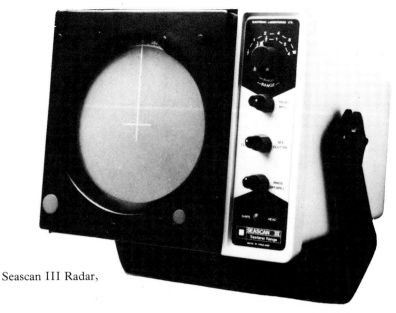

Seascan III Radar,

Hecta M200 DS Echo Sounder,

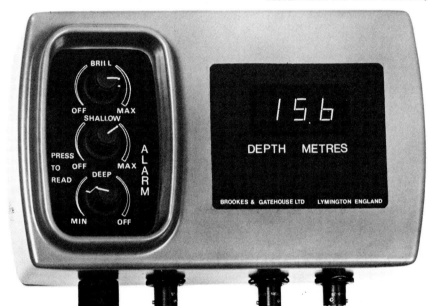

Seascribe II chart recording Echo Sounder.

much as two-fifths if the hull is $\frac{1}{2}''$ thick at the point of mounting. Apart from the oil interface between the transducer and the hull the reduction in depth potential is caused by the density of the glass mat in the resin – the greater the amount of glass the more the depth potential is reduced.

Bearing in mind both cost and requirements the best choice of echo sounder for the average cruising yacht is undoubtedly one of the battery-operated instantaneous reading type.

Logs Any cruising yacht which makes passages of more than a few miles must be able to plot a D.R. position at any time, and it is therefore important quickly to be able to establish 'distance run'.

At present there are a variety of logs available – in fact the choice is surprisingly wide. One of the earliest logs in common use was the Dutchman's Log and it is worth remembering the principle against the time when the modern instrument may fail. Briefly, all that is required is a piece of wood, which is dropped over the bows and timed over a set distance alongside the vessel. If the distance is say twenty feet then the speed can easily be calculated (100 feet per minute = 1 knot). Reasonably accurate results can be obtained by careful observation and timing.

Modern logs may be divided into the following groups:
Walker towed log.
Impeller-type mechanical logs.
Impeller-type electrical logs.
Electro-magnetic logs.
Doppler logs.
The Walker log is one of the oldest types which is still in use. It is simple in operation, robust and most unlikely to fail, and

consists of an impeller towed on the end of a special line, the latter operating a mechanical counting device which measures distance run and speed. It has the great advantage that if the impeller is fouled by seaweed it can be quickly hauled aboard and cleaned. It is an extremely reliable piece of equipment, although perhaps by electronic standards a slightly cumbersome one. The disadvantage is that it does not register accurately at speeds of less than about 2 knots as the impeller tends to sink and may under-register with a heavy following sea. Mechanical impeller logs have a small rotator or impeller mounted on the outside of the hull below the waterline, the impeller drives a steel wire cable (like a speedometer cable) which operates a meter showing speed and distance run. This is another useful and reliable type of instrument which is comparatively inexpensive, but it suffers from the disadvantage that weed or barnacles etc. may adversely affect its performance and, generally speaking, it is necessary to slip the boat to clear it – unless one is prepared to do some diving. Later and more expensive types have the facility of withdrawal into the vessel whilst afloat. Basic types are priced from £50. The impeller-type electrical log consists of a very small nylon impeller containing a magnet, the rotation of which induces electrical pulses in a small coil mounted in the body of the underwater unit. The impulses are fed into an amplifier which operates the speed and distance meters. Messrs. Brookes and Gatehouse 'Harrier' speedometer and log is a good example of this type of unit with retractable impeller. The 'Stowe' electronic log uses

the same principle of operation but its impeller is towed on the end of an electrical cable, which avoids the necessity for any skin fittings and thereby reduces the cost of installation.

Electro-magnetic logs work on the principle of measuring the voltage between two sensors in an electrical field, the sensors being mounted at the extremity of a transducer which is mounted in an insulating skin fitting and is retractable. It has the obvious advantage of having no moving parts and forming a very small protuberance on the outside of the hull. A good example of this type is the 'Seafarer' log manufactured by Electronic Laboratories.

The most recent development in the field of logs is the utilization of the 'doppler principle' for speed measurement. This works on the principle that the frequency of a sound wave transmitted from a moving object appears to alter as it passes a fixed point. Theoretically the principle probably offers the best solution to speed measurement as it is completely unaffected by any influence except the movement of the vessel relative to the sea bed, and therefore completely eliminates the need for any drift calculations.

Wind Speed and Direction Indicators These instruments are not as necessary for the average cruising yacht as they are for the offshore racer whose fine sail-trimming may mean the difference between success and failure, and where the information is part of the basic data required for feeding into a sailing performance computer. Wind direction indication is very useful to the cruising man when he is on a dead run down-wind and enables him to

Seafarer Electro Magnetic Log

weigh up the chances of a gybe. On the other hand, however, it could be argued that a cruising yacht in these circumstances should not be running dead before the wind . . . but sufficiently off the wind to bring it comfortably on the quarter – in other words tacking downward.

Wind speed indication is useful in connection with sail changes. For example, as a result of experience it may be decided to change down from the No. 1 genoa at Force 4, and so this becomes a routine matter. Now, occasions may arise when conditions are particularly good, with bright sunshine, and unless the routine is observed, the genoa may be carried until a change down is long overdue and which becomes correspondingly difficult. . . . Wind speed and direction indicators are therefore helpful, but they are not as essential as a good log. Taking into account the exposed position of this gear and its inaccessability, it is better to wait until you can afford to buy good equipment rather than settling for the cheapest early on. Messrs. Brooks and Gatehouse manufacture a complete range of equipment covering all likely requirements, but – the average cruising man will probably

regard a wind speed indicator as a luxury to be acquired when all other demands on his wallet have been satisfied.

Auto-Pilots During the last few years auto-pilots have come into fairly general use in comparatively small cruising yachts. The impetus for this development probably came from the wind-operated self-steering systems developed by the long-distance single-handed yachtsmen of the last few decades. There is much to be said for a device which enables the skipper of a weakly-crewed

family cruiser to leave the tiller for lengthy periods to carry out his other jobs on board, knowing that the boat will remain on course whilst he is otherwise engaged.

In the size of yacht we are dealing with there are two types of unit: the single-piston type for use with a tiller only and the motorised-drum type which can be used to operate either tiller or wheel steering. Both systems have a magnetic sensor for steering a magnetic course and usually have a wind vane sensor for maintaining a

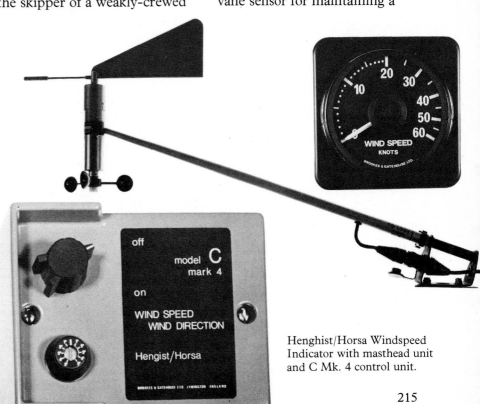

Henghist/Horsa Windspeed Indicator with masthead unit and C Mk. 4 control unit.

course relative to wind direction as an optional extra.

The magnetic sensor unit can encompass a wider sphere of operations as it will perform perfectly well in a flat calm, while under the auxiliary, when the wind vane would be useless of course. The simplest and most easily-fitted type for tiller steering is the piston type, a good example of which is the 'Autohelm 1000' made by Nautech Ltd. This model is suitable for yachts up to about 35 ft L.O.A. whilst a larger unit, the '2000', is made for tiller-steered yachts of any size. Electronic Laboratories also produce a very effective model called the 'Seacourse', and have recently introduced a smaller model, the 'Mini-Seacourse', suitable for tiller-steered yachts up to 30 ft in length.

The drum type of unit is needed where the vessel has wheel steering. A separate drum is fixed to the wheel and two lines from the motorised drum of the pilot are attached to it. Due to its complexity this type tends to be more expensive than the piston type used for tillers, although it can be employed with the equal success on a tiller. An example is the Sharp 'Tillermate', with the facility for using a wind vane sensor if required.

One of the points to consider when purchasing an autopilot is the electrical load on the ship's battery. The power requirement obviously varies according to the conditions, but a drain of 2 amps must be budgetted for and it will be necessary to ensure that the battery is of adequate capacity and that recharging facilities are provided on board.

Electronic Equipment - General comments Ever-accelerating developments in the electronic world, including the rapid development and use of microprocessors, lead to the most modern equipment becoming out-dated in a comparatively short space of time and nowhere is this more in evidence than in the sphere of direction-finding equipment. As well as improvements in in range and capacity, the physical bulk of the equipment is becoming smaller and reliability is increasing. There is little doubt that D.F. sets utilizing satellite navigation will be common place in a few years and they will probably cost no more than a good electro-magnetic log does now relatively speaking.

When he is selecting electronic gear the novice may be puzzled by the wide variation in price of equipment with apparently similar performance. In some cases the reason is obvious even to the inexperienced eye but in others it is less so. Some manufacturers have no overseas agents and, therefore, their operating costs under guarantee are much less than others who offer a good guarantee service which is effectively world-wide – and for which, quite rightly, one has to pay extra. The yacht cruising to several foreign countries is obviously in a much better position 'repair-wise' if equipment is bought from a manufacturer with agents in those countries. Therefore, if you are only cruising in a fairly limited area it would be reasonable to consider purchasing less expensive equipment. Another point to look into is weather-proofing – a good hermetically-sealed unit which will not suffer with internal condensation under any conditions will obviously cost more than an instrument which is not so well constructed and which will obviously have a shorter life. Finally, when you are buying equipment and have decided that a particular service meets your requirements both technically and in price, ask yourself 'does it look well made and sufficiently robust to work in a testing environment?'

Opposite top: Seacourse Auto-pilot.
Opposite right: Mini Seacourse Auto-pilot.

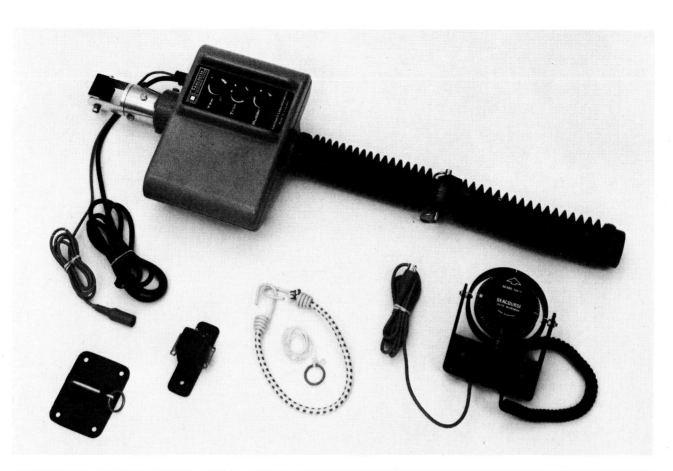

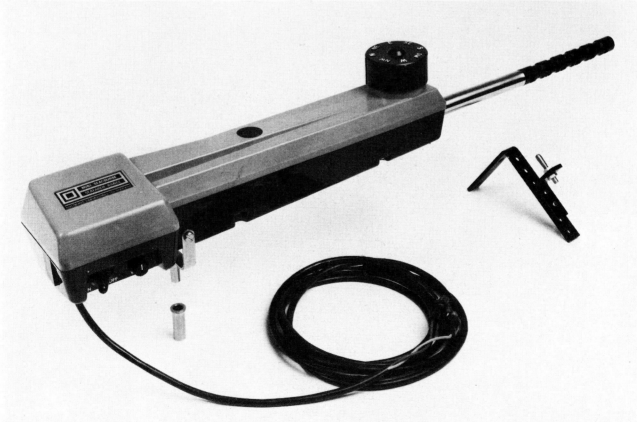

Self Steering Self steering in various forms was developed by the early single-handed, long-range cruising yachtsmen, and from the small yacht's point of view it has one very big advantage – there is no electrical load to drain the battery. . . .

There are three basic types of self-steering gear: the simple wind vane, the trim tab and the pendulum servo system. The simple wind vane system is the most elementary form of control and consists of a vertically-pivoted wind vane which is directly connected by lines to the tiller. Its disadvantages are that a very large vane is required to exert a reasonable amount of power and that it develops little power when close on course. The second generation wind vane system employs a horizontally-hinged wind vane, which is much more responsive and develops more power, still considerably less than a pendulum servo system, but it has the advantage that a competent handyman could construct one for himself.

The trim tab servo can only be fitted to a boat with a counter-hung rudder or one that protrudes beyond the stern. The trim tab is, in effect, a small rudder hung on the back end of the main rudder. The wind vane, producing a comparatively small force, moves the trim tab which in turn alters the direction of the main rudder, thus altering the vessels's course. By this means a much greater force is applied to the main rudder than would be the case if the wind vane was coupled directly to it.

The principle of the independent servo blade system was originally developed by the well-known yachtsman Col. 'Blondie' Hasler. Called the

pendulum servo system, it is one of the best-known types in use today. The pendulum or servo blade is suspended over the stern of the vessel and is free to swing from side to side, the prime mover is again a wind vane which is coupled to the servo blade. When an alteration in course is required the wind vane moves the servo blade in the same manner as it

would a rudder, but as the servo blade is pivoted at its top end only, it immediately swings to one side or the other, depending upon the direction required. This movement is then transmitted to the tiller and thereby operates the rudder, the power produced being in direct ratio to the vessel's speed through the water. This type of equipment can be used

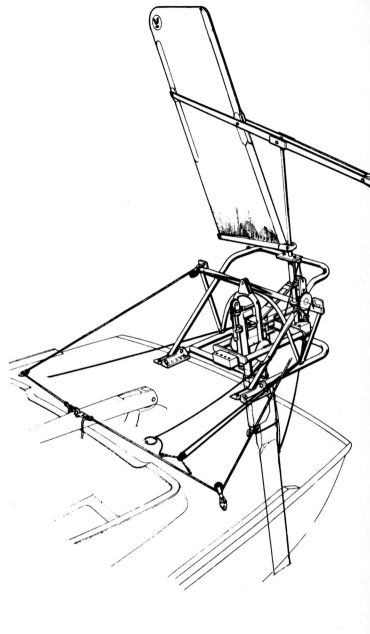

to control the vessel under all conditions, the limiting factor being the mechanical strength of the gear.

A fourth type, which is really a development of standard wind vane gears, has an additional rudder mounted on the stern and controlled by a pendulum servo system. The rudder is smaller than the main rudder and is balanced to

assist the servo system.

There are a number of makes of self-steering gear but provided you understand the basic principles it should not be difficult to choose one that will prove to be a great boon to the short-handed cruising man.

Left: Type Sp Hasler self steering gear.
Above: Hasler Vane small pendulum–servo gear for yachts up to 9m (30ft) long.

Appendix 2 - Ships Husbandry

Ship's Papers

Legal requirements regarding ship's papers vary from country to country but all countries will require seeing some statement of official ownership and country of origin when a foreign yacht is visiting their waters. Any vessel which is officially registered in its home country will find its registration certificate acceptable everywhere. It is not, however, necessary to be officially registered to obtain papers enabling you to sail abroad without hindrance; the International Certificate for Pleasure Navigation issued by the Royal Yachting Association in England, and by comparable authorities in other countries, for unregistered yachts is universally acceptable. In some cases ownership certificates issued by well-known yacht clubs (such as the Cruising Association) are also accepted abroad.

At present it appears that certain countries may require Certificates of Competence to be held by owners of yachts, particularly if they are sailing in inland waterways. In view of the damage that an incompetent helmsman of a power boat may do, you can appreciate some authorities feeling that it is not unreasonable to require some proof of reasonable ability in boat handling before they permit navigation in their waters.

However, irrespective of whether it is officially required or not, a certificate is a useful piece of paper to have about you when dealing with foreign maritime authorities. Facilities to obtain Certificates of Competence exist in most countries. In England the R.Y.A. have prescribed courses, both theoretical and practical, leading up to such awards as the National Motor Launch and Power Boat Certificate and Yachtmaster Certificates, both offshore and Ocean. Apart from the possible necessity for possessing a Certificate of Competence it is obviously sound practice to improve one's knowledge of sailing in all its aspects – which should be the aim of every yachtsman. Incidentally, some insurance companies grant a premium discount to holders of the Yachtmaster's Certificate.

Insurance

To its owner a yacht probably represents years of hard saving, and possibly a financial commitment second only to his house. Therefore the importance of adequate insurance as a financial life-belt against accidents due to the owner's or third parties' short-comings, cannot be stressed too highly. Marine underwriting in the United Kingdom began in Edward Lloyd's Coffee House in Lombard Street in the City of London in the seventeenth century, and much of the wording used in marine policies today has derived from that time; hence its old-world quaintness and apparent obscurity to the layman. In fact the owner who has read his policy will no doubt be impressed to find that he is insured against perils of the sea, including action by 'Enemies, Pirates, Rovers' etc. and 'Detachments of all Kings, Princes and Peoples'. . . . However, when it comes to ascertaining his coverage in more mundane matters the position is sometimes far from clear!

A simple initial approach to the problem of insuring one's yacht is to obtain proposal forms from one or two companies, which normally include a summary of the general cover and they will assist you in deciding the extent of the cover which seems desirable.

The owner will probably have a fair idea of the market value of his vessel, but it would be a prudent step to check this annually and, at the same time, to make an inventory of all its equipment – tenders, outboard motors, radio equipment, and so on. This procedure should enable you to avoid the risk of finding yourself under-insured, bearing in mind that, with inflation at its present rate, the value of certain types of yacht can double in as little as five years. . . . The under-insured owner runs the risk of the insurers applying the policy condition of 'average' which briefly means that if his yacht is insured for 50% of value, he will only receive 50% of the cost of any losses, whether for a small knock or a total loss.

Liability to third parties can, in certain circumstances, be limited by Section 503 of the Merchant Shipping Act to the value of the vessel. However, it is strongly recommended that the policy has a third party indemnity, and liability to passengers should not be over-looked either.

General points which should be considered, and the policy extended accordingly, include:

1. Will cruising be restricted to coastal and inland waters?
2. Should transit by trailer on land be covered?
3. Will there be participation in racing?
4. Is cover required for out-board engines lost over the side?
5. Is it intended to charter the yacht to other persons?

On the question of the cost of the marine policy, it is advisable to obtain more than one quotation, and employing the services of a marine insurance broker should save much time and confusion. When the quotations have been obtained the broker can advise which is the most favourable, balancing the extent of cover offered against the premium demanded. Costs can be reduced if the owner is prepared to accept an 'excess clause' by which he pays, for example, part of every claim. Most insurers will also offer a 'No Claims Bonus' which will help to reduce insurance costs over the years of loss-free cruising. Finally, when the policy is received you should read it carefully, and any points which you don't understand should be referred to the broker for clarification. It is far better for the owner to have a reasonable knowledge of the policy's scope and its limitations, than to find out about it after a loss which it does not cover.

Tools

The owner who is a good 'D.I.Y.-type' will need little advice on the subject of tools. He will probably have an excellent kit already and probably feels competent to tackle any job that does not actually require a salvage tug.

The newcomer to sailing should consider the full implications of off-shore cruising. One day he may have to carry out an unaided and immediate repair to some part of his gear, and there is no assistance at sea except in the ultimate emergency when the Life-boat Services have been alerted. The best advice on tool kits for boats applies in any sphere: buy the very best you can afford and look after it properly. A novice will do better with a first-class tool than with an inferior one. There is no consolation in having saved money on a tool if, when it is put to the test in difficult conditions, it proves miserably inadequate. Before setting out to buy the tool kit first consider the type of sailing that is to be done and hence the size of kit that is needed. The vessel that is only going to be used for week-end sailing – possibly never going out of sight of land – will only need a fairly basic kit, whereas a serious off-shore cruiser must take the matter more seriously and be prepared to cope with a far greater range of jobs than the week-ender.

Two suggested lists are given below:

Basic kit

1. Hammer.
2. Set of spanners for auxiliary engine.
3. Pliers.
4. Screwdrivers.
5. Adjustable spanner.
6. If petrol-fuelled auxiliary – spanner and wire cleaning brush for plugs.

Additional Tools for the Off-shore Cruiser

1. Hand drill.
2. Six assorted twist drills.
3. Assorted files – say two round and two flat.
4. Small hacksaw with spare blades.
5. Padsaw handle and blade.
6. Longnose pliers.
7. Cold chisel.
8. Combination saw.
9. Large Stillson Wrench.
10. Small vice mounted on a board.
11. Soldering iron, flux and solder.
12. Molegrips.

If funds permit a small electrical test set, (combined voltmeter and ohm-meter) can save hours in tracing electrical faults, making it a worthwhile investment when you consider the ever-increasing amount of electrical equipment to be found even on a small boat.

The area where most thought is probably needed is in connection with spanners. A modern cruising boat will probably only need metric, A.F., and possibly B.A. spanners, whereas a boat with older equipment may require Whitworth, and B.S.F. as well. This sounds rather complicated and expensive, but basically the requirement is to have a really good set of the appropriate set spanners for the auxiliary (if these have not been provided by the manufacturer) and good adjustable spanners for other equipment where practicable. Adjustable spanners must be of the best quality – poorly-made ones will quickly ruin nuts. At least two sizes of standard screwdrivers are required, together with the necessary Phillips-type screwdrivers to deal with the various sizes of Phillips screws on board. A good hand-drill with, say, six assorted twist drills, together with a couple of round files to enable you to enlarge holes where the largest drill is not quite big enough. A small hacksaw (with spare blades) is an important piece of equipment, while a padsaw handle to hold broken hacksaw blades can be very useful in an emergency. Remember that you may have some very large nuts on board (on the stern gland for example) for which a Stillson wrench is really the only answer. Pliers of course are necessary items and a pair of the long-nose variety can be extraordinarily useful for getting into difficult corners. A few assorted files will be required sooner or later, and, together with one of the combination saws' that will cut anything, should complete the kit apart from one final item: a vice. A small vice, mounted on a board which can be fixed somewhere, between cockpit seats, for example, is an invaluable 'third hand'.

Ship's Stores

Anyone who has cruised for some years in either sail or power usually has his own definite ideas on what should be carried as ship's stores (including provisions and medical stores). Assuming the term 'stores' to include deck and engine spares the amount to be carried should, like tools, be related to the type of cruising you intend to carry

out. The week-ender need only carry spares which might be classified as 'first-aid', whereas the off-shore cruiser which may leave its home port for two or three weeks should carry equipment able to cope with any reasonably foreseeable eventuality.

In view of the multiplicity of engines it is impossible to give explicit advice on what 'spares' should be carried. Perhaps the best course of action is to ask the particular manufacturer of the engine in your boat for his recommendations and, in fact, many manufacturers supply packs, already made-up, of the more commonly-used spares required for their engines. It may happen that some part, such as the impellor for the water pump, is needed but, because there is no local agent in the port where you happen to be, lengthy delays occur while it is obtained. This is a good reason for carrying spares abroad. Suggestions of stores for a sail-boat or a motor cruiser are listed below in case the owner may not feel competent to fit them himself.

Engine

1. One set of spares as recommended by the manufacturer.
2. One spare dynamo (or alternator) drive-belt.
3. Lubricating oil.
4. Gearbox oil.
5. Stern gland grease.
6. Cylinder-head jointing compound
7. Dismantling fluid (Plus gas or similar proprietory fluid).

The electrical stores on a modern cruiser, with a wide range of equipment, should contain a number of items but fortunately these are light-weight and occupy little space.

Electrical

1. Spare fuses for all circuits.
2. Spare bulbs for lights including navigation lights.
3. Wire and connector blocks for circuit repairs.
4. Spare batteries for: radio, echo sounder, torch etc.
5. Water-proofing aerosol (WD 40, Holts Anti-damp or equivalent).
6. Insulating tape.

Deck Stores

1. Sufficient rope for reeving a spare halyard.
2. Whipping twine.
3. 3 mm line for lashings.
4. Two or three 'D' shackles.
5. Four Crosbie clips and a twenty foot (5 m) lenth of rigging wire (will probably never be used but rather a comfort to have on board).
6. One spare bottlescrew.
7. Assorted split pins.
8. Assorted nuts and bolts.
9. Monel wire for seizings.
10. P.V.C. tape.
11. Spares for inflatable dinghy (patches and solution).
12. G.R.P. repair pack including resin, glass mat and gel-coat.
13. Bedding-down compound (silicone rubber or equivalent).
14. Spare aerosols for Fog-horn.

The lists above do not claim to be comprehensive but they are intended to stimulate thoughts as to what you should carry on your own boat. In addition to deck stores there should also be spares for the lavatory and the cooker. Should the latter be of the gas-type mounted in gimbals, the stores should certainly include a spare length of flexible gas pipe.

Safety equipment

It has been said that the emergency for which you have

prepared rarely happens. On this basis any money spent on safety equipment is a good investment! Regulations regarding safety equipment vary from country to country – in the United Kingdom for example the Department of Trade and Industry makes recommendations for yachts up to 45 ft in length, and lays down compulsory requirements for boats in excess of that length. You should however adopt the attitude that safety on a yacht is of paramount importance and thus should never look upon the Recommendations and Regulations merely as irksome restrictions. Remember that when you are at sea, whether it is 'fire-on-board' or 'man-overboard' – you are alone. *And as Skipper you are solely responsible for the lives of your crew – and also for your own. . . !*

The following summary of safety equipment taken from the Department of Trade and Industry (D.T.I.) Recommendations for Safety Equipment on Pleasure Craft 5.5 m to 13.7 m (18 to 45 ft) should be regarded as a good basic list of equipment to be carried on any yacht, irrespective of any local 'home port' regulations which may be less thorough. Certain items – charts for example – are such a fundamental part of the equipment of any well-found sea-going yacht that it may seem strange to see them listed as 'Safety Equipment'. . . .

Personal Safety Equipment
One lifejacket to B.S.I. specification for each crew member (not accepted if wholly dependent on oral inflation). One safety harness to B.S.I. specification for each crew member on a sailing yacht and one or two more as necessary

for use on deck in a motor-cruiser.

Rescue Equipment for man overboard At least two life-buoys, one within easy reach of helmsman and fitted with a self-igniting light if sailing at night. One hundred feet (20 m) buoyant line, within easy reach of helmsman (minimum breaking strain 250 lbs = 115 kg).

Other Flotation Equipment if Vessel sails more than 3 miles off-shore Inflatable life-raft capable of carrying all on-board. Should be of D.T.I. accepted type or equivalent, carried on deck or in a locker opening directly on deck. To be serviced annually.
OR
Rigid dinghy with permanent (not inflatable) buoyancy complete with oars and rowlocks, carried on deck.
OR
Inflatable dinghy built with two compartments, one of which must be kept fully inflated, with oars and rowlocks secured.

Fire-fighting Equipment For vessels with cooking facilities and engines – two fire extinguishers each of not less than 1.4 kg (3 lb) capacity dry powder or equivalent. Alternatives to dry powder extinguishers are CO^2 or foam extinguishers, B.C.F. or B.T.M. extinguishers may be carried but fumes given off are toxic and dangerous in confined spaces.
Two buckets with lanyards.
One bag of sand – useful for containing burning fuel spillage.

General Equipment Anchors – two with appropriate size warp or chain (if warp used at least 5.5 m (3 fathoms) of chain between anchor and warp).
Bilge pump.
Efficient compass (and spare).
Charts (covering intended area

of operations).
Distress flares – 6 with 2 of the rocket/parachute type.
Daylight distress smoke signal.
Tow rope – of adequate size and length.
First Aid box – with anti-sea sickness tablets.
Radio receiver – for weather forecasts.
Water-resistant torch.
Radar reflector of adequate performance, as large as can conveniently be carried, preferably mounted at least 3 m (10 ft) above sea level.
Life lines.
Engine tool kit.
Name or number painted prominently on the vessel or on the dodgers in letters or figures at least 22 cm (9 in) high.

This extract from the D.T.I. Recommendations contains the basic items with which any well-found yacht will be equipped, but there are a few points worth mentioning about them. The buoyant line suggested will be more useful if one end is secured to the vessel and the other has a small float or buoy attached to it, and the whole fitted up so that it can be quickly released by the helmsan. An addition to the flares list should be at least four hand-held 'mini flares' to be carried by each crew member for use in a 'man-overboard' emergency at night.

An additional item of equipment which should be carried (if space permits) is a small rigid boarding ladder (see page 104). Alternatively, if the transom design permits it, fixed let-down steps could be a godsend in an emergency.

A medical handbook or first aid book should always be available on board. *Reed's Nautical Almanac* contains a first aid section written by a doctor with very extensive long-range cruising experience in yachts, and it gives full details of the first aid cabinet requirements (including drugs) together with the relevant information for diagnosing and dealing with the type of cases likely to be met at sea.

Remember – medical advice can always be quickly obtained via a Shore Station if you have V.H.F. If you haven't, then flying the International Code Flag 'W', or sending the morse signal 'dot, dash, dash' meaning 'I require medical assistance', may help if it is seen or heard by a passing vessel. Depending on the size of the yacht, a dan-buoy (a 6-foot staff with flotation and a flag on the top), if it could be accommodated, would be extremely useful for marking the spot in a 'man-overboard situation' should there be any sea running.

Regarding fire-fighting equipment: powder-type extinguishers are efficient and safe in operation, only if the seat of the fire can be attacked directly. In other words, the stream of powder will not go round corners into restricted spaces. Whereas a motor-cruiser with a large engine installation may well have an automatic foam extinguisher, the average sailing yacht will normally be equipped with only two hand-held extinguishers and it is here that the owner must decide for himself what type he should settle for. The dry powder type is absolutely safe but has certain disadvantages which could, in certain circumstances, add considerably to the difficulties of the predicament. The alternative, of course, is a vapourising liquid-type – such as the B.C.F. (bromo-chloro-difluoro-methane) extinguisher.

The danger with this type is that when the vapour comes into contact with flames, toxic gases are given off – in confined spaces with no ventilation this is naturally dangerous. In the average yacht of up to say 10m or about 35 ft in length, there is little chance of anyone being in a confined space, shut off from the open atmosphere. Taking these factors into consideration the B.C.F. extinguisher has definite advantages over the dry powder type. For full information on the D.T.I. Recommendations and Regulations see 'Safety in Small Craft', published by Her Majesty's Stationery Office; or Reed's Nautical Almanac.

First Aid
There are many excellent handbooks and pamphlets on first aid at sea available written by well-qualified medical people. Suffice to say that anyone who is cruising off-shore may be out of reach of medical aid for perhaps twenty-four hours or even more, and it is therefore important for a first aid cabinet to be kept on board and for someone to have some rudimentary first aid knowledge. Inevitably the skipper will at some time have to deal with cuts and burns, and possibly even a broken limb, and the correct treatment early on will materially speed the patient's recovery.

Apart from incidents such as these the most difficult conditions that may have to be dealt with are apparent death by drowning, hypothermia (exposure to cold) and shock.

A case of apparent death by drowning is, of course, easily recognisable and must be dealt with IMMEDIATELY using the mouth-to-mouth method of

artificial resuscitation. It is vital to begin AT ONCE – SECONDS COUNT. A card of instructions on the procedure should always be displayed in the immediate vicinity of the First Aid box.

Hypothermia, i.e. exposure to cold, is dangerous, and many who die following immersion do so from hypothermia, not from drowning. Immediate and correct treatment is vital. Similarly, shock following an accident may considerably complicate matters if it is not dealt with properly.

Sea sickness may not perhaps be regarded as an emergency but, if it is allowed to continue for a prolonged period, it too is dangerous. Anyone susceptible to sea sickness should find out as soon as possible which particular type of anti-sea sickness pills suits them best and make sure that one is taken in good time – say one hour before the advent of bad weather.

Basic First Aid Box
Sterile non-adhesive dressing.
Gauze packs – five large and five small.
Cotton wool.
One triangular bandage.
One crêpe bandage.
Roll of adhesive plaster.
Transparent waterproof tape.
Rolls of 1 in and 2 in bandage.
Assorted safety pins.
Clinical thermometer.
Scissors.
Sea sickness tablets.
Splints.
Reflective blanket (space type).
Regarding drugs, the selection should be made after consulting the appropriate medical first aid guide, or the first aid section of Reed's Nautical Almanac.

Clothing
For comfortable cruising, good

wet weather clothing is an essential item of personal equipment and it pays to buy the best, which is not necessarily the most expensive. (Keep in mind that although some of the fashionable lightweight nylon suits are attractive they are not always suitable for sustained spells of bad weather.) A yacht chandler is not necessarily the best person to advise on the subject and, if you are buying for the first time, probably the best line of action is to ask several experienced yachtsmen for their opinions. It is unlikely that they will all agree but at least the knowledge gained will help you in making a sensible choice.

Regarding personal clothing the golden rule, unless one is sailing in the tropics, is to have plenty of warm clothing aboard. Stowage is always a problem in little ships but a supply of strong plastic bags (dustbin liners) can ease it. For example if all shirts are packed in one bag, socks in another and so on, it is much easier to find things, to keep them dry and also to stow them, as they can be thrust into places which would not normally be used.

The Galley
Cookers and Cooking The longer the cruises that are undertaken the more important becomes the galley in its role as the nerve centre of the ship. To the weekender the galley is primarily the place for the preparation of hot drinks and simple hot meals, some of which will undoubtedly have been prepared ashore. All the same, demands will be heavy on the galley of a small family cruiser (probably complete with two children) off on a two or three week cruise. In these

circumstances a well-designed galley is a 'must'. Even if the boat's designer was a little casual in his approach to the problem, quite often a modest amount of work by the owner can transform the galley into a useful centre of activity. The work normally consists of modifying, or adding to, the stowage of equipment as most shortcomings occur due to the mistaken apprehension that a frying pan is the sole item of equipment needed.

The galley preferably should be located amidships where the motion is least but it must also be so situated that ventilation is adequate and, ideally, it should be placed apart, where the cook can pen himself or herself in and be out of the way of anyone moving about in the cabin. The latter point depends on the size of the yacht of course and in a small family cruiser usually it represents unattainable luxury. The minimum requirements in the galley, apart from stowage space, should be regarded as a small hand-pump fed from a jerrican, together with a cooker having two burners and a grill – if the cooker has an oven then the arrangements can almost be regarded as the ultimate in vessels up to say 10m (30ft) in length.

In deciding upon the type of cooker to be installed in a thirty foot (10m) yacht the choice lies between calor gas, methylated spirit or paraffin. For obvious reasons solid fuel or electricity are impracticable except in very large yachts.

First take the **methylated spirit** (or alcohol) cooker. With its low fire risk it has attractions and is most favoured in the United States of America due to its being approved by the U.S. Coastguard. Cookers of

this type have the merit of being clean and silent in operation, together with a comparatively low capital and installation cost and no vices, but the running costs are probably higher than with parafin.

Cookers using **paraffin** under pressure have the great advantage of comparatively cheap fuel that is universally available, combined with no great fire risk and no danger of explosion. The main disadvantages with most of the cookers is the necessity for carrying a separate preheating fuel (methylated spirit) and the tendency for the burners to carbon up if they are run at very low flame level for any length of time. In addition, if preheating is not properly carried out there is always the possibility of an alarming-looking flare-up. There are now some cookers in which the preheating is carried out with paraffin and which thus avoid the necessity of carrying a second fuel on board.

Calor gas is sometimes regarded as a dangerous fuel because of the risk of explosion if it is not properly installed and correctly used, but it probably offers the greatest attraction to yachts cruising in Continental and United Kingdom waters. Apart from the obvious advantages of no preheating and complete controllability, the fuel is readily available, always bearing in mind that the Calor gas system will need an adaptor to accommodate Continental Camping Gaz bottles. When Calor gas is the cooking medium the installation must be properly carried out and operated in a sensible manner, when the possible explosion risk may be regarded as negligible. The gas, being

225

heavier than air, will sink into the bilges and it may be argued that the small spillage that occurs when ever a burner is lit may accumulate and form an explosive mixture in the bilges. However, this risk can be eliminated by pumping the bilges every few days. Similarly if a burner has blown out unnoticed for a little while, it would be prudent to pump the bilges before relighting the stove. The installation should be carried out in solid drawn annealed copper tubing using compression type joints, together with any flexible tubing connections manufactured to the appropriate national specification. Gas bottle accommodation should be so arranged that the bottles are above water level and any gas leakage drains over the side and not into the bilges. The gas should be turned off when not in use so that ideally the bottle should be placed in an easily accessible position.

Many small 'production line' cruisers are not fitted with gimballed cookers the reason given being that gimballing requires additional space for the cooker in which to swing and also that in any case the crew of such a boat do not normally cook under way. Both contentions contain some truth but, even if you do not propose to cook under way, it is good practice to have the cooker gimballed if possible. Remember that when you are at anchor or moored the close passage of a motor launch driven with more enthusiasm than consideration, may have painful results if a kettle of boiling water is suddenly shot from the cooker. Cookers should of course have fiddles, preferably with adjustable sections to hold saucepans in position. If the

latter are not fitted, a useful alternative can be made with curtain springs with the plastic covering stripped off, fitted with a hook at each end and tightly stretched between the fiddle rails.

Meals When you start sailing it is easy to assume that meals on board will be identical with those at home or else that the menus will be limited to fried beef burgers, with an occasional dish of curry. Neither alternative is strictly true. Admittedly if one has an oven on board it is possible to live exactly as one does at home but is this necessarily desirable? Cruising should be a change and the cook should be able to join in any pre-dinner drinks with an easy conscience and no worry about the meal.

The following notes on provisioning ship cooking may perhaps be of some help to those starting cruising. It is assumed that the vessel does not have a refrigerator and that too much reliance is not placed on an ice box.

Equipment: The minimum requirements in a good basic galley are:
One thick frying pan (large as possible).
One thick saucepan (large – with lid).
One small saucepan.
One kettle (whistling).
Egg whisk.
Cheese grater.
Can opener (wall mounting).
Chopping board.
One or two cook's knives.
One wooden spoon.
At least two thermos flasks (one with a wide neck).
Plastic containers for dried foods.
Aluminium foil.
Paper kitchen roll.
Washing-up liquid and brush.

Until one becomes reasonably experienced provisioning a ship may present one or two problems, and the omission of some vital item cannot always easily be corrected by dashing out to the nearest supermarket. The following list is suggested as basic ship's stores, possibly bulk purchased at the beginning of the season (depending on storage space). If the stocks are maintained at a reasonable level it means that a weekend trip can be quickly arranged without doubts about food stocks, except fresh provisions (with the list suggested these could even be omitted).

Provisions
Canned Meats
Stewed beef.
Beef burgers.
Pork burgers.
Minced meat (beef).
Corned beef.
Steak pies.
Ham.
Steak and kidney pies.
Canned Vegetables
Celery hearts.
Peppers.
Tomatoes.
Mushrooms.
Baked beans.
Peas.
Asparagus.
Canned Fish
Tuna.
Dried Vegetables
Onions.
Potatoes.
Beans.
Peas.
Rice.
Butter beans.
Miscellaneous
Tomato Purée.
Plain flour.
Pepper.
Salt.
Dried Milk.
Spaghetti.
Spices.
Digestive and dry biscuits.

Margarine.
Bovril and Oxo cubes.
Dried soups.
Cloves of garlic.
Eggs.
Cooking oil.
Canned pineapples.

The list may appear inordinately long and too bulky, but obviously it must be trimmed to fit the boat. Packets of dried vegetables for example can be substituted for canned peas and beans and will effect big economies in space. It is also surprising what can be packed into odd corners which would not otherwise be used, even some bilge compartments remain dry and enable heavy tinned goods to be stowed at low level, leaving higher level stowage for light goods and thus not upsetting the trim of the ship. Speaking of trim – watch the inclinometer when stowing heavy goods, its surprising how easy it is to upset the trim by a few degrees in a small boat. Incidentally you will note that none of the tinned meats contain vegetables as they are almost invariably less tasty than separately canned meat and vegetables mixed in the cooking pot. When you are actually on the point of departing for a cruise the necessary fresh fruit, vegetables, cheese and so on can be put on board (margarine incidentally keeps much better than butter though the latter can be bought in small quantities when required for cooking).

The first cruise It is unlikely that any passages will be undertaken which will exceed twenty-four hours in length and from a cook's point of view in these circumstances the preparation of a main meal at sea is not essential or even desirable. However, it is important to have readily available a good supply of hot drinks, soup and such items as chocolate, fruit cake, cheese and also glucose sweets. The thermos flasks are now invaluable – they will have been filled with hot water before starting out (one of them preferably with soup) and this will reduce the necessaity for heating water whilst on passage. Incidentally, any hot water left in the kettle should always be stored in a thermos flask – it saves fuel and helps with the washing-up. From the outset the cook must make it clearly understood that, from the start of sailing, meals will consist of breakfast, a snack lunch (cheese and biscuits) and a main meal in the evening, even when the ship is in harbour. The family cruise usually seems to start with a rush down to the boat the night before, complete with a surprising quantity of last minute items – don't try and prepare an elaborate meal that night – bring down a prepared meal such as steak and mushroom pie with suet crust, followed by fruit and cheese.

The first day Have a really good breakfast before getting underway, with a minimum of liquid for anyone who is prone to seasickness.

Mid morning – cups of soup or Oxo with biscuits (tea or coffee best avoided by queasy stomachs).

Mid-day – Chicken joints and ham sandwiches (prepared previous day and wrapped in cling film), knob of cheese, fruit etc., coffee.

Mid afternoon – Fruit cake or chocolate, drink of choice.

Evening meal – Hopefully taken in harbour. If not, and conditions permitting, heat up casserole with meat and vegetables in it (prepared previous day). Serve in bowls and eat with spoons. If conditions are bad, cups of soup again (with sherry in if possible).

The general pattern of eating on board depends on several variables: individual requirements, facilities in the galley, weather conditions etc. (and of course the expertise of the cook). Bearing in mind the necessity for one good meal a day apart from breakfast, the following recipes are included to give ideas for the main meals. A couple of hints to the first-time cook – get all your materials ready before starting to cook, and don't forget that food should be served on hot plates, easily done over a saucepan in which something is cooking. When mixing things in a sauce-pan always use a wooden spoon.

Recipes
Potatoes Potatoes are a good basic vegetable and, whereas instant potato is extremely useful, when time permits the fresh vegetable should be used. A much better flavour will result if, instead of peeling, they are well scrubbed, eyes cut out, pierced several times with a skewer and boiled for twenty minutes with a teaspoon of salt. They may then be served with skins on or mashed. If an oven is available potatoes baked in their jackets are a welcome change.

Batter Batter is required for various dishes – pancakes, corned beef fritters for example and it should always be prepared at least an hour before use. Pancakes can be made in advance and stored until the following day (interleaved with sheets of greaseproof paper). Batter for pancakes is thinned down with water or milk.
Ingredients: Four heaped

dessertspoons of plain flour; two heaped dessertspoons of dried milk powder; one egg, pinch of salt; *Method*: mix all dry ingredients in basin, make well in centre, drop in one egg and stir in gently, gradually adding a little water to keep mixture smooth and creamy (just thick enough to cover the back of the spoon). For corned beef fritters do not make batter too thin – it will not adhere sufficiently to the meat.

Corned Beef Fritters

Ingredients: batter; one tin of corned beef. *Method*: slice corned beef into four. Have a saucepan or deep frying pan of very hot cooking oil. Dip slices into batter, drain off surplus, drop into hot oil and cook until golden brown. (Surplus batter may be used for pancakes – thinning batter down a little for if it is too thick it will not roll easily).

Cheese and Ham Risotto

Ingredients: one oz butter or margarine; one chopped onion; four oz long grain rice; one chicken stock cube; four oz diced (chopped) cooked meat (corned beef, ham, tongue etc.); four oz grated cheese; salt and pepper. *Method*: Make chicken stock by dissolving cube in one pint of water. Melt butter in saucepan add onion and fry until tender (not brown). Add rice, stir well over heat, then add stock, simmer for 15–20 minutes. Add chopped cooked meat, simmer 5 minutes. Add grated cheese just before serving *Note*: Vegetables to choice; if canned use liquid for making the chicken stock.

Savoury Pancakes *Ingredients*:

batter or ready prepared pancakes; one tin minced beef; one onion; one tin mushrooms. *The sauce*: one heaped dessert spoon powdered milk; one heaped dessertspoon plain flour; one oxo cube; one knob of margarine or butter (walnut size); liquid from mushrooms in tin made up to half a pint by adding water. *Method*: Prepare pancakes (or heat previously prepared ones). Slice and fry onion until almost brown, slice mushrooms (keep liquid) and stir in minced beef and cook until all hot. Spread thickly on pancakes, roll up and place in heat–proof dish with joined side on bottom – keep hot while making sauce. To make sauce mix milk powder, flour and broken oxo cube with margarine in saucepan, stir in mushroom liquid made up to half a pint adding water, place pan on low heat, stirring constantly until a smooth sauce results, (not too thin). Pour over pancakes and heat (in oven) until all ingredients thoroughly hot. *Note*: If no mushroom liquid – add just water. A clove of garlic added with the minced beef improves flavour. Grated cheese could be sprinkled over dish before final heating.

Sweet Stuffed Pancakes

Ingredients: Batter or previously made pancakes; one jar mincemeat (fruit). *Method*: Spread mincemeat thickly on pancakes, roll and place joined side on bottom of heat-proof dish, and warm gently until hot in oven.

Ham or Pork Burgers – with pineapple rings *Ingredients*:

one tin of pork burgers; one tin of pineapple rings. *Method I: using the oven*. Separate pork burgers and place pineapple ring on top of each. Put in oven for twenty to twenty-five minutes. *Method II: using frying pan*. Separate pork burgers and lightly brown on each side in frying pan, brown one side and when turned over to brown the under side, place on top of each a pineapple ring.

Note: if using canned ham use the round tins of sweet cured shoulder and cut across into four round steaks, place on tray (fire-proof), on top of each place one pineapple ring, cook in oven for approximately twenty minutes, being careful not to dry up the ham.

Serve with peas and potatoes boiled in their jackets; potatoes will take twenty to twenty-five minutes. If using dried peas these will cook more quickly if soaked first unless they happen to be those which only need boiling water poured over them, left one minute and strained off.

Ham and Celery with Cheese Sauce

Ingredients: one can ham; one can of celery hearts; four oz of cheese (cheddar); one dessertspoon of dried milk; one knob of butter (walnut size); one-half pint of liquid from celery; one dessertspoon of plain flour. *Method*: Carve ham into very thin slices. If celery hearts are large divide them up. Place celery onto one thin slice of ham, roll up and lay joined side down, in fire-proof dish, continue until all ham and celery needed is ready. *Sauce*: place dried milk, plain flour and knob of butter in saucepan. Stir in liquid slowly until smooth, place on heat, cook slowly stirring all the time, when thick and inclined to bubble, remove from heat and stir in grated cheese, pour this sauce over the ham and celery rolls. Put in oven or under grill until thoroughly warmed through. If using liquid from tinned vegetables, don't add salt as liquid is quite salty enough and cheese and ham have sufficient saltiness in themselves.

Glossary

Translations are given under the following headings:

1a	Types of Vessels (Private)	10	Fuel Etc.
1b	Types of Vessels (Commercial)	11	Lights
2	Dimensions	12	Chandelry
3	Materials	13	Tools
4	Parts of Vessels	14	Ships Papers
5	Masts and Spars	15	Below Deck
6a	Rigging (Standing)	16	First Aid
6b	Rigging (Running)	17	Food
7a	Sails (Types of)	18	In Harbour
7b	Sails (Parts of)	19	Shops and Places Ashore
8a	Engines (Parts of)	20	Navigation Equipment
8b	Engines (Accessories)	21	Radio and Aural Aids
9	Electrics	22	Chart Terms – Light Characteristics
		23	Colours of Aids
		24	Buoys
		25	Shape
		26	Type of Marking
		27	Chart Dangers
		28	Structures and Floats
		29	Description
		30	Weather
		31	Tides

English	French	German	Spanish	Dutch
1a Types of Vessels (Private)				
Cutter	Cotre	Kutter	Cúter	Kotter
Dinghy	Youyou – prame	Beiboot	Balandro	Jol
Ketch	Ketch	Ketsch	Queche	Kits
Launch	Chaloupe	Barkasse	Launcha	Barkas
Life-boat	Bateau, or canot, de sauvetage	Rettungsboot	Bote salvavidas	Reddingsboot
Motor-boat	Bateau a moteur	Motoryacht	Motora, bote a motor	Motorboot
Motor-sailer	Bateau mixte	Motorsegler	Moto-velero	Motorzeiljacht
Schooner	Coélette	Schoner	Goleta	Schoener
Sloop	Sloop	Slup	Balandra	Sloep
Yawl	Yawl	Yawl	Yola	Yawl
1b Types of Vessels (Commercial)				
Ferry	Transbordeur, bac	Fähre	Transbordador	Pont. veerboot
Merchantman	Navire marchand	Handelsschiff	Buque mercante	Handelsman
Tanker	Bateau-citerne	Tanker	Petrolero	Tankschip
Trawler	Chalutier	Fischereifahrzeug	Pesquero	Stoomtreiler
Tug	Remorqueur	Schlepper	Remolcador	Sleepboot
2 Dimensions				
Breadth	Largeur, de large	Breite	Ancho, anchura	Breedte
Depth	Oreux	Raumtiefe	Puntal	Holte
Draught	Tirant d'eau	Trefgang	Calado	Diepgang
Height	Tirant d'air	Durchfahrtshöhe	Alturza	Doorvaarthoogte
3 Material				
Aluminium	Aluminium	Aluminium	Aluminio	Aluminium
Brass	Laiton	Messing	Latón	Messing
Bronze	Bronze	Bronze	Bronce	Brons
Concrete	Béton	Betom	Hormingón	Beton
Copper	Cuivre	Kupfer	Cobre	Koper
Galvanised iron	Fer galvanise	Galvanisiertes Eisen	Hierro galvanizado	Galvaniseerd Yzer
Iron	Fer	Eisen	Hierro	Ijzer
Metal	Métal	Metall	Metal	Metaalachtig
Stainless steel	Acier inoxydable	Rostfreier Stahl	Acero inoxidable	Roestvrijstaal
Steel	Acier	Stahl	Acero	Staal
Stone Masonry	Maqonnerie	Steinern	Silleria	Steuen
Wood	Bois	Holzern	Madera	Hauten

English	French	German	Spanish	Dutch

4 Parts of Vessels

English	French	German	Spanish	Dutch
Bilge pump	Pompe de cale	Bilgepumpe	Bombas de achique de sentina	Lenspomp
Bilges	Cale	Bilge	Sentina	Kim
Bulkhead	Cloison	Schott	Memparo	Schot
Bunk	Couchette	Koje	Litera	Bank
Cabin	Cabine	Kajüte	Camarote	Kajuit
Chain Locker	Puits à chaînes	Kettenkasten	Caja de cadenas	Kettingbak
Chartroom	Salle des cartes	Kartenraum	Caseta de derrota	Kaartenkamer
Cockpit	Cockpit	Cockpit	Cabina	Kuip
Engine room	Chambre des machines	Maschinenraum	Cámara de máquinas	Motorruim
Forecastle (fo'c's'le)	Gaillard d'avant	Vorschiff, back	Castillo de proa	Vooronder
Fore peak	Pic avant	Vorpiek	Pique de proa	Voorpiek
Freshwater tank	Reservoir d'eau douce	Frischwassertank	Tanque de agua potable	Drinkwatertank
Galley	Cuisine	Kombüse	Cocina	Kombuis
Gunwale	Plat-bord	Schandeck	Borda, regala	Dolboord
Hatch	Ecoutille	Luk	Escotilla	Luik
Keel	Quille	Kiel	Quilla	Kiel
Lavatory	Toilette	Toilette	Jardines	W.C.
Locker	Coffre	Schrank	Taquilla	Kastje
Pipe cot	Cadre	Gasrohrkoje	Catre	Pijpkooi
Propeller	Hélice	Propeller	Hélice	Schroef
Pulpit	Balcon avant	Bugkorb	Púlpito	Preekstoel
Pushpit	Balcon arrière	Heckkorb	Púlpito de popa	Heckstoel
Rubbing strake	Bourrelet de défense	Scheuerleiste	Verduguillo	Berghout
Rudder	Gouvernail	Ruder	Timón	Roer
Sail locker	Soute a voiles	Segellast	Panol de velas	Zeilkooi
Saloon	Salon	Messe	Salon (Camara)	Salon
Stanchions	Chandelier	Reelingstutze	Candelero	Steun voor zeereling
Stem	Etrave	Vorsteven	Roda	Voorsteven
Stern	Poupe	Heck	Popa	Achtersteven
Tiller	Barre	Ruderpinne	Caña	Helmstok

5 Masts and Spars

English	French	German	Spanish	Dutch
Boom	Bome	Baum	Botavara	Giek
Bowsprit	Beaupré	Bugspriet	Baupres	Boegspriet
Bumpkin	Bout-dehors	Ausleger, achtern	Pescante amura trinquete	Papegaaistok
Cross trees	Barres de flèche	Salinge	Crucetas	Dwarszaling
Derrick	Grue	Ladebaum	Pluma de carga	Dirk of Kraanlijn
Foremast	Mât de misaine	Grossmast	Trinquete	Fokkemast
Gaff	Corne	Gaffel	Pico (de vela cangreja)	Gaffel
Hollow	Creaux	Hohl	Hueco	Hol
Jumper struts	Guignol	Jumpstagstrebe	Contrete	Knikstagen
Mast	Mât	Mast	Palo	Mast
Mizzen mast	Mât d'artimon	Besanmast	Palo mesana	Besaans mast
Roller reefing	Bôme à rouleau	Patentreff	Rizo de catalina	Patentrif
Slide	Coulisseau	Rutscher	Corredera	Sleetjes
Solid	Massif	Voll	Macizo	Massief
Spinaker boom	Tangón de spi	Spinnakerbaum	Tangon del espinaquer	Nagel-of spinnakerboom
Truck	Pomme	Topp	Tope (galleta)	Top
Worm gear	Vis sans fin	Schneckenreff	Husillo	Worm en wormwiel

6a Rigging (Standing)

English	French	German	Spanish	Dutch
Aft stay	Etai arrière	Preventer	Stay de popa	Achterstag
Backstay	Galhauban	Achterstag	Brandal	Bakstagen
Bob stay	Sous-barbe	Wasserstag	Barbiquejo	Waterstag
Forestay	Etai avant ou de trinquette	Vorstag	Estay de proa	Voorstag

English	French	German	Spanish	Dutch
Guy	Retenue	Achterholer	Retenida (cabo de retenida viento)	Bulletaije
Shrouds	Haubans	Wanten	Obenques	Want
Stay	Etai	Stag	Estay	Stag

6b Rigging (Running)

English	French	German	Spanish	Dutch
Burgee halyard	Drisse de guidon	Standerfall	Driza de grimpola	Clubstandaardval
"D" Shackle	Groupille "D"	"U" Schäkel	Grillete en D	Rechte sluiting
Double block	Pouile double	Zweischeibenblock	Motón de dos cajeras	Zweeschijfsblok
Foresail halyard	Drisse de misaine	Vorsegelfall	Driza de trinquetilla	Voorzeil val
Foresail sheet	Ecoute de misaine	Vorschot	Trinquetilla (escota de)	Voorzeil of fokke-schoot
Halyard	Drisse	Fall	Driza	Val
Kicking strap	Hale-bas de bôme	Niederholer	Trapa	Neerhouder
Main sheet	Ecoute de grande voile	Gross-Schot	Escota mayor	Grootschoot
Peak halyard	Drisse de pic	Piekfall	Driza de pico	Piekval
Pin	Goupille	Bolzen	Perno, cabilla	Bout
Rope	Cordage	Tauwerk	Cabulleria	Touw
Shackle	Manille	Schäkel	Grillete	Sluiting
Sheave	Réa	Rolle	Roldana	Schijf
Single block	Pouile simple	Einscheibenblock	Motón de una cajera	Einschijfsblok
Snap shackle	Manillerapide	Schnappschäkel	Grillete de escapè	Patent sluiting
Throat halyard	Attache de drisse	Klaufall	Driza de boca	Klauwval
Topping lift	Balanoine	Dirk	Amantillo	Dirk

7a Sails (Types of)

English	French	German	Spanish	Dutch
Foresail	Voile de misaine	Vorsegel	Vela trinquete	Voorseil
Genoa	Génois	Genua	Foque génova	Genua
Jib	Foc	Klüver	Foque	Fok
Lugsail	Voile de fortune	Luggersegel	Vela al tercio	Emmerzeil
Mainsail	Grand voile	Gross-Segal	Vela mayor	Grootzeil
Mizzen sail	Artimon	Besan	Mesana	Bruil of bazaan
Spinnaker	Spinnaker	Spinnaker	Espinaquer (foque balón)	Spinnaker
Stormjib	Tourmentin	Sturmklüver	Foque de capa	Stormfok
Topsail	Flèche	Toppsegel	Gavia	Topzeil
Trysail	Voile de cape	Trysegel	Vela de cangrejo	Stormzeil

7b Sails (Parts of)

English	French	German	Spanish	Dutch
Batten	Latte	Latte	Enjaretado	Zeillat
Batten pocket	Etui, ou gaine de latte	Lattentasche	Bolsa del sable	Zeillatzak
Clew	Point d'ecoute	Schothorn	Puño de escota	Schoothoorn
Cringle	Anneau, patte de Bouline	Kausch	Garruncho de cabo	Grommer
Foot	Bordure	Unterliek	Pujamen	Onderlijk
Head	Point de drisse	Kopf	Puño de driza	Top
Leech	Chute arrière	Achterliek	Apagapenol	Achterlijk
Luff	Guindant	Vorliek	Gratil	Voorlijk
Peak	Pic	Piek	Pica	Piek
Roach	Rond echanorure	Rundung des Achterlieks	Alunamiento	Gilling
Sailbag	Sac à voile	Segelsack	Saco de vela	Zeilzak
Seam	Couture	Naht	Costura	Naad
Tack	Point d'amure	Hals	Puño de amura	Hals
Throat	Gorge	Klau	Puño de driza	Klauw

8a Engines (Parts of)

English	French	German	Spanish	Dutch
Carburettor	Carburateur	Vergaser	Carburado	Carburateur
Clutch	Embrayage	Kupplung	Embrague	Koppeling
Diesel engine	Moteur diesel	Dieselmotor	Motor diesel	Dieselmotor

English	French	German	Spanish	Dutch
Exhaust pipe	Tuyau déchappement	Auspuffrohr	Tubo de escape	Uitaatpijp
Four stroke	A quatre temps	Viertakt	Cuatro tiempos	Viertakt
Fuel pump	Pompe à combustible	Brennstoffpumpe	Bombade alimentación	Brandstofpump
Fuel tank	Reservoir de combustible	Brennstofftank	Tanque de combustible	Brandstoftank
Gear box	Bôite de vitesse	Getriebekasten	Caja de engranajes	Versnellingsbak
Gear lever	Levier de vitesse	Schalthebel	Palanca de cambio	Versnellingshandel
Petrol engine	Moteur à essence	Benzinmotor	Motor de gasolina	Benzinemotor
Stern tube	tube d'étambot, arbre	Stevenrohr	Bocina	Schroefaskoker
Throttle	Accélérateur	Gashebel	Estrangulador	Manette
Two stroke	a deux temps	Zweitakt	Dos tiempos	Tweetakt

8b Engines (Accessories)

English	French	German	Spanish	Dutch
Asbestos tape	Ruban d'amiante	Asbestband	Cinta de amianto	Asbestband
Bolt	Boulon	Bolzen	Perno	Bout
Copper pipe	Tuyau de cuivre	Kupferrohr	Tubo de cobre	Koperpijp
Cylinder head	Culasse	Zylinderkopf	Culata	Cilinderkop
Jointing compound	Pâte à joint	Dichtungsmasse	Junta de culata	Vloeibare pakking
Nut	Ecrou	Schraubenmutter	Tuerca	Moer
Plastic pipe	Tuyau de plastique	Plastikrohr	Tubo de plastico	Plastikpijp
Split pin	Coupille fendue	Splint	Pasador abierto	Splitpen
Washer	Rondelle	Unterlegsscheibe	Arandela	Ring

9 Electrics

English	French	German	Spanish	Dutch
Amp	Ampères	Ampere	Amperio	Ampère
Battery	Accumulateur	Batterie	Bateria	Accu
Bulb	Ampoule	Glühbirne	Bombilla	Lampje
Contact breaker	Interrupteur	Unterbrecher-kontakt	Disyuntor	Contactonder-breker
Copper wire	File de cuivre	Kupferdraht	Cable de cobre	Koperdraad
Distilled water	Eau distillée	Destilliertes wasser	Agua destilada	Gedistilleerd water
Dynamo	Dynamo	Lichtmaschine	Dinamo	Dynamo
Dynamo belt	Courroie de dynamo	Riemen fur lichtmaschine	Correa de dinamo	Dynamoriem
Fluxite	Flux	Flussmittel	Flux	Smeltmiddel
Fuse box	Boite à fusibles	Sicherungskasten	Caja de fusibles	Zekeringskast
Insulating tape	Ruban isolant	Isolierband	Cinta aislante	Isolatieband
Magneto	Magnéto	Magnetzündung	Magneto	Magneet
Solder	Soudure	Lötmetall	Soldadura	Soldeer
Sparking plug	Bougie	Zündkerze	Bujia	Bougie
Switch	Commutateur	Schalter	Interruptor	Schakelaar
Voltage	Tension	Stromspannung	Voltaje	Spanning

10 Fuel Etc.

English	French	German	Spanish	Dutch
Diesel Oil	Gas-oil	Diesel Kraftstoff	Gasoil	Dieselolie
Grease	Graisee	Schmierfett	Grasa	Vet
Lubricating oil	Huile	Schmieröl	Aceite de lubricacion	Smeerolie
Methylated spirit	Alcool à brûler	Denaturierter spiritus	Alcool desnaturalizado	Spiritus
Paraffin	Pétrole lampant	Petroleum	Petroleo	Petroleum
Penetrating oil	Huile penetrante ou degrippant	Rostlösendes Öl	Aceite penetrante	Kruipolie
Petrol	Essence	Bensin	Gasolina	Benzine
T.V.O.	Pétrole carburant	Taktoren kraftstoff	T.V.O. petroleo	Tractor-petroleu
Two stroke oil	Huile deux temps	Zweitakter Öl	Aceite de motor 2 tiempos	Tweetaktolie

11 Lights

English	French	German	Spanish	Dutch
Cabin lamp	Lampe de cabina	Kajütslampe	Lámpara de camarote	Kajuitlamp
Lamp glass	verre de lampe	Glaszylinder	Lámpara de cristal	Lampeglas
Mast head light	Feux de tête de mât	Topplicht	Luz del tope de proa	Toplicht
Navigation lights	Feux de position	Positionslampen	Luces de navegacion	Navigatie lichten

English	French	German	Spanish	Dutch
Port light	Feux de babord	Backbordlampe	Luz de babor	Bakboordlicht
Spreader light	Feux de barre de flèche	Salinglampe	Luz de verga	Zalinglicht
Starboard light	Feux de tribord	Steuerbordlampe	Luz de estribor	Stuerboordlicht
Stern light	Feux arrières	Hecklicht	Luz de alcance	Heklicht
Wick	Mèche	Docht	Mecha (para engrase)	Kous

12 Chandelry

English	French	German	Spanish	Dutch
Anchor	Ancre	Anker	Ancla	Anker
Anchor chain	Chaîne d'ancre	Ankerkette	Cadena del ancla	Ankerketting
Boat hook	Gaffe	Bootshaken	Bichero	Pikhaak
Burgee	Guidon	Klubstander	Grimpola	Clubstandaard
Cleat	Taquet	Klampe	Cornamusa	Klamp
Courtesy flag	Fanion de courtoisie	Gastlandflagge	Pabellón extranjero	Vreemde natievlag
Ensign	Pavillon	Nationalflagge	Pabellón	Natie vlag
Eye bolt	Piton de filière	Augbolzen	Cáncamo	Oggbout
Fair lead	Chaumard	Lippe	Guía	Verhaalkam
Fender	Défense	Fender	Defensa	Stootkussen
Foghorn	Corne de brume	Nebelhorn	Bocina de niebla	Misthoorn
Glass paper	Papier de verre	Glaspapier	Papel de lija	Schuurpapier
Hawser	Cable d'acier	Drahttauwerk	Estacha, amarra	Staaldraadtouw
Hemp rope	Cordage de chanvre	Hanftauwerk	Cabullería de cañamo	Henneptouw
Life buoy	Bouée de sauvetage	Rettungsboje	Guindola	Redding boei
Nylon rope	Cordage de nylon	Nylontauwerk	Cabulleria de nylon	Nylon touw
Oar	Aviron	Ruder	Remo	Riem
Paint	Peinture	Farbe	Pintura	Verf
Q flag	Fanion	Quarantäneflagge	Bandera Q	Quarantaine Vlag
Rope	Cordage	Tanwerk	Cabulleria	Touw
Signal flag	Pavillon (alphabétique)	Signalflagge	Bandera de señales	Seinvlag
Synthetic rope	Cordage synthétique	Synthetisches tauwerk	Cabullería sintetica	Synthetisch touw
Terylene rope	Cordage de Tergal	Terylentauwerk	Cabullería de terylene	Terylene touw
Varnish	Vernis	Lack	Barniz	Lak
Winch	Winch	Winde	Chigre	Lier

13 Tools

English	French	German	Spanish	Dutch
Adjustable spanner	Clé Anglaise	Verstellbarer Schraubenschlüssel	Llave adjustable	Verstelbare sleutel
Cold chisel	Ciseau à froid	Meissel	Cortafrio	Koubeital
File	Lime	Feile	Lima	Vijl
Hacksaw	Scie à métaux	Metallsäge	Sierra para metal	Metaalzaag
Hammer	Marteau	Hammer	Martillo	Hamer
Hand drill	Chignolle à main	Handbohrmaschine	Taladro de mano	Handboor
Pliers	Pinces	Zange	Alicantes	Buigtang
Saw	Scie	Säge	Sierra	Zaag
Screwdriver	Tournevis	Schraubenzieher	Destornillador	Schroevedraaier
Spanner	Clé	Schraubenschlüssel	Llave para tuercas	Sleutel
Wire cutters	Pinces coupantes	Drahtschere	Cortador de alambre	Draadschaar
Wood chisel	Ciseau à bois	Stemmeisen	Formón	Beitel
Wrench	Tourne-à-gauche	Schraubenschlüssel	Llave de boca	Waterpomptang

14 Ships Papers

English	French	German	Spanish	Dutch
Certificate of Registry	Acte de Francisation	Schiffsmessbrief	Patente de Navegacion	Zeebrief
Customs clearance	Dédouanement	Zollpapier	Despacho de aduana	Bewijs van klaring door douane
Insurance certificate	Certificat d'assurance	Versicherungspolice	Poliza de seguro	Verzekeringsbewijs
Passport	Passeport	Reisepass	Passaporte	Paspoort
Pratique	Libre-pratique	Verkehrserlaubnis	Plática	Verlof tot Ontscheping
Ship's log	Livre de bord	Schiffstagebuch	Cuaderno de bítacora	Journaal

English	French	German	Spanish	Dutch

15 Below Deck

English	French	German	Spanish	Dutch
Blanket	Couverture	Decke	Manta	Wollen deken
Cabin	Cabine	Kajüte	Camarote	Kajuit
Coffee pot	Cafetière	Kaffekanne	Cafetera	Koffiepot
Cooker	Cuisinière	Kocher	Fogón	Kockpan
Corkscrew	Tire-bouchon	Korkenzieher	Sacacorchos	Kurketrekker
Forks	Fourchettes	Gabel	Tenedores	Vorken
Frying pan	Poêle à frire	Bratpfanne	Sartén	Braadpan
Galley	Cuisine	Kombüse	Cocina	Kombuis
Kettle	Bouilloire	Kessel	Caldero	Ketel
Knives	Couteaux	Messer	Cuchillos	Messen
Lavatory paper	Papier hygiénique	Toilettenpapier	Papel higiénico	Toilet-papier
Matches	Allumettes	Striechhölzer	Cerillas	Lucifers
Mattress	Matelas	Matratze	Colchón	Matras
Saucepan	Casserole	Kochtopf	Cacerola	Steelpan of stoofpan
Sheet	Drap	Bettlaken	Sábana	Laken
Sleeping bag	Sac de couchage	Schlafsack	Saco de dormir	Slaapzak
Soap	Savon	Seife	Jabón	Zeep
Spoons	Cuillers	Löffel	Cucharas	Lepels
Tea pot	Théière	Teekanne	Tetera	Theepot
Tin opener	Ouvre-boites	Dosenöffner	Abrelatas	Blikopener
Toilet	Toilette	Toilette	Retretes	W.C.
Towel	Serviette	Handtuch	Toalla	Handdoek
Washing-up liquid	Détergent	Abwaschmittel	Detergente	Afwasmiddel

16 First Aid

English	French	German	Spanish	Dutch
Anti-seasickness pills	Remède contre le mal de mer	Antiseekrankheite mittel	Pildoras contra el mareo	Pillen tegen zeeziekte
Antiseptic cream	Onguent antiseptique	Antiseptische Salbe	Pomada antiséptica	Antiseptische zalf
Aspirin tablets	Aspirine	Aspirintabletten	Pastillas de aspirina	Aspirine
Bandage	Bandage	Binde	Venda	Verband
Calamine lotion	Lotion à la calamine	Zink-Tinktur	Locion de calamina	Anti-jeuk middel
Cotton wool	Quate	Watte	Algodón	Watten
Disinfectant	Désinfectant	Desinfektionsmittel	Desinfectante	Desinfecterend middel
Indigestion tablets	Pillules pour l'indigestion	Tabletten gegen Darmstörungen	Pastillas laxantes	Laxeertabletten
Laxative	Laxatif	Abführmittel	Laxante	Laxeermiddel
Lint	Pansement	Verbandsmull	Hilacha	Pluksel
Safety pin	Epingle de sûreté	Sicherheitsnadel	Imperdibles	Veiligheidsspeld
Scissors	Ciseaux	Schere	Tijeras	Schaar
Sticking plaster	Pansament adhesif	Heftplaster	Esparadrapo	Kleefpleister
Stomach upset	Mal à l'estomac	Magen-und Darmbeschwerden	Corte de digestión	Last van de maag
Thermometer	Thermomètre	Thermometer	Termómetro	Thermometer
Tweezers	Pince à échardes	Pinzette	Pinzas	Pincet
Wound dressing	Pansement stérilisé	Verbandzeug	Botiquin para heridas	Noodverband

7 Food

English	French	German	Spanish	Dutch
Bacon	Lard fúme	Speck	Tocino	Spek
Beef	Boeuf	Rindfleisch	Carne de vaca	Rundvless
Bread	Le pain	Brot	Pan	Brood
Butter	Le beurre	Butter	Mantequilla	Boter
Cheese	Fromage	Käse	Queso	Kaas
Eggs	Oeufs	Eier	Huevos	Eieren
Fish	Poisson	Fisch	Pescado	Vis
Fresh water	Eau douce	Süsswasser	Agua dulce	Zoetwater
Fruit	Fruits	Obst	Frutas	Fruit
Ham	Jambon	Schinken	Jamón	Ham

English	French	German	Spanish	Dutch
Jam	La confiture	Marmelade	Compota	Jam
Marmalade	Confiture d'oranges	Orangen marmelade	Mermelada	Marmelade
Meat	Viande	Fleisch	Carne	Vlees
Milk	Du lait	Milch	Leche	Melk
Mustard	Moutarde	Senf	Mostaza	Mosterd
Mutton	Mouton	Hammelfleisch	Carne de cernero	Schepevlees
Pepper	Poivre	Pfeffer	Pimienta	Peper
Pork	Poro	Schweinefleisch	Carne de cerdo	Varkensvlees
Salt	Sel	Salz	Sal	Zout
Sausages	Saucisses	Würstchen	Embutidos	Worstjes
Vegetables	Légumes	Gemuse	Legumbres	Groenten
Vinegar	Vinaigre	Essig	Vinagre	Azijn

18 In Harbour

English	French	German	Spanish	Dutch
Anchoring prohibited	Défense de mouiller	Ankern verboten!	Fondeadero prohibido	Verboden ankerplaats
Canal	Canal	Kanal	Canal	Kanaal
Customs Office	Bureau de douane	Zollamt	Aduana	Douanekantoor
Ferry	Bao	Fähre	Transbordador	Veer
Fishing harbour	Port de pêche	Fischereihafen	Puerto pesquero	Vissershaven
Harbour	Bassin	Hafen	Puerto	Haven
Harbour Master	Capitaine de Port	Hafenkapitän	Capitan de puerto	Havenmeester
Harbour Master's Office	Bureau de Capitaine de Port	Büro des Hafenkapitäns	Comandancia de puerto	Havenkantoor
Harbour steps	Escalier du quai	Kaitreppe	Escala Real	Haventrappen
Immigration Officer	Agent du service de l'immigration	Beamter der Passkontrolle	Oficial de immigracíon	Immigratie Beamte
Lifting bridge	Pont basculant	Hubbrücke	Puente levadizo	Hefbrug
Lock	Ecluse	Schleuse	Esculusa	Sluis
Mooring place	Point d'accostage	Liegeplatz im Bojenfeld	Amarradero	Meerplaats
Mooring prohibited	Accostage interdit	Anlegen verboten	Amarradero prohibido	Verboden aan te leggen
Movable bridge	Pont mobile	Bewegliche brücke	Puente móvil	Beweegbare brug
Prohibited Area	Zone interdit	Verbotenes gebiet	Zona prohibida	Verboden gebied
Swing bridge	Pont tournant	Drehbrücke	Puente giratorio	Draaibrug
Yacht harbour	Bassin pour hachts	Yachthafen	Puerto de yates	Jachthaven

19 Shops and Places Ashore

English	French	German	Spanish	Dutch
Baker	Boulanger	Bäcker	Panadero	Bakker
Bank	Banque	Bank	Banco	Bank
Bus	L'autobus	Bus	Autobús	Bus
Butcher	Boucher	Metzger	Carnicero	Slager
Chemist	Pharmacien	Apotheke	Farmaceútico	Apotheek
Dentist	Dentiste	Zahnarzt	Dentista	Tandarts
Doctor	Médecin	Arzt	Medico	Dokter
Fishmonger	Marchand de poisson	Fischhändler	Pescadero	Vishandel
Garage	Garage	Garage	Garaje	Garage
Greengrocer	Marchand de légumes	Gemüsehändler	Verdulero	Groente handelaar
Grocer	L'épicier	Krämer	Tendero de comestibles	Kruidenier
Hospital	Hôpital	Krankenhaus	Hospital	Ziekenhuis
Ironmonger	Quincaillerie	Eisenwarenhändler	Ferretero	Ijzerwarenwinkel
Market	Marché	Markt	Mercado	Markt
Post Office	Poste	Postamt	Correos	Postkantoor
Railway station	Gare	Bahnhof	Estación	Station
Sailmaker	Voilier	Segelmacher	Velero	Zeilmaker
Supermarket	Supermarché	Supermarkt	Supermercado	Supermarkt
Yacht chandler	Fournisseur de marine	Yachtausrüster	Almacén de efectos navales	Scheepsleverancier

English	French	German	Spanish	Dutch

20   Navigation Equipment

English	French	German	Spanish	Dutch
Binoculars	Jumelles	Fernglas	Gemelos	Kijker
Chart	Cartes marines	Seekarte	Carta náutica	Zeekaarten
Chart table	Table à cartes	Kartentisch	Planero	Kaartentafel
Compass	Compas	Kompass	Compás	Kompas
Direction finding radio	Récepteur goniométrique	Funkpeiler	Radio goniómetro	Radio peil-toestel
Dividers	Pointes seches	Kartenzirkel	Compas de puntas	Verdeelpasser
Echo sounder	Echosondeur	Echolot	Sondador acústico	Echolood
Hand-bearing compass	Compass de relèvement	Handpeilkompass	Alidada	Handpeilkompas
Parallel ruler	Règles parallèles	Parallel-lineal	Regla de paralelas	Parallel liniaal
Patent log	Loch enregistreur	Patent log	Corredera de patente	Patent log
Pencil	Crayon	Bleistift	Lápiz	Potlood
Protractor	Rapporteur	Winkelmesser	Transpartador	Gradenboog
Radio receiver	Poste récepteur	Empfangsgerät	Receptor de radio	Radio-ontvangtoestel
Rubber	Gomme	Radiergummi	Goma	Vlakgom
Sextant	Sextant	Sextant	Sextante	Sextant

21   Radio and Aural Aids

English	French	German	Spanish	Dutch
Bell	Cloche	Glooke	Campana	Mistklok
Diaphone	Diaphone	Kolbensirene	Diafono	Diafoon
Explosive	Explosion	Nebelknallsignal	Explosivo	Knalmistsein
Gong	Gong	Gong	Gong	Mistgong
Horn	Nautophone	Nautofon	Nautofono	Nautofoon
Radiobeacon	Radiophare	Funkfeuer	Radiofaro	Radiobaken
Reed	Trompette	Zungenhorn	Bocina	Mistfluit
Siren	Sirene	Sirene	Sirena	Mistsirene
Whistle	Sifflet	Heuler	Silbato	Mistfluit

22   Chart Terms (Light Characteristics)

English	French	German	Spanish	Dutch
ALT.	Alt.	Wels	Alt.	ALT.
F.	Fixe	F.	F.	V.
F. FL	Fize…ecalats	Mi.	F.D.	V. & S.
F. GP. FL.	Fixe…gr. cligns	Mi.	G. Gp. D.	V. & GS.
FL.	ECLAT	Blz.	D.	S.
GP. FL.	Gr. Cligns	Blz. Grp.	Gp. D.	GS.
GP. OCC.	Gr. Occ.	Ubr. Grp.	Gp. Oc.	GO.
INT. QK. FL.	Scint. dis.	Fkl. unt.	Gp. Ct.	INT. FL.
ISO.	Isophase	Glt.	Iso.	Iso.
MO.		Mo.	Mo.	
OCC.	Occ.	Ubr.	Oc.	O.
QK. FL.	Scint.	Fkl.	Ct.	Fl.

23   Colours of Aids

English		French	German		Spanish	Dutch	
Blue	Bl.	bl.	blau	bl.	Azul	Blauw	B.
Black	B.	Noir	schwarz	S.	Negro	Zwart	Z.
Brown		Brun	braun		Moreno	Bruin	
Green	G.	v.	grün	gn.	V.	Groen	Gn.
Grey		Gris	grau		Gris	Grije	
Orange	Or.	org.	orange	or.	Onaranjado	Oranje	Or.
Red	R.	r.	rot	r.	r.	Rood	R.
Violet	Vi.	Vio.	viol.		Vi.	Violet	Vi.
White	W.	b.	weiss	w.	bl.	Wit	W.
Yellow	Y.	jaune	gelb	g.	Amarillo	Geel	Gl.

24   Buoys

English	French	German	Spanish	Dutch
Bell buoy	Bouée sonore à cloche	Clockentonne (Gl-Tn)	Boya de campana	Belboel (Bel)
Can buoy	Bouée plate, cylindrique	Stumpttonne	Boya cilindrica	Stompe ton

English	French	German	Spanish	Dutch
Conical buoy	Bouée conique, cône	Spitztonne	Boya cónica	Spitse ton
Light buoy	Bouée lumineuse	Leuchttonne	Boya luminosa	Lichtboel
Mooring buoy	Coffre d'amarrage	Festmachetonne	Boya de amarre	Meerboel
Pillar buoy	Bouée à foseau	Bakentonne	Boya de huso	Torenboel
Spar buoy	Bouée a espar	Spierentonne	Boya de espeque	Sparboel
Spherical buoy	Bouée sphérique disque	Kugeltonne	Boya estérica	Bol ton
Whistle buoy	Bouée sonore à siffler	Heultonne (Hl-tn)	Boya de silbato	Brulboel (brul)

25 Shape

English	French	German	Spanish	Dutch
Cone	Cone	Kegel	Cono	Kegel
Conical	Conique	Kegelformig	Conico	Kegelvormig
Diamond	Rhombe	Raute	Rombo	Ruitoormig
Round	Circulaire	rund	Redondo	Rond
Square	Carré	Viereck	Cuadrangular	Vierkaut
Triangle	Triangle	Dreieck	Triangulo	Driehook
Triangular	Triangulaire	dreieckig	Triangular	Driehockig

26 Type of Marking

English	French	German	Spanish	Dutch
Band	Bande	waagerechtgestreift	fajas horizontales	Horizontaal gestreept
Chequered	à damier	gewurfelt	Damero	Geblokt
Stripe	Raic	senkrecht gestreift	Fajas verticales	Vertikaal gestreept
Top mark	Vogant	Toppzeichen	Marea de Tope	Topteken

27 Chart Dangers

English	French	German	Spanish	Dutch
Dries	Assèche	Trockenfallend (tr)	Que vela en bajamar	Iroogvallend
Isolated danger	Danger isolé	Einzelliegende gefahr	Peligro islado	Losliggend gevaar
Obstruction	Obstruction (Obs)	Schiffaharts-Hindemis (Sch-H)		Belemmering van de vaarts, hindernis (Obstr)
Overfalls	Remous et clapotis	Stromk abbelung	Escarceos, hileros	Stroomrafeling
Shoal	Haut fond (Ht Fd)	Untiefe (Untf)	Bajo (Bo)	Droogte, ondiepte (Dre)
Sunken rock	Roche submergée	Unterwasserklippe (Klp)	Roca siempre cubierta	Blinde klip
Wreck	Épave	Wrack	Naufragro (Nauf)	Wrak

28 Structures and Floats

English	French	German	Spanish	Dutch
Beacon	Balbise	Bake	Baliza	Baken
Column	Colonne	Laternenträger	Columna	Lantaarnpaal
Dolphin	Dauphin	Dalben	Duge de alba	Ducdalf
Dwelling	Corps de logis	Wohnhaus	Casa	Huis traliemast
House	Bâtiment	Haus	Casa	Huis
Hut	Cabane	Hutte	Caseta	Huisje
Light	Feu	Leuchtfeuer	Luz	Licht
Light float	Feu flottant	Leuchtfloss	Luzflotante	Lichulot
Light vessel	Feu (ou phare)	Leuchtschiff	Faro flotano	Lichtschip
Lighthouse	Phare	Leuchtturm	Faro	Lichttoren
Mast	Mat	Mast	Mastil	Mast
Post	Poteau	Laternenpfahl	Poste	Lantaarnpaal
Tower	Tour	Turm	Torre	Toren

29 Description

English	French	German	Spanish	Dutch
Destroyed	Détruit	zerstört	Destruido	Vernield
Extinguished	Éteint	gelöscht	Apagada	Gedoofd
Occasional	Feu occasionnell	gelegentlich	Ocasional	Facultatict (Fai)
Temporary	Temporaire	votübergehend	Temporal	Tijdelijk

237

English	French	German	Spanish	Dutch
30 Weather				
Fog	Bruillard	Nebel	Niebla	Mist
Gale	Coupe de vent	Stütmischer wind	Duro	Stormachtig
Mist	Brume légère ou mouillée	Feuchter dunst, diesig	Neblina	Nevel
Squall	Grain	Bö	Turbonada	Bui
Weather forecast	Previsions météu	Wettervorhersage	Previsión meteorológica	Weersvoorspelling
31 Tides				
Current	Courant	Strom	Corriente	Stroom
Ebb	Marée decendante	Ebbe	Vaciante	Eb
Flood	Marée montante	Flut	Entrante	Vloed
High water	Pleine mer	Hochwasser	Pleamar	Hoogwater
Low water	Basse mer	Niedrigwasser	Bajamar	Laagwater
Mean	Moyen	Mittlere	Media	Gemiddeld
Neap tide	Morte eau	Nipptide	Aguas muertas	Doodtij
Range	Amplitude	Tidenhub	Repunte	Verval
Sea level	Niveau	Wasserstand	Nivel	Waterstand
Spring tide	Vive eau	Springtide	Marea viva	Springtij
Stand	Étale	Easserstand	Margen	Stilwater

Acknowledgements List

P. 10/11: George Taylor; p. 14: Barry Pickthall; p. 15: Barry Pickthall; p. 16: David Eglise; p. 18: Beken of Cowes; p. 19 *top*: Arthur Somers; p. 19 *bottom*: Colin Jarman; p. 23: Colin Jarman; p. 26/7: Barry Pickthall; p. 28: Prout Catamarans Ltd; p. 38 *left* and *centre*: Barry Pickthall; p. 39: Barry Pickthall; p. 42 *left* and *right*: Colin Jarman; p. 43 *left*: Colin Jarman; p. 43 *right*: George Taylor; p. 44 *left*: Gordon Hammond; p. 44 *right*: Colin Jarman; p. 45 *left*: Colin Jarman; p. 45 *right*: Gordon Hammond; p. 46/47: Barry Pickthall; p. 54/55: Barry Pickthall; p. 58/59: Barry Pickthall; p. 62/63: George Taylor; p. 67: George Taylor; p. 71: Brian Trodd; p. 76 *left* and *right*: Colin Jarman; p. 77: George Taylor; p. 81: Colin Jarman; p. 82: Brian Trodd; p. 82/83: John Watney; p. 90/91: George Taylor; p. 100: George Taylor; p. 101: Alistair Black; p. 102: John Watney; p. 102/103: Beken of Cowes; p. 104: Colin Jarman; p. 106/7: George Taylor; p. 108: Colin Jarman; p. 110: Hamlyn Group; p. 121: Jonathan Eastland; p. 126/127: Colin Jarman; p. 131: Brian Trodd; p. 143: Brian Trodd; p. 146/147: Gil Montalaverne; p. 154 *top left*: Meteorological Office (M.O.) (R.H. Hughes); p. 154 *top right*: M.O. (D. Limbert); p. 154 *centre left*: M.O. (R.K. Pilsbury); p. 154 *centre right*: M.O. (D.E. Pedgley); p. 154 *bottom*: M.O. (R.I. Campbell); p. 155 *top*: M.O. (R.H. Highes); p. 155 *centre left*: M.O. (R.K. Pilsbury); p. 155 *centre right*: M.O. (W.G. Pendelton); p. 155 *bottom*: M.O. (Miss D.J. Wandsworth); p. 162: Beken of Cowes; p. 186: Brian Trodd; p. 187: Beken of Cowes; p. 198: Beken of Cowes; p. 199 *left* and *right*: George Taylor; p. 200/201: John Watney; p. 203: Beken of Cowes; p. 205: Jonathan Eastland; p. 210 *top*: Electronic Laboratories Ltd., p. 210 *bottom*: Brookes and Gates; p. 212: Electronic Laboratories Ltd., p. 213 *top* and *bottom*: Electronic Laboratories Ltd; p. 213 *centre*: Brookes and Gates; p. 215: *top right* and *bottom*: Brookes and Gates; p. 215 *top left*: Electronic Laboratories Ltd; p. 216 *top and bottom*: Electronic Laboratories Ltd; p. 218/219: M.S. Gibb Ltd.

Book designed and illustrated by Bob Mathias.

Index

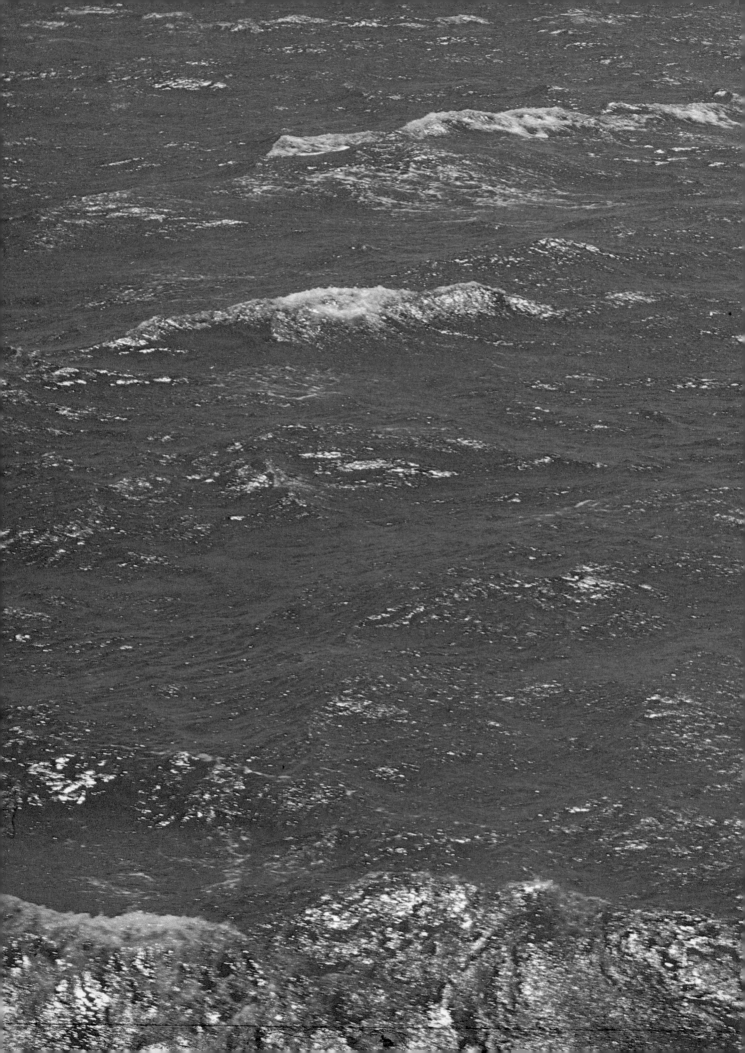